POLITICAL
HYPOCRISY

POLITICAL HYPOCRISY

THE MASK OF POWER, FROM HOBBES TO ORWELL AND BEYOND

DAVID RUNCIMAN

PRINCETON UNIVERSITY PRESS · PRINCETON AND OXFORD

Copyright © 2008 by Princeton University Press
Published by Princeton University Press, 41 William Street, Princeton,
New Jersey 08540

In the United Kingdom: Princeton University Press,
6 Oxford Street, Woodstock, Oxfordshire OX20 1TW

Library of Congress Cataloging-in-Publication Data

Runciman, David.
Political hypocrisy : the mask of power, from Hobbes to
Orwell and beyond / David Runciman.
p.   cm.
Includes bibliographical references and index.
ISBN: 978-0-691-12931-0 (hardcover : alk. paper)   1. Political ethics.
2. Hypocrisy—Political aspects.   3. Political Science—philosophy.
I. Title.

JA79.R7819 2008
320.101—dc22   2007046793

British Library Cataloging-in-Publication Data is available

This book has been composed in Palatino

Printed on acid-free paper. ∞

press.princeton.edu

Printed in the United States of America

1 3 5 7 9 10 8 6 4 2

The Mask Hypocrisie's flung down,
From the great Statesman to the Clown;
And some, in borrow'd Looks well known
Appear'd like Strangers in their own.
—Mandeville, "The Grumbling Hive," 1705

Contents

Preface

This book is based on the Carlyle lectures that I delivered at Oxford University during February-March 2007. Each of the chapters is a substantially revised and expanded version of the original lectures, but I have tried to retain the style of the lectures in the written version, and have kept references to the scholarly literature to a minimum. Each chapter deals with a different aspect of the problem of hypocrisy in modern politics: respectively power, virtue, freedom, language, party politics, empire and contemporary democracy. The subjects of these chapters are connected by a number of inter-related themes, but I hope that they can also be read as separate essays in their own right. It is one of the central claims of this book that there is a tradition of thinking about the problem of hypocrisy in politics that runs from Hobbes to Orwell, and connects to the problems of the present day. I do not claim that this is an entirely unified or coherent tradition, nor that these authors were necessarily worrying about the same things as each other, never mind the same things that we are worried about now. But I do believe that there is enough of a connection between them to suggest that there is an alternative way of thinking about the problem of political hypocrisy to the counsels of cynicism or despair that we so often hear. My hope is that this connection emerges over the course of the book as a whole.

The chapter on Jefferson and American independence was not part of the original lecture series. The focus of the final chapter on the lessons of this story for contemporary politics has tried to take account of the shifting political scene both in Britain and the United States (it has only been a few months since I delivered the lecture on which it is based, but a few months is a long time in politics). Political hypocrisy is a difficult subject to pin down, because there is so much of it about, and because hypocrites, being hypocrites, can't be relied on. That is why a historical perspective is so important.

Acknowledgments

I am very grateful to the Carlyle Lectures committee for the invitation to give the course of lectures on which this book is based, and I would particularly like to thank George Garnett for all his encouragement and support. While in Oxford, Nuffield College provided me with a quiet and comfortable room in which to work. Kinch Hoekstra, Noel Malcolm and Patricia Williams were very generous with their time and hospitality. Between them they made what might have been a daunting experience an extremely enjoyable one.

At Princeton University Press, Ian Malcolm has been a superb and tireless editor and I am very grateful for all his hard work, as I am for the support of Caroline Priday and the rest of the Princeton UK office; Jodi Beder offered much useful advice during the copyediting stage. I would also like to express my thanks to two anonymous readers for their very helpful comments, to Richard Tuck for his pointers about Hobbes and sincerity, and to Miranda Landgraf, for kindly agreeing to read and comment on the bulk of the manuscript. My colleagues in the Politics Department at Cambridge and at Trinity Hall generously covered for me during the term's leave I took to write and deliver the lectures. I would particularly like to thank Helen Thompson for her friendship and conversation over the years, about hypocrisy and much else besides.

The initial reading for and thinking about the themes of this book was done during a two-month fellowship at the Research School of Social Sciences at the Australian National

University in Canberra. Bob Goodin was an exceptionally generous and tolerant host, and I very much appreciate the freedom that visit gave me to get started on this project. Finally, I would like to say thank you to Bee, Tom and Natasha for coming with me to Canberra, and for making that trip, as everything else, such a joy.

POLITICAL
HYPOCRISY

INTRODUCTION

This is a book about hypocritical politicians, and about some of the ways we might learn to view them. There is a lot of hypocrisy at work in contemporary politics—no doubt we all have our favourite examples, from the moralising adulterers to the mudslinging do-gooders. But although it is fairly easy to point the finger at all this hypocrisy, it is much harder to know what, if anything, to do about it. The problem is that hypocrisy, though inherently unattractive, is also more or less inevitable in most political settings, and in liberal democratic societies it is practically ubiquitous. No one likes it, but everyone is at it, which means that it is difficult to criticise hypocrisy without falling into the trap of exemplifying the very thing one is criticising. This is an intractable problem, but for that reason, it is nothing new, and in this book I explore what a range of past political thinkers have had to say about the difficulty of trying to rescue politics from the most destructive forms of hypocrisy without simply making the problem worse. The thinkers that I discuss—from Thomas Hobbes to George Orwell—are not the usual ones who are looked to for guidance on matters of hypocrisy and duplicity. This is because as champions of a straight-talking approach to politics they can appear either naively or wilfully cut off from the fact that hypocrisy is something we have to learn to live with. But in fact, I believe these are precisely the thinkers who can help us to understand the role that hypocrisy does and ought to play in political life, because they saw the problem of hypocrisy in all its complexity, and were torn in their responses to it. In

1

this introduction, I will explain why I think these particular authors can serve as a guide to our own concerns about political double standards, and why they are better suited to that task than the writers—from Machiavelli to Nietzsche—who are more often assumed to be telling us the truth about the limits of truthfulness in politics.

Hypocrisy: an "ordinary" vice

One of the best places to begin any discussion of the problem of hypocrisy in liberal democratic politics is with the classic treatment of this question in Judith Shklar's *Ordinary Vices* (1984). In that book, Shklar makes the case for ranking the vices according to the nature of the threat that they pose to liberal societies. The vice that emerges as the worst of all, and by far, is cruelty. The other vices, Shklar suggests, are therefore not so bad, and this includes the one with which she begins her discussion: the vice of hypocrisy. She wants us (the inhabitants of liberal societies) to stop spending so much time worrying about hypocrisy, and to stop minding about it so much. But it is difficult not to mind about hypocrisy, for two reasons. First, it is so very easy to take a dislike to it—on a basic human level, there is something repulsive about hypocrisy encountered at first hand, since no one enjoys being played for a fool. Second, for everyone who does take a dislike to it, it is so very easy to find. "For those who put hypocrisy first," Shklar writes ("first" here meaning ranked worst among the vices), "their horror is enhanced precisely because they see it everywhere"; and this means, in particular, that they see it everywhere in politics.[1]

The specific political problem is that liberal societies are, or have become, democracies. Because people don't like hypocrisy, and because hypocrisy is everywhere, it is all too tempting for democratic politicians to seek to expose the inevitable double standards of their rivals in the pursuit of power, and votes. Take the most obvious contemporary instance of this temptation: negative advertising. If you wish to do the maximum possible damage to your political opponent in thirty seconds of airtime, you should try to paint him or her as a hypocrite: you must highlight the gap between the honeyed words and the underlying reality, between the mask and the person behind the mask, between what they say now and what they once did. And negative advertising works, which is why it proves so hard to resist for any politician, particularly those who find themselves behind in the polls, and certainly including those who have promised to foreswear it. Shklar does not discuss negative advertising, but she does say this, which is almost impossible to dispute: "It is easier to dispose of an opponent's character by exposing his hypocrisy than to show his political convictions are wrong."[2]

Shklar thinks we have got all this the wrong way around, that we are worrying about hypocrisy when we should be worrying about our intolerance for it. She highlights the risks for liberal democracies of too great a reliance on "public sincerity," which simply leaves all politicians vulnerable to charges of bad faith. We should learn to be more sanguine about hypocrisy, and accept that liberal democratic politics are only sustainable if mixed with a certain amount of dissimulation and pretence. The difficulty, though, is knowing how to get this mixture right. The problem is that we do not want to be sanguine about the wrong kinds of hypocrisy. Nor ought we to assume that there is nothing we can do if mild forms of hypocrisy start to leach into every corner of public life. In some places, a tolerance for hypocrisy can do real harm. After all, some forms of hypocrisy are inherently destructive of liberalism itself, even in Shklar's terms. For example, allowing people to treat government-sanctioned torture as a necessary resource of all political societies *in extremis*, no matter how liberal their public principles, would simply let in cruelty by the back door. Equally, it would be counter-productive to tolerate hypocrisy about our tolerance for hypocrisy: it hardly makes sense to permit politicians to get away with renouncing negative advertising while their underlings carry on spreading poison about their opponents behind the scenes. Yet negative advertising only works because it works on *us*; so politicians caught out in this way might legitimately claim that we are the ones being hypocritical about our tolerance for hypocrisy, since the reason they keep coming back to the well of poison is because it is the only reliable way to get our attention. Clearly, a line needs to be drawn somewhere between the hypocrisies that are unavoidable in contemporary political life, and the hypocrisies that are intolerable. But it is hard to see where. Shklar does not offer much advice about where and how to draw this line, except to remind us that it will not be easy, because, as she puts it, "what we have to live with is a morally pluralistic world in which hypocrisy and antihypocrisy are joined to form a discrete system."[3]

This book is an attempt to tease apart some of the different sorts of hypocrisy at work in the morally pluralistic world of modern politics, using the history of political thought as a guide. It is not unusual to see the history of ideas as an appropriate place to look for guidance on these matters. Shklar herself does it in *Ordinary Vices*, where she draws not just on philosophers (such as Hegel) but also playwrights (above all Molière, the man who gave us "tartuffery") and novelists (including Hawthorne and Dickens) for insights into the intricate dance of hypocrisy and anti-hypocrisy, the constant round of masking and unmasking that makes up our social existence. Other authors have sought to supplement Shklar's account by going back to the great scourges of well-meaning sanctimony in the history of political thought, such as Machiavelli and Rousseau, who together provide the inspiration for Ruth Grant's *Hypocrisy and Integrity* (1997); or Rousseau and Nietzsche, who provide two of the main sources for Bernard Williams's meditation on the perils of authenticity in *Truth and Truthfulness* (2002). But what is much rarer is an attempt to seek some answers in the classic liberal tradition itself. Indeed,

Grant argues that the liberal tradition is precisely the wrong place to look. "The appreciation of the necessity for political hypocrisy," she writes, "and the perspective of the liberal rationalist are simply at odds with each other."[4] She goes on: "Liberal theory does not take sufficient account of the distinctive character of political relations, of political passions, and of moral discourse and so underestimates the place of hypocrisy in politics."[5] By liberal rationalists, Grant says she means writers like Hobbes, Locke, and Adam Smith. The reason she thinks we must go back to Machiavelli when considering the role of hypocrisy in political life is that in her view none of these other authors have anything of use to tell us on the subject. But Grant is wrong about this, and she is therefore wrong about the failures of liberal theory to make sense of hypocrisy. In this book I hope to show why.

There is a weak and a strong version of the case Grant makes. The weak version says that because liberal rationalists are precommitted to the importance of truthfulness in politics, they simply don't understand why hypocrisy is inevitable. The strong version says that they do understand, but are simply pretending not to, which makes them the worst hypocrites of all. This is often what people mean when they talk about hypocrisy as the English vice, so it is easy to see why English liberals often strike outsiders as the very worst of hypocrites, particularly when their liberal rationalism turns into liberal imperialism. In this book, I will be looking at a broadly liberal rationalist tradition of English political thought starting with Hobbes, and stretching up to Victorian imperialism and beyond. Of course, by its very Englishness it cannot be taken to be definitive of what Grant calls liberal rationalism (for example, I will only be discussing Scottish Enlightenment thinkers like Adam Smith and David Hume in passing). Moreover, it is not the whole of English liberal rationalism, since I will be bypassing John Locke as well. It includes one Anglicised Dutch writer (Mandeville) and one American detour, into the arguments surrounding American dependence and independence at the end of the eighteenth century, since these were in their own ways arguments about the nature of English hypocrisy, and about whether there was a nonhypocritical way of confronting it. The authors discussed in this book constitute a highly selective sample in what is a broad field. But what connects them is the fact that they have important things to say about the nature of political hypocrisy, and this is related to the fact that they were often thought to be the worst of hypocrites themselves.

Certainly it is hard to think of any political thinkers who have faced the charge of hypocrisy more often than the ones I will be discussing in what follows: Hobbes, Mandeville, Franklin, Jefferson, Bentham, Sidgwick, Orwell are some of the great anti-hypocrites of the liberal tradition, which makes them in many people's eyes its arch-hypocrites as well. But this is unfair, as well as inaccurate: their anti-hypocrisy was much more subtle and complicated than that would suggest. These authors have some of the most interesting and useful things to say about hypocrisy, precisely because they were conscious of its hold on political life, even as they tried to escape it. In other words, they were struggling with the problem from the inside, and could see that it was a problem, unlike those (Machiavelli, Rousseau, Nietzsche) who have looked at the hypocrisy of liberal (or in an earlier guise, "Christian") politics from the outside, and saw only how easy it would be to pull aside the mask, which is what they did.

The writers that I will be discussing in this book are the ones who were willing to keep the mask in place, despite or because of the fact that they were also truth-tellers, committed to looking behind the mask, and revealing what they found there. Keeping the mask in place while being aware of what lies behind the mask is precisely the problem of hypocrisy for liberal societies; indeed, it is one of the deepest problems of politics that we face. These writers were also specifically concerned with problems of language, and the difficulty of saying what you mean in a political environment in which there are often good reasons not to mean what you say. They are therefore the people we should be looking to for help in thinking about the puzzle that Shklar leaves us with, because it was a puzzle for them too, and there are no easy answers to be found here. Thinkers like Machiavelli make it too easy for us to dismiss hypocrisy as a political problem altogether. What's much harder to make sense of is why it remains such a problem for us in the first place.

THE VARIETIES OF HYPOCRISY

Something else that connects the writers I will be discussing in this book is that they all understood that hypocrisy comes in a variety of different forms, which is why it is so important to separate them out, rather than lumping them all together. There is always a temptation to sweep a range of different practices under the general heading of hypocrisy, and then condemn them all out of hand. But in reality the best one can ever do with hypocrisy is take a stand for or against one kind or another, not for or against hypocrisy itself. We might regret the prevalence of hypocrisy, but if we want to do anything about it we have to get beyond generalised regret, and try instead to identify the different ways in which hypocrisy can be a problem. As a result, I am not going to try to provide a catch-all definition of what hypocrisy is, nor of how it must relate either to sincerity on the one hand or to lying on the other. A variety of different forms of sincerity, hypocrisy, and lies will emerge over the course of this book, and a variety of different relationships between them. But I do want to offer a preliminary account of how the concept of hypocrisy is able to sustain such a range of different interpretations, in order to set these later discussions in context. To do so, it is necessary to go back to the origins of the term.

The idea of hypocrisy has its roots in the theatre. The original "hypocrites" were classical stage actors, and the Greek term (*hypokrisis*) meant the playing of a part. So in its original form the term was merely descriptive of the theatrical function of pretending to be something one is not. But it is not difficult to see why the idea should have acquired pejorative connotations, given the various sorts of disapproval that the theatrical way of life has itself attracted over the centuries. People who play a part are potentially unreliable, because they have more than one face they can display. The theatre sets some limits to this unreliability by its own conventions (the stage is a space that provides us with some guarantees that what we are seeing is merely a performance, though a good performance will try to make us forget this fact). But actors encountered off the stage may have the ability to play a part without their audience being aware of what is going on. To play a part that does not reveal itself to be the playing of a part is a kind of deception, and hypocrisy in its pejorative sense always entails a deception of some kind.

However, this deception, once it is not bounded by the conventions of the stage, can take many different forms. The earliest extension of the term was from theatre to religion, and to public (and often highly theatrical) professions of religious faith by individuals who did not actually believe what they were saying.[6] The act here is an act of piety. But hypocrisy has also come to describe public statements of principle that do not coincide with an individual's private practices—indeed, this is what we most often mean by hypocrisy today, where the duplicity lies not in the concealment of one's personal beliefs but in the attempt to separate off one's personal behaviour from the standards that hold for everyone else (as in the phrase "It's one rule for them, and one rule for the rest of us"). But this is by no means the only way of thinking about hypocrisy. Other kinds of hypocritical deception include claims to knowledge that one lacks, claims to a consistency that one cannot sustain, claims to a loyalty that one does not possess, claims to an identity that one does not hold. A hypocrite is always putting on an act, but precisely because it is an act, hypocrisy can come in almost any form.

Because hypocrisy always involves an element of pretence, it might be said that all forms of hypocrisy are a kind of lie. But it certainly does not follow that all lies are therefore hypocritical. Some lies are simply lies—telling an untruth does not necessarily involve putting on an act, because an act involves the attempt to convey an impression that extends beyond the instant of the lie itself. A lie creates the immediate impression that one believes something that happens to be false, but that does not mean that one is not what one seems (indeed, people who have a well-deserved reputation for lying may by telling a lie be confirming exactly who they are). Hypocrisy turns on questions of character rather than simply coincidence with the truth. Likewise, though hypocrisy will involve some element of inconsistency, it is not true that inconsistency is itself evidence of hypocrisy. People often do, and often should, change their minds about how to act, or vary their principles depending on the situation they find themselves in. It is not hypocrisy to seek special treatment for one's own children—to arrive, say, in a crowded emergency room with an ailing child and demand immediate attention—though it may be unrealistic or even counter-productive to behave in this way; it is only hypocrisy if one has some prior commitment not to do so. It is the prior commitment not to be inconsistent, rather than the fact of inconsistency, that generates the conditions of hypocrisy. That, of course, is one reason why hypocrisy is such a problem for politicians.

Broadly speaking, then, hypocrisy involves the construction of a persona (another word, as we shall see in the next chapter, with its roots in the theatre) that generates some kind of false impression. Thus one consistent way of thinking about hypocrisy, and one that will recur throughout this book, is as the wearing of masks. But the idea of hypocrisy as mask-wearing leaves open the question of what it is that is being masked. It also leaves open the nature of the relationship between hypocrisy and bad behaviour, or vice. The most common way of thinking about hypocrisy is *as* a vice—that is, to take it for granted that it is always a bad thing to seek to conceal whom one really is. But another way of thinking about hypocrisy is as a coping mechanism for the problem of vice itself, in which case it may be that hypocrisy is not a vice at all. One way to cope with vice is to seek to conceal it, or to dress it up as something it is not. This sort of act—the passing off of vice as virtue—makes it possible to consider hypocrisy in two very different lights. From one perspective the act of concealment makes things worse—it simply piles vice on top of vice, which is why hypocrites are often seen as wickeder than people who are simply, and openly, bad. But from another perspective the concealment turns out to be a form of amelioration—it is, in Rochefoucauld's timeless phrase, "the tribute that vice pays to virtue." Hypocrites who pretend to be better than they really are could also be said to be better than they might be, because they are at least pretending to be good.

This does not exhaust the range of possible attitudes to vice of which hypocrisy may be a symptom. Sometimes individuals may find it necessary to pretend to be worse than they really are, for the sake of appearances. A democratic politician might feel the need to conceal some of her moral refinements of character for fear of appearing holier-than-thou and putting off the electorate—this is the curious democratic tribute that virtue occasionally plays to vice. Equally, it is possible for someone to believe that the categories of vice and virtue are meaningless in themselves, but nevertheless to wish to give the appearance of taking them seriously. This does not require dressing up vice as virtue; instead, it means dressing up morally arbitrary actions as though they had their own moral character, for better or for worse. As we shall see, the difference between concealing the fact of vice and concealing the fact that vice can be hard to distinguish from virtue turns out to be of deep political significance for a body of liberal rational thought that can be traced all the way back to Hobbes.

Finally, there remains the question of whether hypocrisy depends on the intention behind the action—that is, whether hypocrites need to know that what they are doing is hypocrisy for it to count as such. One view is that hypocrisy must involve the deliberate intention to deceive, and that the more deliberate the deception, the worse the hypocrite. But many people conceal aspects of their true natures not out of malice or from other designing motives, but simply because it is the easy option, and one that may even be required by basic standards of social conformity. It is common to see this latter sort of hypocrisy—if hypocrisy is what it is—as essentially benign. Indeed, it is possible to understand many socially useful conventions as hypocrisy of this kind—politeness, for example, is by definition a dressing up of one's true feelings (of course, it is possible to be motivated by a sincere desire not to hurt someone else's feelings, but if one is sincerely motivated by concern for another, one is being something more than merely polite).[7] It seems absurd to view good manners as on a par with the more malicious forms of hypocrisy. But precisely because hypocrisy can take these very different forms, it also follows that well-meaning hypocrisy may lack one of the qualities that is unavoidable among those individuals whose hypocrisy is of their own design: self-knowledge. Hypocrites who know what they are doing at least know that what they are doing is hypocrisy. But hypocrites who lack the sense that they are responsible for the part that they are playing can also lack a sense of responsibility for its consequences. In large groups, this absence of self-awareness can turn into a kind of collective self-deception. The least one can say for the nastier kind of hypocrites is that they are not self-deceived.

If hypocrisy is a kind of deception, therefore, it is still very important to distinguish within hypocritical behaviour between the different kinds of deception for which it allows: deliberate and inadvertent, personal and collective, self-deceptions and other-directed deceptions. And these distinctions are the ones that turn out to be of the greatest political significance in the story I will be telling in this book, of greater significance than broader distinctions between hypocrisy and

sincerity, or between truth-telling and lies. Once we acknowledge that some element of hypocrisy is inevitable in our political life, then it becomes self-defeating simply to try to guard
against it. Instead, what we need to know is what *sorts* of hypocrites we want our politicians to be, and in what sorts of com-
binations. Do we want them to be hypocrites like us, so that
they can understand us, or to be hypocrites of a different kind,
so that they can manage our hypocrisy? Do we want them to
be designing hypocrites, who at least know what they are doing, or do we want them to be more innocent than that? Do we
want them to expose each other's hypocrisy, or to ameliorate
it? These are the sorts of questions that concerned the authors
I will be discussing in this book, and in their attempts to answer them they tell us something about what it makes sense to
wish for in the hypocritical world of politics.

HYPOCRISY THEN AND NOW

I began this introduction by remarking that there is a lot of
hypocrisy about in contemporary politics. But it would be a
mistake to assume that there is *more* hypocrisy around than
ever before; there is just more political exposure, in an age of
24-hour news, which makes hypocrisy easier to find. It
may be that some of the hypocrisies of the contemporary
world are relatively new, and potentially very dangerous—
the hypocrisies surrounding the politics of global warming,
for example. Others, though, are all too familiar. As religion
returns as a central category of political and intellectual engagement, the question of the authenticity of the religious beliefs of both politicians and citizens is once again an issue, in
domestic politics (particularly in American presidential politics, a subject to which I will return in the final chapter) and in
the international arena (for example, in the exchanges between President Bush and President Ahmadinejad of Iran).[8] In
this book I will try to use history to provide some insight into

these current preoccupations, and to get a sense of the extent to which we have been here before.

Nevertheless, it is always a mistake to treat the history of ideas as a repository of timeless wisdom for us to draw on when we run out of ideas of our own, and to assume that past authors are talking directly to us, and wanting to help us with our particular difficulties.[9] The historical period covered by this book is a broad one, and there are inevitably substantial differences between the kinds of politics being considered by the different authors under discussion. Many aspects of our politics would be unrecognizable to them, just as much of their politics has become deeply unfamiliar to us. In the chapters that follow, I will highlight the different contexts in which the various authors were writing, and seek to identify some of the particular historical controversies with which they were concerned. Nevertheless, I do want to try to draw some broader lessons that cut across these differences of context. The final chapter of this book attempts to bring the story up-to-date, and to explore what the history of hypocrisy in liberal rationalist thought can tell us about politics at the beginning of the twenty-first century. The focus of this chapter is on American politics, because it is in the United States that many of the themes of this predominantly English story are now on most prominent display: hypocrisy and power, hypocrisy and virtue, hypocrisy and empire. This is not to claim that the United States has replaced the United Kingdom as the repository for much of the world's hypocrisy. Rather it is to note that the questions at the heart of this book tend to be most acute at the centres of power. It would perhaps be fair to say that hypocrisy is currently perceived by much of the rest of the world as the American vice, which from an American perspective simply serves to emphasise the far deeper hypocrisy of America's critics.[10]

I believe that the history covered in this book can help us with some of these arguments; if nothing else, it shows us that many of them have deep roots in the intellectual tradition from which our politics derives. I also think it can provide us with a sense of perspective on some of our more immediate concerns, including our endless worries about the way that politicians use empty words to conceal what they are up to. Here too we may discover that, for all our heightened awareness of and exposure to spin and counter-spin, the basic problem of fraudulent political language is nothing new, and it stands at the heart of the liberal tradition. Spin, like hypocrisy, is pretty repulsive encountered at first-hand, and it tends to make people angry, which is one good reason why it is sometimes helpful to approach it from a more tangential direction. In the great dance of hypocrisy and anti-hypocrisy that is democratic politics, it is all too easy to get wrapped up in the constant back-and-forth and to lose sight of the wider picture. Using a history stretching back over three hundred years to gain a sense of that wider picture can be hazardous—to ask, as I do in the final chapter, what a philosopher like Thomas Hobbes might think of a politician like Hillary Clinton is perhaps stretching the limits of the historical evidence. But it is nonetheless the central claim of this book that there is a line of thought about sincerity, hypocrisy, and lies in politics that runs all the way back from our own time to that of Hobbes.

Moreover, this line of thought shows much more obvious continuity with our current political concerns than does the body of writing that is usually taken to give us insights into the nature of political hypocrisy. Hypocrisy is a subject that lends itself to maxims—Rochefoucauld's *Maxims* is sometimes taken to be the definitive text on the subject—and it is to maxims that we often look to discover the timeless truth about what it is for a politician to dissemble and deceive. Truths tend to look more timeless when they come in neat little packages. But these maxims, almost by definition, are taken out of context (Rochefoucauld's book, for example, is about French courtly hypocrisy and its relationship to Jansenist philosophy). Of course, context isn't everything, and there may be times when philosophers wish to abstract away from the circumstances in which ideas were first generated. Indeed, there is a view—often associated with the philosopher and historian of ideas Leo Strauss, himself often associated with current strands of neo-conservative political thinking—that the deep truths about politics exist beyond and beneath immediate context, which serves merely as a mask for these timeless ideas. Straussians see a line of thought that runs from Plato through Machiavelli and Hobbes up to the present, containing certain truths about the need for political lies. The idea is that these truths can be passed on to those in the know, while remaining hidden from anyone who sees only the surface concerns in which they are dressed up. In this book, I have deliberately avoided getting bogged down in the fraught methodological disputes that swirl around Strauss and the history of ideas more generally. But in offering a story that begins with Hobbes, that separates Hobbes off from Machiavelli, and that takes the surface concerns of political philosophers seriously, I hope it is clear that I take a different view.

Certainly, I believe that the idea that political morality can be boiled down to a set of all-purpose maxims is itself an illusion. We are better off looking to the past for help with our present concerns if it exhibits a deep continuity with the political ideas and institutions that we have inherited, in all their complexity. Too many participants in the world of contemporary politics, with all its duplicity and double-dealing, think they need to read Machiavelli's *Prince*, or Sun Tzu's *Art of War*, or any one of the other hackneyed manuals of managerial *Realpolitik*, in order to understand the nature of the game they are playing. If they really wanted to understand the nature of the game they are playing, they would be better off starting with Hobbes's *Leviathan*.

⊷ 1 ⊶

HOBBES AND THE MASK OF POWER

Hypocrisy and sovereignty

Throughout his long writing career, Thomas Hobbes (1588–1679) displayed a striking consistency on his central political concerns: the scope and content of the laws of nature (which boil down to "the Fundamentall Law of Nature, which is *to seek Peace, and follow it*"); the unfettered power of the sovereign to decide on questions of "security" (including what was to count as a question of security); the threat posed to any lasting peace that comes from allowing individuals to exercise their private judgment on such questions; and the horrors of the civil war that might result.[1] But he also shifted his attitude in relation to a number of important issues: the role of rhetoric in political discourse, and its possible uses in the dissemination of "civil science"; the Erastian implications of the sovereign's supreme authority over all questions of religious doctrine; the function of the concept of representation in building up the idea of the state. All of these areas of his thought have been the subject of considerable scholarly interest in recent years, and I will come back to them.[2] But another matter on which Hobbes appears to have altered his position, and one which has attracted far less attention than these others, concerns the dangers of hypocrisy in political life. The apparent shift can be illustrated by looking at the scope

Hobbes gives to the problem of hypocrisy in three of his major works on politics: *De Cive* (1642), *Leviathan* (1651), and *Behemoth* (completed in 1668, but only published posthumously in 1682).[3] In *De Cive*, though Hobbes has things of importance to say about the need for sincerity on the part of the sovereign, he has nothing at all to say about hypocrisy; he does not seem to have considered it a problem. In *Behemoth*, by contrast, Hobbes is obsessed with hypocrisy: it is everywhere in that book, not least in its opening lines, which blame hypocrisy (something Hobbes characterises as "double iniquity") along with self-conceit ("double folly") for the catastrophe of the English civil war.[4] Between these two books comes *Leviathan*, where Hobbes is neither as sanguine about hypocrisy as he is in *De Cive*, nor as troubled by it as he is in *Behemoth*. Rather, it is here that he provides his clearest indications of where he thinks the limits of acceptable hypocrisy in political life might lie.

Before exploring what *Leviathan* has to say about the necessary hypocrisies of a civil existence, I want to discuss the wide gap between his treatment of the subject in the other two works. Part of the explanation for the different approaches taken in these two books lies in the kinds of books they are: *De Cive* is a work of philosophy (or "science" as Hobbes would call it); *Behemoth* is a history, designed to tell the story of, but more importantly to apportion the blame for, the civil war. It is much easier to be untroubled by hypocrisy when considering it philosophically, in the abstract or in the round; much harder, when thinking about an actual sequence of political events in which hypocrisy is on conspicuous display. Hobbes is by no means alone in this. David Hume (1711–1776), who was Hobbes's intellectual successor in so many ways, also has a split attitude to hypocrisy in his different modes of writing: calmly and clinically dismissive of its apparent wickedness in his philosophical oeuvre, and even more so in some of his private letters,[5] he is nevertheless deeply exercised by the hypocritical behaviour of some of the leading protagonists in his

History of England, particularly in the chapters that deal with the period 1640–1660. Above all, Hume was unable to resist harping on what he saw as the brazen hypocrisy of Oliver Cromwell, a subject to which we shall return.[6] This serves as an important reminder when thinking about the problem of hypocrisy: however much one might recognise its essential triviality as a vice, it is impossible to avoid its potential significance as a motor of political conflict, given its capacity to provoke people beyond measure. Hobbes and Hume also show how hard it is, even for the most clear-headed political thinkers, to keep their cool when it comes to the hypocrisy of people they thoroughly dislike or distrust (as Hume both disliked and distrusted what he knew of Cromwell's personality, even as he acknowledged the hold it gave him over his followers). *Behemoth* is perhaps Hobbes's angriest piece of political writing, and while it is true that the hypocrisy he sees at work among those who took their part against the king helps to fuel his anger, it is equally true that his anger serves to fuel his obsession with their hypocrisy. Hobbes would have us believe that the reason he cannot stand the Presbyterians (the primary focus of his fury in *Behemoth*) is because they are hypocrites; but it is just as likely that the reason he thinks they are hypocrites is because he simply cannot stand them.

Nevertheless, the difference between *De Cive* and *Behemoth* is not simply one of genre or provocation. It is also the case that Hobbes is making different kinds of arguments in the two books, though by no means incompatible ones. One way to capture this difference, and thereby to see the wider continuity in Hobbes's view of hypocrisy, is to look at what he has to say in *De Cive* about the role of sincerity and good intentions in political life. In a striking note at the end of chapter III, which follows his lengthy itemisation of the various laws of nature, Hobbes offers this summary: "Briefly, in a state of nature, Just and Unjust should be judged not from actions but from the intention and conscience of the agents."[7] In other words, a just action is one that is sincerely intended to be just.

18

One implication of this is Hobbes's famous contention that the laws of nature, though they bind internally (*in foro interno*), do not always do so externally (*in foro externo*)—that is, an action performed with the intention to seek peace is just, even if it does not accord with the outward observance of the laws of nature. So, for example, "to steal from Thieves" is, in Hobbes's terms, "to act reasonably," because it is consistent with a desire to seek peace: although natural law says we should behave towards others with consideration—"the fourth precept of nature is that *everyone should be considerate of others*"—treating thieves in this way would just encourage them.[8] But more importantly for our purposes here, in chapter III of *De Cive* Hobbes also draws the countervailing inference: that to act in accordance with the natural law without meaning to do so is *injustice*. "Laws which bind the conscience," he writes, "may be violated not only by an action contrary to them but also an action consonant with them, if the agent believes it to be contrary. For although the act itself is in accordance with the laws, his conscience is against them."[9] In other words, if you happen to do the right thing, that is not enough; unless you intended it to be the right thing, what you did was still wrong.

Is this emphasis on the inner motives of political actors a veiled warning against the dangers of hypocrisy in politics, of not being on the inside what you appear to be on the outside? I think not, for two reasons. First, the injunction against insincerity in effect only applies to those who remain subject in their actions to the laws of nature; that is, it only applies to sovereigns. On Hobbes's understanding of politics, sovereigns are the sole agents who persist in a state of nature; everyone else is subject to the civil laws.[10] So the scope of this injunction is in political terms pretty narrow. It is true that Hobbes allows for the possibility that all the members of a state could collectively form the sovereign body, in what he, and we, would call an absolute democracy. In that case, everyone would be part of the sovereign power. But it certainly would not follow that everyone would be living under the laws of nature. Individual citizens would still be subject to the civil law. Sovereignty would reside with the artificial body of the citizens, assembled together to act by majority rule. It is hard to know what it would mean to insist that an artificial body of this kind should be sincere in all it does. Part of the problem is that it is not clear what the inner life of the assembly would consist in—an assembly does not have thoughts of its own beyond those expressed in its collective decisions. But the deeper problem, certainly for Hobbes, is that sincerity is the last thing one would expect of the individual members of such a body, given the kind of politics they were bound to be engaged in. Democracies were places of posturing, rhetorical dissimulation, and grandstanding—"nothing but an aristocracy of orators," as he witheringly puts it in *The Elements of Law* (1640).[11] This was one of the lessons Hobbes learned from Thucydides, whose translator he had been. The reason monarchies were to be preferred to democracies is precisely because the institutions of popular rule made political sincerity practically impossible. Such sincerity could never therefore be a widespread value in Hobbes's view of the world.

The second point to make here is that Hobbes's claim about insincerity does not straightforwardly translate into an argument against hypocrisy. What Hobbes says is that an action which *happens* to coincide with natural law is unjust if it is nothing more than that: pure chance. For example (and this is my example, not Hobbes's, but it is probably the sort of thing he had in mind), if a sovereign ruler declares war on a rival power for entirely capricious reasons—boredom, avarice, cruelty—it may be that the result is to cement peaceful relations between the two states; perhaps the threatened state, terrified by the prospect of war against such a capricious opponent, surrenders straight away. Still, in Hobbes's terms, the act of aggression that produced this outcome is an unjust one, because the aggressor did not care about peace; mindless aggression is wrong whatever its consequences. But aggressive acts that produce peaceful outcomes are not strictly speaking hypocritical, because hypocrisy requires more than the coincidence of an ill-intended act with a desirable result. If I commit a burglary, say, with the result that its victim ends up better off than before thanks to an insurance payout, that does not make me a hypocrite. It might make me a fool, if my intention was to do the victim harm; but fools, like liars, are by no means always hypocrites. Hypocrisy is not about a mismatch between intentions and outcomes. Rather, hypocrisy is an ill-intended act *dressed up* to look like a well-intended one (or, very occasionally, a well-intended act dressed up to look like an ill-intended one).

Hobbes has nothing to say about this sort of hypocrisy in *De Cive*. Indeed, how sovereigns choose to dress up their actions in their relations with each other is not really an issue for Hobbes. They may well see the need to pretend to be abiding by the outward demands of the laws of nature even when they have no intention of doing so—signing a peace treaty they have no intention of keeping, for example. This would be no different than stealing from thieves, and may be the rational thing to do in the treacherous world of international relations, if it is the only way to achieve security. Certainly, Hobbes had no great expectations that sovereigns would be open with each other.[12] But sovereigns who sign a treaty they have no intention of keeping because they have no interest in peace or security are behaving unjustly, whether they try to conceal their real motives or not. Let me illustrate with a more recent example—was Hitler a hypocrite for signing Neville Chamberlain's little piece of paper at Munich in 1938, pledging himself to a peace he had no real intention of upholding? Not really, because he hardly made any efforts to conceal his underlying contempt for what he was doing. But on this account, that is not the point—what matters is that if Hitler wanted war for war's sake, then he was an unjust ruler in Hobbes's terms, whatever the outcome of his actions, and however he dressed them up. Hypocrisy is not the issue for Hobbes. The issue is justice.

But if hypocrisy is not the issue in the world of sovereigns, neither is it the issue in the world of subjects, for entirely opposite reasons. Intentions, which are all important under natural law, cease to count under civil law, because what matters is outward conformity to the will of the sovereign. Conscience, which may be the test of natural justice, is not the test of what Hobbes calls "right," i.e., justice under the laws of a commonwealth. Indeed, it is a large part of Hobbes's polemical purpose throughout his political writings to reconfigure how people understand the language of "conscience," so that they might come to accept that conscientious action simply means acting in accordance with the will of the sovereign.[13] A subject's internal beliefs or convictions are irrelevant here. So, Hobbes says in chapter XII of *De Cive*, "I am not acting unjustly if I go to war at the order of my commonwealth though I believe it is an unjust war; rather, I act unjustly if I refuse to go to war, claiming for myself the knowledge of what is just and unjust that belongs to a commonwealth."[14] And he goes on: "Those who teach that subjects commit sin in obeying a command of their Prince which seems to them unjust, hold an opinion which is not only false but one of those opinions which are inimical to civil obedience."[15] Under these conditions, subjects may have to do things that would fall under the broad heading of hypocrisy: they may have to perform actions, or profess beliefs, that are suggestive of an underlying set of convictions that they do not hold. So it is hardly surprising that Hobbes does not choose to categorise this sort of behaviour as hypocrisy, with all the pejorative connotations that the term brought with it (which was at least as true then as it is now). Instead, he wants to emphasise that the concealment of one's inner motives on the part of subjects may be not merely inevitable, but essential to the survival of the state.

THE HYPOCRISY OF DISOBEDIENCE

In the world of sovereigns and subjects described in *De Cive*, there is no real space for worrying about hypocrisy. It is more or less irrelevant for sovereigns, and more or less unavoidable for subjects, which is why in neither case does Hobbes label it as such. How then does hypocrisy become Hobbes's central worry by the time he writes *Behemoth*? The answer is that *Behemoth* is about a third category of political actor, beyond sovereigns and subjects: it is about the perpetrators of sedition. Of course, throughout his political writings, Hobbes has plenty of things to say about disobedient subjects, and how they should be dealt with. In *De Cive*, he categorises "the CRIME OF LÈSE-MAJESTÉ," which is punishable by death, as "the deed or word" by which citizens reveal that they no longer intend to obey their sovereign. "A citizen reveals such an intention by his action when he inflicts or attempts to inflict violence against those who hold the sovereign power or are carrying out their orders; such are traitors, Regicides, those who bear arms against their country or desert to the enemy in wartime. People reveal the same intention in words when they plainly deny that they or the other citizens are obligated to offer such obedience."[16] But the seditious individuals Hobbes is concerned with in *Behemoth* do not simply belong in one or other of these categories. The reason is that they did not reveal their intentions in so "plain" or self-evident a manner, certainly not until the civil war was well under way—indeed, Hobbes writes, some of them "did not challenge the sovereignty in plain terms, and by that name, till they had slain the king."[17] Instead, they sought to conceal their true intentions behind the mask of their supposed piety. It is this that made them hypocrites. What is more, it was their hypocrisy, Hobbes suspected, that enabled them to get away with it. "Who would think," he writes, "that such horrible designs as these could so easily and so long remain covered by the cloak of godliness?"[18]

23

This deliberate concealment is what makes hypocrisy "double iniquity" as Hobbes understands it: first there is the sin, then there is the sin of attempting to cover it up. It is also what distinguishes hypocrisy from what Hobbes calls the "double folly" of self-conceit, which constitutes a form of self-deception. For Hobbes, the ways in which human beings were capable of deceiving themselves were many and various. In *Leviathan*, his preoccupation is with "Vain-glory," which arises whenever men set store by the flattery of others, and glory in what it suggests about their own power and ability. What makes this glorying "vain" is that it does not survive the test of experience: "Vain-glorious men, such as estimate their sufficiency by the flattery of other men, or the fortune of some precedent action . . . are enclined to rash engaging; and in the approach of danger or difficulty, to retire if they can."[19] In other words, once they have to put up, the vainglorious tend to shut up: this is a sense of self that crumbles under pressure. But the enemies of the king did not crumble, despite the fact that they too had an absurdly puffed up sense of their own importance. As such, they suffered from a heightened form of self-conceit, which adds to the folly of setting store by the opinions of others the folly of acting consistently on those opinions. In *Behemoth*, Hobbes makes clear that vanity (as we might now understand it) was a large part of the problem in the political insurrection of the 1640s—the king's enemies tended to be men, Hobbes says, "such as had a great opinion of their sufficiency in politics, which they thought was not sufficiently taken notice of by the king."[20] But this was not simply vainglory, in that the illusion was not exposed by acting on it; rather, it was a form of self-deception, because the illusion generated the carapace of unjustified and ultimately self-destructive actions needed to sustain it. These were people who had come to believe their own publicity. Hypocrisy and self-conceit are thus two sides of the same coin: they are both the result of a gap between appearance and reality. What distinguishes them is that hypocrites are seeking to conceal the truth about themselves from other people, whereas those whose conceit has turned into self-deception are concealing the truth from themselves.

What, though, was it that the hypocrites who brought about civil war had been deliberately concealing about themselves? For Hobbes's audience, hypocrisy would have meant one sort of concealment in particular: hiding one's true religious beliefs—or more specifically, the lack of them—behind a façade of public religious observance. The problem is that it is not clear that this is the kind of hypocrisy that Hobbes wants to attack. Nor is it clear that he is in a position to attack it, since this was precisely the hypocrisy that Hobbes and his followers were themselves being accused of at the time he wrote *Behemoth*, on the basis of views he had spelled out in *Leviathan*, but had certainly not concealed in his earlier political writings, that subjects were not only allowed but obliged to put on an act of faith for the sake of conformity to the will of the sovereign. Had *Behemoth* been published when it was written—in 1668— its readers would undoubtedly have been struck by the fact that Hobbes, the arch-hypocrite, was now accusing others of hypocrisy (and part of the reason it could not get published is that this would have inflamed further Hobbes's already volatile political reputation). For Hobbes to accuse others of hypocrisy would have looked to his many critics like the ultimate act of hypocrisy in itself. Would they have been right?

This is not a straightforward question to answer. Part of the problem is that Hobbes is not entirely consistent about what should be considered culpable hypocrisy in *Behemoth*, and at times he gives his critics ammunition for supposing that he has changed his tune. For example, here he is on the plight of Charles's wife, Queen Henrietta Maria, at the hands of the king's Puritan enemies, who wished her to renounce her faith:

> The Queen was a Catholic by profession, and therefore could not but endeavour to do the Catholics all the good she could: she had not else been truly that which she professed to be. But

it seems they meant to force her to hypocrisy, being hypocrites themselves. Can any man think it a crime in a devout lady, of what sect soever, to seek the favour and benediction of that Church whereof she is a member?[21]

It is hard to imagine that Hobbes ever penned a less convincing passage than this one. For a start, one man who might think it a crime for someone, however devout, to place sincere religion above all other considerations was Hobbes himself, given his previously expressed views about the irrelevance of personal conviction when the security of the state is at issue. It could be argued that this case is an exception, because he is talking about the family of the sovereign, and the sincerity of sovereigns does trump other considerations. But of course, the queen herself was not sovereign, only the king was, and again it is central to Hobbes's political philosophy that sovereignty should never be divided. The one genuinely Hobbesian defence of the queen's religious practices would be that the king had permitted them, but that is not what he says here; instead, he says that the queen was sincere, and therefore had no choice. Finally, it is hard to make sense of Hobbes's claim that the reason her enemies wished to force her to renounce her faith is that they were hypocrites themselves. Why should hypocrites wish hypocrisy on others? Being hypocrites, they are free to confound their own principles as they wish, and act to their own best advantage; in this case that would surely have meant having the queen continue in her ostentatiously Catholic ways in order to stir up the people against the king.

So weak is Hobbes's argument at this point, that some explanation is needed. One possibility is that he simply lost sight of what he was doing: after all, even the greatest political philosophers can have their heads turned by a queen in revolutionary distress—compare Edmund Burke's notorious loss of judgment when it came to Marie Antoinette ("Never, never more, shall we behold that generous loyalty to rank and sex, that proud submission, that dignified obedience, that subordination of the heart, which kept alive, even in servitude itself, the spirit of an exalted freedom!" etc., etc.). But Hobbes is not Burke, and though he was an old man when he wrote *Behemoth* (1668 was his eightieth year), it is a lucid and deeply unsentimental book. Moreover, it is a dialogue, and the dialogue form allows for a certain distance to open up between an author's intentions and the words on the page. The words about the hypocrisy of the Queen's enemies are spoken in *Behemoth* by "*B*," who is second fiddle to "*A*," from whom "*B*" is receiving instruction about the causes of the war.[22] Thus a more likely explanation is that this passage is not to be taken entirely seriously; that it is just window-dressing, designed to act as cover for the book's more deliberately provocative passages (Queen Henrietta Maria was, after all, mother to Hobbes's then sovereign, Charles II, and she was still alive in 1668).

The view that this passage is not to be taken at face value also makes sense, given Hobbes's own position on hypocrisy: as someone who has previously shown himself unconcerned by it, he is free to affect concern when it suits him, since sincerity has no special premium for him. In fact, this was something that struck many contemporaries as an unavoidable consideration when thinking about how to read Hobbes—if he is serious about the justifiability of dissimulation, then there is no reason to take at face value the things he himself says, including what he has to say on this score. As Kinch Hoekstra has put it in an essay on Hobbes's attitude to the truth: "His justification of simulation and dissimulation was notorious among his early readers for destabilizing any attempt to interpret the intention of Hobbes and his followers."[23] Indeed, there is a paradox of a sort at work here, which became a recurring theme in the political thought of the period: advocates of hypocrisy may find it hard to be taken seriously, because if they really believe what they say, then it serves to render what they say hard to believe.[24]

But this does not mean that nothing Hobbes has to say about hypocrisy is reliable, nor that his underlying political message is unclear. Hobbes's primary concern in *Behemoth*, as elsewhere in his writings, is to distinguish between the kinds of duplicity that matter and the kinds of duplicity that do not. For these purposes, the issue of the queen's devoutness of faith is indeed just a sideshow. "*A*," the lead voice in the dialogue, does not bother with it—his only concern is what this antipathy towards the queen's religion revealed about the intentions of the king's enemies (essentially, it showed that they wished to tar the king with the brush of the queen's "Popery," to such an extent "that some of them did not stick to say openly, that the King was governed by her").[25] On the central question of whether the state should worry about individuals who merely pretended to believe what they professed to believe, Hobbes's position does not shift in *Behemoth*—what other people called hypocrisy (i.e., pretended religious faith) was not his concern. He held to the view that it was not the state's business, nor anyone else's, to pry into the realm of personal faith, simply in order to highlight a mismatch between outward behaviour and what may lie in someone's heart. What's more, it would be futile. As he says in *Behemoth*, "Hypocrisy hath this great prerogative above other sins, that it cannot be accused [i.e., proved]."[26] More importantly still, he accepts that this feature of hypocrisy cuts both ways. If it does not make sense to question whether those who obey the law really believe what they are required to profess, neither does it make sense to ask whether religious firebrands and other dissenters who challenged the authority of the king really believed that they were acting on God's instruction. That's what they said—that, as Hobbes puts it, what they preached was "as they thought agreeable to God's revealed will in the Scriptures." And he goes on: "How can any man prove they thought otherwise?"[27]

If religious hypocrisy was not really the issue for Hobbes in *Behemoth*, what is more striking about the account he gives is his acknowledgment that it was not really the issue for the firebrands either. He makes this clear in an extended passage in which he discusses how Presbyterian preachers sought to stay on the right side of their congregations. Hobbes highlights their readiness to tolerate merely the outward conformity to respectable behaviour. They were careful in their sermons not to inveigh against what he calls "the lucrative vices": "such as are feigning, lying, cozening, hypocrisy or other uncharitableness, except want of charity to their pastors or to the faithful; which was a great ease to the generality of citizens and the inhabitants of market-towns, and no little profit to themselves."[28] This was pure politics on the preachers' part—they were aware of how important it was to retain the support of their public, both moral and financial, and therefore they did nothing that might jeopardise that support. Indeed, they were behaving in just the astute way that Hobbes believed anyone who was serious about power ought to behave—tough on the primary loyalties of their congregations, but lax about their private failings. The only difference, of course, was that the sole person Hobbes believed should be behaving in this way was the sovereign.

Yet it was precisely this astuteness on the part of the Presbyterian pastors that revealed the true nature of their hypocrisy, because it demonstrated that they knew what they were doing. By constructing an image for themselves that furthered their political ambitions, the Puritan leaders showed that they understood the nature of politics perfectly well. The clichéd view of Puritan hypocrisy (particularly of Puritan sexual hypocrisy) that lingers to this day is that it meant imposing impossibly high standards of public morality, which no one could possibly meet, including the Puritans themselves. What is so distinctive about Hobbes's account is his view that they actually set quite low standards (except, perhaps, in sexual matters, which Hobbes does not mention), both for themselves and others, and it was *this* that confirmed their hypocrisy, because it revealed that they knew exactly what they were about; they were not self-deceived.

In other words, these were consummate political operators. What made them hypocrites was that they had to cloak their political understanding behind a façade of political naivety. They had to present themselves as innocent of the implications of the doctrines of subversion that they preached. "You may count this among their artifices," Hobbes writes, "to make the people believe they were oppressed by the King, or perhaps the bishops, or both."[29] Did they themselves believe what they preached, that the king and/or the bishops were oppressors? Who can say, since it is impossible to be certain what anyone truly believes. Perhaps they did believe it in their hearts. What mattered was that even if they did believe it, they also ought to have known that they could not act on it, any more than a sincere atheist could act on his atheism. The hypocrisy of the Presbyterians (or as Hobbes calls it here, their "artifice") lay not in concealing their true feelings about the king or the bishops, but in concealing the fact that they must have known what such feelings were really worth.

COLOURING AND CLOAKING

One way of bringing out the wider implications of what Hobbes is saying here about political hypocrisy is to look away from *Behemoth*, and to turn instead to his treatment throughout his writings of the problem of *paradiastole*, or what Quentin Skinner has called "rhetorical redescription." Rhetorical redescription is the practice of deploying terms of moral approval to describe certain types of actions in order to present them in a more favourable light (or alternatively terms of disapproval, in order to present them unfavourably). So, for example, to call an action courageous is not merely to describe it but to commend it; and to call the same action foolhardy is to condemn it; the result is that in both cases, though it remains the same action, it is the descriptive epithet that determines its character.

In the Renaissance and early modern literature in which this practice is discussed, there are two main metaphors used to capture what is being attempted. The first talks about concealing vices under the mantle of virtues—as one sixteenth-century poet put it, "[using] the nearest virtue to cloak away the vice."[30] These are what Skinner calls "the metaphors of masking and concealment," and clearly they stand close to the idea of hypocrisy, which has always had some connection with the business of hiding behind a mask. By contrast, the other metaphor used for rhetorical redescription is that of "colour," or the "colouring" of an action, meaning to give it a particular moral hue. It is true that this can be understood as another version of masking—for example, by painting an action, or indeed a face, to hide its true appearance—and some early modern definitions of hypocrisy run the ideas of colouring and cloaking together (an *OED* source from 1555 speaks of "no coulor nor cloked hipocrisie"). But the metaphors of cloaking and colouring are not necessarily interchangeable. An alternative way to think of "colouring" is as the giving of a moral glow to something that is otherwise morally arbitrary or colourless. No vices are being hidden here, because there is nothing to hide (the canvas is effectively blank); rather, the redescription is designed to introduce moral criteria where previously there were none.

Of these two ways of conceiving the problem of *paradiastole*, Hobbes's primary concern is clearly with the second, not the first—with colouring, not cloaking. When he repeatedly points out, as he does across his political writings, the dangers of words being used in effect at random to signify either the approval or the disapproval of certain actions, he is not worried that as a result some vices will remain concealed. In the arbitrary world of the state of nature as Hobbes understands it (the celebrated "war of all against all"), there are no vices to hide; instead, there is simply the endless attempt by individuals to redescribe what they happen to prefer as virtue, and what others happen to prefer as vice. As Hobbes puts it in *Leviathan*: "For one man calleth Wisdome, what another calleth feare; and one cruelty, what another justice . . . [and so on]. Therefore such names can never be the true ground of any ratiocination."[31] It hardly makes sense to call this hypocrisy, since it is entirely natural to behave in this way when there are no fixed standards. What is needed to escape this arbitrary existence is a sovereign to fix the meaning of such words, and any other terms over which men might disagree, by the wholly artificial determination of his political authority.

Yet there is still a clear sense in which *paradiastole* understood as the colouring of morally arbitrary actions counts as a form of concealment in Hobbes's terms. One way to illustrate why this is so is to consider how Hobbes uses morally loaded terms in his own writing to highlight their relative arbitrariness, and thereby expose their essential superficiality. Take, for example, a word like "conscience," which Hobbes deploys in the highly unusual sense of meaning a willingness to act in conformity with the judgment of one's sovereign (see above). Clearly, Hobbes is taking issue with all those who use the language of conscience to ground the right of an individual to ignore sovereign judgments of which they happen to disapprove. But so unusual is Hobbes's understanding of the term that it seems hard to believe that this is what he thinks it really means—if "conscience" is just outward conformity, then surely it doesn't mean anything at all? And that, of course, is Hobbes's point. He is not trying to redefine conscience so much as show that it is just a word—the moral substance of an action is determined by its political character as obedience or disobedience, not by the label that you put on it. In Skinner's terms, what Hobbes is doing is "satirising" those who put too much weight on a word like conscience, and he does so by sticking the label onto something entirely unfamiliar while indicating that nothing about it has really changed.

He does the same with perhaps the most contested term in the entire modern political lexicon—"democracy."[32] Hobbes uses the language of democracy in his own writing to describe what might otherwise be understood as arbitrary rule—that is, he treats democratic regimes as on a par with monarchies and aristocracies in their reliance on absolute sovereign power in order to function successfully. This has led some commentators to suppose that Hobbes himself can be understood as a kind of democrat.[33] But it is much more plausible to see him as suggesting that it is a mistake to overvalue such labels as "democracy," since the essential character of the regimes they describe is unaffected by the terms being used. Indeed, in *De Cive* he goes so far as to imply that the words associated with democracy and monarchy are more or less interchangeable: as he puts it, in a monarchy "(though it may seem a paradox) the *King* is the *people*."[34] His point is that the more usual democratic claim that "the *people* is *king*" is essentially empty—the word that comes first does not matter; what matters is that the underlying political reality remains unaltered. In this sense, Hobbes is showing that words like "conscience" and "democracy" are just colour. But he is also showing how that colour can be used to conceal certain basic political truths, if the word is taken to be the substance of the practice of which it is merely a gloss. This can be understood as *paradiastole*, but not in the sense that Hobbes is practising rhetorical redescription; rather, he is exposing it, and thereby seeking to render it redundant.[35] Hobbes is trying to prevent colourful political language from being used to mask political reality. He does so by showing that a mask is all that it is.

Here, then, is the point at which the business of colouring links to the hypocritical practice of cloaking. And this is what Hobbes was trying to expose in *Behemoth*. If the moral arbitrariness of the state of nature produces the need for sovereign power, then the need for that power is the one thing that no one should try to hide behind the colourful language of vice and virtue. For the one thing that colour terms might mask is the fact of moral arbitrariness itself, i.e., the fact that there are no virtues and vices, except on the say-so of the sovereign. It was colouring of this kind that generated the political hypocrisy of the 1640s as Hobbes saw it. Throughout *Behemoth* he uses the term "colour" to describe the attempts by the parliamentarians to justify their disobedience to the king. To seek to colour the king's actions as unjust or cruel was hypocritical because it deliberately sought to hide the fact that without the king, there would be no such thing as injustice or cruelty, because the words would lack meaning. Another way to put this is to say that for Hobbes there is only one certain virtue in a morally arbitrary world, that of seeking peace, which means obeying the law. And there is only one vice, which is to deny that justice means obeying the law. Therefore, there is only one kind of hypocrisy that matters— concealing the vice of sedition behind the language of godliness, piety, and other supposed virtues. Hobbes is not objecting to people who try to pass off political disobedience as political obedience, since in Hobbes's terms you cannot really fake political obedience—the outward show is the essence of the act. Instead, he is objecting to those who seek to pass off political disobedience as obedience to a set of higher values than mere politics, given that without mere politics obedience has no lasting value at all.

Hobbes believed that in the period leading up to civil war, the vice of disobedience was concealed behind the mask of patriotism as well that of piety: this was a time, as he puts it at the beginning of *Behemoth*, when "disobedient persons [were] considered the best patriots."[36] Patriotism, in this sense, is just another colour term for Hobbes, one that can be used by hypocrites to hide the truth about politics. But the climate that successfully sustained its hold on the public imagination was one of collective self-deception—"the people," Hobbes goes on to insist, "were corrupted generally."[37] The evidence for the strength of the delusion is that so many of them were willing to fight and die on the parliamentary side for the cause of cod patriotism: they did not run away when they realised that they had been duped by fine words. Yet Hobbes remained convinced that there was a core of hypocrisy at the heart of the madness. It is one of the themes of *Behemoth* that hypocrisy and self-deception can feed off each other, so that the same individuals who use language to gloss reality can lose sight of the fact that the language is just a gloss. Nevertheless, some of those ultimately responsible for the war understood exactly what they were doing—they knew it was vice they were trying to conceal, which is why they were at such pains to conceal it. The best evidence for this is that before the war began they played the game of rhetorical redescription for all it was worth; but after the conflict came out in the open, they dropped the pretence that they were ignorant of the basic rules of politics. Some of them became the pure politicians they had been, but had been pretending not to be, all along.

Thus once Parliament was in a position to set its own arbitrary terms to the king, then it was done, as Hobbes himself says, with "plain-dealing and without hypocrisy."[38] Things were called by their proper names: power was power, and obedience, obedience. Parliament told the king what they wanted, and they expected him to obey. The king was informed that "treason cannot be committed against his person, otherwise than as he is entrusted with the kingdom and discharges that trust; and that they [Parliament] have a power to judge whether he shall have discharged this trust or not"; moreover, "they [Parliament] may dispose of the king when they will."[39] In the end, when the king refused to comply, they did indeed dispose of him (though the Presbyterians, being the ultimate hypocrites, opposed the execution; it was Cromwell who had to carry it through, which is something that I will pick up on in the chapters that follow, where I consider various responses to the vexed question of Cromwell's own hypocrisy). By killing the king the parliamentarians reaped the consequences of their hypocrisy and self-deception. But at the point when they did so, they ceased to be either hypocrites or self-deceived.

HYPOCRITES AND PERSONS

I want to consider now the question of how this conception of political hypocrisy relates to the wider argument I have only touched on to this point: the account Hobbes gives in *Leviathan* of the character and purposes of sovereign power. Overall, what Hobbes says in *Leviathan* about hypocrisy and sincerity is broadly consistent with the themes I have drawn on already. He makes clear that it is not the business of the commonwealth to reconcile the public statements of belief made by individuals with their private convictions; when it comes to this form of concealment, all a sovereign need concern himself with is outward conformity to the law. As Hobbes says in his discussion of excommunication in chapter 42 of *Leviathan*: "A true and unfeigned Christian is not liable to Excommunication: Nor he also that is a professed Christian, till his Hypocrisy appear in his manners; that is, till his behaviour bee contrary to the law of his Soveraign."[40] Professing religion without believing is characterised here as hypocrisy; but Hobbes's whole point is that it is nonetheless harmless on this account, and of no account, unless it leads to political dissent. Nowhere could it be clearer that Hobbes does not think anything can be decided simply by calling something hypocrisy—everything depends on what sort of hypocrisy it is. Hobbes was particularly keen to press this point in *Leviathan* because the book was published at a time when England was subject to the government of the new parliamentary regime, and Hobbes was adamant that politics should continue to take priority over religion on all doctrinal and ecclesiastical questions. As various commentators have pointed out, this strict Erastianism was a large part of what Hobbes wanted to convey in *Leviathan* (indeed, it was one of the reasons he wrote the book rather than simply producing an English translation of *De Cive*): regime change gave him an opportunity to emphasise that state religion in England did not mean Anglicanism, but instead whatever the state determined it to be.[41] All that loyal subjects, even convinced Anglicans, had to do was obey.

The determination of the new regime to impose its will on questions of religion—and the fact, as Hobbes welcomed at the time, that they appeared to favour a policy of Independency, or toleration—meant that the earlier hypocrisy of some of its leading lights also ceased to matter. They were sovereign now, and what counted was simply that they had a will to impose. But in *Leviathan*, Hobbes reiterated the point that as sovereign their sincerity still mattered. Sovereigns ought to seek peace sincerely, and also to advertise their sincerity, particularly in matters of religion. This did not mean that they should let people know what they really believed. Rather, it meant that they should make it plain that they were sincere about the relationship between religious conformity and peace. "Power," Hobbes states towards the end of *Leviathan*, "is preserved by the same virtues by which it is acquired; that is to say, by Wisdome, Humility, Clearnesse of Doctrine, and sincerity of Conversation; and not by suppression of the Naturall Sciences, and of the Morality of Natural Reason; nor by obscure Language; nor by Arrogating to themselves more Knowledge than they make appear; nor by Pious Frauds, nor by such other faults, as in the Pastors of Gods Church are not only Faults, but scandals."[42] Moreover, among the pastors of God's Church who stray into politics, these things are not only scandals; they are also the worst kind of hypocrisy, because, as Hobbes says, "none should know this better than they."[43]

But if pious frauds in politics are hypocrisy, it is because of the piety, not because of the fraud. Hobbes has no problem in *Leviathan*, any more than elsewhere in his work, with political fraud *per se*. Sovereigns must be prepared to dissemble, cheat, and lie if necessary, in order to do what they think best for their own security, and the security of their state. They may even lie about religion—Hobbes admired "the First Founders, and Legislators of commonwealths amongst the Gentiles," who pretended that their authority came from God, and who made sure "that the same things were displeasing to the Gods, which were forbidden by the laws."[44] This was sincerely done, because it was in the cause of "keeping the people in obedience, and peace."[45] What was intolerable was to dress up any deceptions in the language of some higher virtue—some "piety"—that muddied the necessary connection between the prerogatives of the sovereign and natural justice. In other words, the only intolerable hypocrisy for Hobbes is hypocrisy about the basic principles of political life itself.

What Hobbes has to say about the imperatives of sincerity in *Leviathan* is therefore quite consistent with the more general themes of deception and dissimulation that run not just through that work but throughout Hobbes's life.[46] Hobbes never doubted that in politics, it may be necessary to conceal the truth—he was, in this respect, a lifelong student of Tacitus.[47] He knew perfectly well that no one should ever expect to be entirely open, least of all the sovereign. But there is one further point to add. In *Leviathan*, Hobbes includes a chapter which has no equivalent in *De Cive*, on the role of representation in politics. The chapter is called "Of PERSONS, AUTHORS, and *things Personated*," and in it Hobbes connects the idea of representation, through the language of "personation," to the theatrical practice of wearing a mask. As he puts it, "*Persona* in latine signifies the disguise, or outward appearance of a man, counterfeited on the Stage; and sometimes more particularly that part of it, which disguiseth the face, as a Mask or Vizard."[48]

Representation is the extension of this practice into the world of politics. The sovereign representative, in personating the commonwealth, puts on a kind of mask: this is the mask of power. After all, to be sovereign is inevitably to engage in a kind of disguise: it is a wholly artificial performance, in which human beings play the part of "mortall gods" while retaining their underlying natural capacities. To be sovereign is to be no different than the rest of us, yet to be utterly different, because of the power sovereigns wield. This remains one of the central insights of modern politics, and the steady advance of democracy has done nothing to diminish its significance. To rule in a modern state is by definition to play a kind of double role—that of the everyman who is also the only person with real power. Throughout *Leviathan*, Hobbes is at pains to spell out how important it is to sustain this performance, and not to collapse it. Sovereigns must preserve the appearance of power— "Reputation of power," as Hobbes says, "is Power"—yet must keep their private identities separate, and must behave in a way that is in keeping with the office they hold.[49] But because all personality—whether natural or artificial—is a mask for Hobbes, everyone else has a part to play in the life of the state as well. Being possessed of "natural" personality in Hobbes's terms does not mean being genuinely or truly oneself, as we might understand the idea today. It simply means that individuals are personally responsible for whatever they say and do— i.e., that responsibility attaches to people "naturally" rather than "artificially"—which is why it is so important that each individual should construct a persona that can survive anything the world might throw at it. Therefore, natural persons must also put on the appearance that best suits their role as subjects— individual subjects have an obligation, not to be themselves, but to be a civilly sustainable version of themselves. Politics, as laid out by Hobbes in *Leviathan*, is one giant act.

So we have two terms—*person* and *hypocrite*—both of which have their roots in the theatre, and both of which denote a kind of mask-wearing. But one is essential to political life, and the other is fatal for it. How should we distinguish them? The answer, I think, comes from one further definition of hypocrisy Hobbes offers in *Leviathan*, this time drawn from the Bible. In chapter 44, when attacking those who peddle "daemonology" and other superstitions to scare the public, he refers to them as "such as speak lies in Hypocrisie (or as it is in the originall, 1 *Timothy* 4.1, 2. *of those that play the part of lyars*) *with a seared conscience*, that is, contrary to their own knowledge."[50] To be a hypocrite, then, is to act against your own knowledge, but it is also to play the part of a liar. In some ways, this is an unfortunate formulation, and can't be exactly what Hobbes means, because he is not talking about people *pretending* to be liars (this is by no means impossible—honest people may sometimes need to pretend to be dishonest in order to get their way—but this sort of double bluff is not at all what Hobbes has in mind here).[51] Instead, he means people who play lying parts, or play their parts *as* liars. Perhaps the most accurate, if also the ugliest, way to put it is that Hobbes is talking about people who play their parts *lyingly*. After all, one can play a part honestly, or play it falsely. An honest performance is one that is in keeping with the knowledge that lies behind it, including the knowledge that it is a performance, and the rules that govern that performance. To play a part as a liar is to act in a way that makes a mockery of the performance itself.

Hobbes wanted sovereigns and subjects to play their parts truthfully. This did not mean that he thought they should always, or even often, tell the truth about themselves. Sovereigns might lie, deceive, and dissemble, which was entirely as it should be, so long as it was done in the proper spirit, that is, in the pursuit of peace. Equally, loyal subjects should be willing to conceal the truth about themselves in their public professions of faith if to do otherwise would be to undermine the foundations of civil order. It is not hypocrisy to pretend to be something one is not; indeed, in certain circumstances, that is the definition of loyalty. You do not have to believe in what the sovereign requires you to do; you just have to mean it when you do it—that is, say it as though you mean it—which is different. Of course, it is easier to say something as though you mean it if you also happen to believe in what you are saying, and it seems likely that Hobbes hoped that the gap between these two positions would close over time. In a state successfully organised on Hobbesian principles, subjects ought to become progressively freer to speak the truth as they see it, as sovereigns are able to rely more and more on their subjects' innate understanding of the principles of obedience.[52] But the attainment of that level of understanding, Hobbes knew, would take time. In the interim, everyone is liable to face some choices between what they believe and what they are required to do. The beginning of political wisdom, for Hobbes, was to see that this was no choice at all.

HOBBES, HYPOCRISY, AND MODERN POLITICS

Let me turn, finally, to the issue I raised in the introduction—the question of whether a thinker like Hobbes has anything to teach us about the nature of political hypocrisy today. There is no question from the account I have given here that Hobbes was essentially an anti-hypocrite—that is, when he talks explicitly about hypocrisy in his writings, and calls it by name, it is invariably to condemn it. Ruth Grant is therefore correct when she suggests that Hobbes was both unwilling and unable to embrace political hypocrisy in the manner of a thinker like, say, Machiavelli. But this does not mean that he was unaware of or unable to deal with the inevitable hypocrisies of a political existence—Grant is entirely wrong about that. Rather, Hobbes knew just how important it was to distinguish between different kinds of hypocrisy, to be relatively sparing in how one used the term, and to tolerate all sorts of behaviour that would count as hypocritical on a conventional understanding of it. Hobbes was at pains not to set the bar for sincerity too high, which would let in the most corrosive forms of hypocrisy through the back door. But he also believed that some forms of hypocrisy, unchecked, would render political life impossible. He therefore offers a model for how to deal with the problem of hypocrisy in modern politics (what one might call the "Shklar" problem): what is needed is to tread carefully, to avoid lumping all hypocrisies together, and to decide which are the ones that are worth worrying about. Hobbes does not deny the role that hypocrisy can play in generating political conflict, and he is not immune to its capacity to stir up irrational antipathies. But his work as a whole is an attempt to put hypocrisy, and its attendant emotions, in their proper place.

Yet it does not follow from this that Hobbes provides a way of thinking about hypocrisy than can translate straightforwardly into the politics of today. Two factors in particular serve to render the gap between Hobbes's politics and our own very difficult to bridge. First, though religion is an important factor in contemporary politics, it lacks the absolute centrality it possessed in Hobbes's time. One sign of this is that we don't tend to think of political hypocrisy primarily in religious terms, so that Hobbes's attempt to rescue the language of hypocrisy from an unthinking identification with religious insincerity makes little sense now. We do not need that rescue act. We tend unthinkingly to associate hypocrisy with the double standards of people who do not practice what they preach, and Hobbes is not going to rescue us from that, because it was not his primary concern. Second, Hobbes's views about the one sort of hypocrisy that he believed was worth worrying about derive from his insistence on the supreme virtue of political obedience. This does not sit well with the liberal democratic presupposition in favour of contestation and dissent. It would be hard to make a convincing case now for seeing the exercise of private judgment as the ultimate vice. For most people, finding a public space for conflicting private judgments to be heard constitutes the essence of the liberal way of life. This is one reason why few contemporary liberal political thinkers have much time for Hobbes.

Nevertheless, Hobbes's views on hypocrisy may still have something to teach us. Hobbes's political thought rests on an assumption of human equality, which continues to underlie most forms of modern politics, including our own. Sovereigns must base their power on what they have in common with their subjects, and they cannot rely on external sources of authority, divine or otherwise, to tell them what to do. At the same time, the fact of their power serves to separate them out entirely from their subjects, and make them very different sorts of persons from the people they rule. For Hobbes, the starkest reminder of this difference is that sovereigns should act according to their own conscience, while their subjects should simply abandon the idea that they have a conscience of their own. We have moved a long way from this position. But what we have not moved away from is the fact that any politics founded on the idea of equality will produce politicians who have to be of a type with the people they rule, and yet recognisably different, given the fact that they also have to rule them. All political leaders in these circumstances will need to put on the appropriate mask that allows them to sustain this tricky double act. They need to be familiar enough so that we let them rule us, but no so familiar that we cease to regard what they do as rule.

In these circumstances, Hobbes believed it was absurd to fixate on hypocrisy, since all politics will be a kind of act. But what it did make sense to worry about were the kinds of double standards that might render the entire performance of self-justifying political power unsustainable. In his terms, that meant in particular sovereigns who downplayed the value of their own sincerity, or subjects who overplayed the value of theirs. But his terms are not our terms. We do not think that we should put all our trust in the sincerity of our political rulers, because we believe that the judgments of subjects have value in their own right. We are liberal democrats, and Hobbes was not. As a result, we should have our own worries about the sort of hypocrisy that might render our preferred form of politics unsustainable. Sincerity and hypocrisy have no inherent value in their own terms; they only have value in so far as they suit the form of politics that they are required to sustain. In our politics, hypocrisy abounds, whereas sincerity is in short supply. One possible response to this is to argue for more sincerity, in order to make politics and politicians trustworthy again. But if our politics is hypocritical in its very nature, then calls for more sincerity are themselves hypocritical, and may threaten the entire charade that we, as liberal democrats, are committed to uphold. This will be a theme of the chapters that follow, and I will return to it in the final chapter, when I consider what value, if any, it makes sense to put on the sincerity of democratic politicians today. If there is an enduring lesson from Hobbes on hypocrisy, it is this: it does not matter whether or not our politicians are all wearing masks, if that is what is needed to make our form of politics work. What does matter is if people are hypocritical about *that*.

—+— 2 —+—

MANDEVILLE AND THE VIRTUES OF VICE

Faking virtue

In the history of early modern political thought, three men in particular were thought by their scandalised reading publics to be devils, or as Hobbes might put it, to be playing the devil's part. They were Machiavelli, Hobbes himself, and the author whose literal-minded contemporaries were put on notice of his diabolical intentions just by his name, Bernard Mandeville (1670–1733)—the "Man-devil" as he came to be known. Mandeville's *The Fable of the Bees* (first published in 1714, but only really noticed after a second edition in 1723, at which point it became a major scandal) was for much of the eighteenth century the most notoriously wicked book of them all, wickeder than *Leviathan*, wickeder even than *The Prince*. As John Wesley wrote in his journal in 1756: "Till now I imagined there had never appeared in the world such a book as the works of Machiavel. But de Mandevil goes far beyond it."[1] What connected these writers in the public mind, and gave them their diabolical reputations, was specifically their attitude to hypocrisy, and their apparent willingness to sanction the dissimulation of godless vice behind a mask of pious virtue. Yet when one looks at what they actually had to say about hypocrisy in their writings, rather than simply at their reputations, then the connection between them is much harder to discern.

Machiavelli was not particularly bothered about hypocrisy. It did not feature as a separate category of deception in his writings—dissimulation is an essential part of the armoury of the prince, but it does not acquire a particular moral character simply by being dissimulation; its moral character depends entirely on whether or not it is successfully achieved. Hobbes, as we have seen, did believe that hypocrisy retained its own distinctive character—it was still "double iniquity"—which is why he was at such pains to limit the social practices to which the term could reasonably be applied. Only Mandeville can be said to have actively celebrated certain forms of hypocrisy in his work, using the term itself in relation to social practices of which he clearly approved. That is what made him an especially monstrous figure for his outraged critics. But it also makes him a rather implausible candidate for playing the devil's part, since the devil would never have been so open about what he was up to. Hypocrisy depends for its deleterious effects on its remaining unexposed. Mandeville's name should really have been a clue—the devil would hardly have chosen someone with whom he shared a name to do his dirty work. Playing the devil's part means providing the devil with a name to hide behind, which is why Machiavelli—Old Nick—has always been a much more plausible candidate for that role.

In truth, there is not much that unites Machiavelli with Hobbes and Mandeville, beyond their obvious capacity to shock readers on the lookout for shocks of a particular kind. Neither Hobbes nor Mandeville were Machiavellians in any meaningful sense. But if one leaves Machiavelli out of it, along with the devil, there is a great deal that unites Mandeville with Hobbes. Mandeville, who was born in Holland in 1670 and trained there as a doctor before moving to settle in London in the mid-1690s, was unquestionably a Hobbesian, both as part of his Dutch heritage (Hobbes's influence in the Dutch

Republic was extensive at the time of Mandeville's intellectual formation) and on his own account. Many other writers than Hobbes went into making up Mandeville's distinctive world-view (including the great French student of courtly hypocrisy, La Rochefoucauld, along with various medical writers, Dutch humanists, and assorted fabulists stretching back to Aesop). Nonetheless, Hobbes's influence was as great as any of them. What Mandeville shares with Hobbes are his scepticism, his egoism, his absolute insistence on sovereignty as the basis for all forms of political association ("no form of government can subsist without an arbitrary sovereignty," Mandeville wrote in 1720, though it might as well have been Hobbes talking), and his recognition of the essential theatricality of the modern forms of social existence.[2] He also shares with Hobbes a distinctive approach to the problem of hypocrisy in politics, notwithstanding the far wider role that the term itself plays in Mandeville's thought. Though Mandeville appears at various points to be celebrating hypocrisy in his writings, he is also, at many others, deeply censorious about it. In fact, his attitude to hypocrisy is split, between a recognition of its frequently beneficial social effects, and a desire to circumscribe the potentially baneful consequences if hypocrisy is allowed to run uncontrolled through the sphere of politics. In this, he echoes Hobbes as well.

Where Mandeville goes beyond Hobbes is in the sharpness of the distinction he draws between the ubiquitous social practice of hypocrisy, and hypocrisy *about* that practice; that is, between hypocrisy and hypocrisy about hypocrisy itself. In what follows I will characterise this as the difference between first-order and second-order hypocrisy, though that is not exactly how Mandeville would put it (one of the joys of Mandeville's prose is that he avoids technical language wherever possible). Nevertheless, I believe a distinction of this kind plays a crucial role in Mandeville's thought, and it raises important political questions whose significance we can still recognise, despite the essential unfamiliarity of the terms of the moral argument from which they emerge. In particular, it raises questions about the hypocrisy of politicians, and whether we should think of it as being, and whether we should want it to be, of the first-order or the second-order kind. To make sense of these questions, it is necessary to begin by saying something about Mandeville's moral philosophy, in order to explain how the distinction between first- and second-order hypocrisy arises in the first place.

Perhaps the best place to start is another point of overlap between Mandeville and Hobbes: their shared recognition of the role that vanity plays in human affairs, and its capacity to trump reason unless properly handled. As Mandeville puts it in *The Fable of the Bees*: "If Reason in Man was of equal weight with his Pride, he would never be pleas'd with Praises, which he is conscious he don't deserve."[3] Where Mandeville and Hobbes differ is in the inference they draw from this fact. For Hobbes, it was essential to control the catastrophic political effects of untrammelled pride by making sure that vain-glorious behaviour (that is, actions that respond to the pull of flattery *despite* one's knowledge of one's own shortcomings) didn't spill over into self-deception (the point at which knowledge of one's own shortcomings disappears). The means to achieve this was provided by the institution of a sovereign power designed to remind subjects of their very real limitations as political agents, and certainly not to flatter them. Mandeville, by contrast, saw clearly the social and political uses of pride, and of flattery. He was less worried than Hobbes about the need to hold the line between self-conceit and self-deceit. Instead, he believed that the job of a skilful politician involved playing on every individual's desire for praise, however ill-deserved, in order to ensure that human vanity was put to socially beneficial uses.

The social benefits of the political manipulation of human vanity were summarised by Mandeville in a famous aphorism: "The moral virtues are the political offspring which flattery begot upon pride."[4] In other words, people can be encouraged to behave selflessly if their self-interested desire for praise is harnessed in the cause of suppressing their other desires. But Mandeville was adamant that this should never be understood as virtue in its true sense, because true virtue required the conquest of the selfish passions, not merely the suppression of one selfish passion in the service of a more powerful one. "Passions may do good by chance," Mandeville wrote, "but there can be no merit but in the conquest of them."[5] Nevertheless, the good that the passions may do included the simulation of genuine virtue, under the guise of a praiseworthy selflessness. In order that social behaviour should match the outward standards of virtue, "a Man need not conquer his passions, it is sufficient that he conceals them. Virtue bids us subdue, but good breeding only requires that we should hide, our Appetites."[6]

So Mandeville, unlike Hobbes, relied heavily on a distinction between genuine virtue and the socially useful faking of virtue. For Hobbes, as we have seen, it is effectively impossible to fake the only really useful virtue—that of obedience—since it is only really useful so long as you are actually obeying, and actual obedience is something you cannot fake. But Mandeville did not highlight the social uses of fake virtue in order to distinguish himself from Hobbes. Rather it was to attack those contemporary writers whom he believed had failed to understand the socially disastrous consequences of genuine virtue. The truth about real virtue was that it was very hard to achieve, since it represented a significant constraint on human behaviour—the conquest of the passions. For that reason, any widespread achievement of real virtue would be catastrophic for a commercial society that depended upon the passions—and in particular greed, pride, and avarice—to keeps its economy thriving. This was the original message of the poem "The Grumbling Hive" (1705), which provides the basis for *The Fable of the Bees*: that true virtue was the enemy of national prosperity. Mandeville spells it out at the end of the poem, where he offers this "moral":

> *Then leave Complaints: Fools only strive*
> *To make a Great and honest Hive.*
> *T'enjoy the World's Conveniencies,*
> *Be famed in War, yet live in Ease*
> *Without great Vices, is a vain*
> Eutopia *seated in the Brain.*[7]

Mandeville's particular target in "The Grumbling Hive" was Fénelon (1651–1715), whose widely influential *Telemachus* (1699) championed a return to properly virtuous (and austere) social conduct as a means of economic renewal, which Mandeville saw as a contradiction in terms.[8] If virtue were so obviously socially advantageous, it would be easy to be virtuous, and therefore the virtue could hardly be genuine; if it were genuine (and therefore genuinely self-denying), its social disadvantages would far outweigh its benefits. But, crucially for Mandeville, persuading people to fake virtue *was* relatively easy, because it was consistent with their own selfish interests. Pretending to be virtuous was a way of getting ahead, and it relied on just the same principles of envy and competitiveness that made commercial societies tick. These societies would therefore thrive so long as they could content themselves with vices merely dressed up to look like virtues. Hence the famous Mandeville thesis: private vices, public benefits.

Mandeville did not believe that it had always been easy to persuade people to dress up their vices in this way. In the earliest human societies, it had been necessary to rely heavily on strict codes of honour to condition human behaviour—individuals had to be flattered into making substantial sacrifices, particularly on the battlefield, where they had to be taught to fear dishonour more than death itself. But as societies evolved, so did their codes of honour, which became more relaxed, less martial, and gradually developed into something that the modern world had come to call "politeness." In polite societies, the faking of virtue did not simply rest on fear, but on the other passions as well, including envy and greed. Just as in martial societies people were taught to conquer their fear of death by playing on their fear of dishonour, so in commercial societies people were taught to conquer their greed for other people's possessions by their greed for praise. It is because of the rules of politeness as Mandeville understands them that people will fight each other to be the one who takes the smallest piece of cake, or picks up the bill in a restaurant.

First-order and second-order hypocrisy

The obvious question that follows is this: were the manners of the most prosperous societies, therefore, to be understood merely as a form of hypocrisy? Certainly, sincerity was ruled out as a socially useful virtue in these circumstances, since speaking one's mind would undermine the element of pretence on which all politeness depends. "To be at once well-bred and sincere," Mandeville wrote, "is no less than a Contradiction."[9] Equally, he was clear that hypocrisy played an important part in teaching people how to behave. For example, when discussing the pervasive social stigma attached to appearing envious, which stands in such obvious contrast to our true passions, which are envious through and through, Mandeville suggests: "That we are so generally ashamed of this vice, is owing to that strong Habit of Hypocrisy, by the Help of which, we have learned from our Cradle, to hide even from ourselves the vast Extent of Self-Love, and all its different branches."[10] This is hypocrisy in a distinctive sense: it is not simply the business of pretending to be virtuous, but the business of forgetting that it is just a pretence, which comes close to a form of self-deception. Yet without some self-deception, it is hard to see how society could function at all. Lust, Mandeville writes, untempered by "guile and hypocrisy," would reduce men to the level of beasts; so we turn lust into love, "a product of Nature warp'd by Custom and Education, so the true origin and first motive of it . . . is stifled in well-bred People, and almost conceal'd from themselves."[11] Here, hypocrisy becomes the price we have to pay for going through with the performance of publicly acceptable behaviour. As Mandeville puts it in his essay "A Search into the Nature of Society," which he appended to the 1723 edition of the *Fable*: "It is impossible that Man, mere Fallen Man . . . should be sociable creatures without Hypocrisy."[12]

Nevertheless, as many commentators have noted, and as Mandeville himself made clear in "A Search into the Nature of Society," hypocrisy was also something that he wished to condemn. His particular targets here were Shaftesbury (1671–1713) and those other early-eighteenth-century moralists who professed to believe that men were naturally sociable, and that displays of their sociability were also displays of their inherent virtue. These writers claimed that it was possible to be virtuous by being true to oneself, as opposed to the Mandeville view, which held that virtue was a form of denial of one's true nature as a passionate being. "The imaginary Notions that Men may be virtuous without Self-denial," Mandeville explained, "are a vast inlet to Hypocrisy, which being once made habitual, we must not only deceive others, but likewise become altogether unknown to ourselves."[13] He makes the point even more explicitly in the second volume of *The Fable of the Bees*, which he published in 1729 in response to critics of the earlier volume: "In the Opinion of Virtue's requiring Self-denial, there is greater Certainty, and Hypocrites have less Latitude than in the contrary system."[14] Here, hypocrisy is clearly understood as something to be avoided, as is the self-deception it brings in its wake. It was to free people from the hypocritical doctrines of the likes of Shaftesbury that Mandeville is now insisting that he wrote the *Fable*.

How are we to make sense of the difference between these two types of hypocrisy, one of which appears to be an unavoidable feature of prosperous human societies, and the other an intolerable menace to them? The answer is, in the end, a political one, and not just because it is clear that Mandeville, like Hobbes before him and Hume after him, disliked the hypocrisy of his political opponents (though it is certainly clear that he did). It is also political because it relates to the difference between those whose role it was to police polite societies (the "politicians") and those whose role it was simply to inhabit them. What Mandeville is attacking is the hypocrisy of the people who ought to know better, because their job was to keep on top of the hypocrisy that regulates our social existence. Instead, writers like Shaftesbury (who, as Mandeville pointed out, was noticeably reluctant to take up public office) were abdicating that responsibility.[15] There were two possible explanations for this: either the moralists truly believed the doctrines they preached, in which case self-deception had spread to the ranks of those who job it was to manage it, or they didn't really believe it, in which case they were simply concealing the indulgence of their own passions (in Shaftesbury's case, what Mandeville calls "an Indolent Temper, and unactive Spirit"), in precisely the manner that their own doctrines sought to deny.[16] Either way, the resultant hypocrisy was intolerable because it was unconfined, and the self-deception to which it led was so dangerous because it was so complete—we become, in Mandeville's words, not *almost* conceal'd from," but "*altogether* unknown to" ourselves. If the politicians had succumbed to the thing they were meant to be controlling, then we were all lost.

To move beyond the immediate terms of his dispute with Shaftesbury, one might say that what Mandeville is drawing here is a distinction between first-order and second-order hypocrisy. First-order hypocrisy is the ubiquitous practice of concealing vice as virtue, which makes up the parade of our social existence. Second-order hypocrisy is concealing the truth about this practice, and pretending that the parade itself is a form of genuinely virtuous, and therefore self-denying, behaviour. We may need to hide the truth *about* ourselves in order to get by in this world, but we oughtn't to hide the truth *from* ourselves that this is what we are doing.

But can this distinction be made to stick? The problem is that first-order hypocrisy appears to involve an element of self-deception, as Mandeville makes clear—that is, hypocritical social practices have bite because people come to forget that they are being hypocritical, that their love is in fact concealed lust, and so on—which means first-order hypocrisy leaks into second-order, because thoroughly self-deceived people will believe they really are being virtuous. Likewise, second-order hypocrisy—the moralising of the likes of Shaftesbury—is a social practice in its own right, and therefore contains elements of first-order hypocrisy as well (hence Mandeville's suspicion that Shaftesbury's doctrine of sociability was itself just an act). The simplest way to put this difficulty is to say that while it may be possible to draw a conceptual distinction between first-order and second-order hypocrisy, it is much harder to say who are the first-order and who are the second-order hypocrites.

One possible way round this difficulty is to equate these different orders of hypocrites with the different social orders, or classes. Some commentators have argued that Mandeville is in fact offering a class-based account of hypocrisy—that he is seeking to educate the propertied classes about the true nature of their own supposed virtues, so that they should not hypocritically seek to impose them on the uneducated, thereby rendering the labouring and servant classes unfit for the hard work on which the better-off depend.[17] This is most apparent in the piece of writing that most scandalised Mandeville's contemporaries—his "Essay on Charity and Charity-Schools," which sought to expose the second-order hypocrisy of the do-gooders who aimed to educate the poor in the path of true virtue, while ignoring the fact that true virtue was the last thing that the poor needed, or that their educators were capable of supplying. However, this does not help to fix the distinction between first- and second-order hypocrisy, because Mandeville was not arguing that the poor should be educated in the ways of first-order hypocrisy (or "politeness"). Rather, he wanted them kept in ignorance of all but the basic struggle for existence—as he says at the end of *The Fable of the Bees*, "the Poor should be kept strictly to Work . . . I have named Ignorance as a necessary Ingredient in the Mixture of Society"—so that they should be willing to serve their masters.[18] The people who needed educating were the do-gooders, whose failure to recognise that their own "charitableness" was merely a "vogue" threatened to expose the whole charade of public virtue, by allowing hypocrisy to leak through the entire system. "A servant can have no unfeigned Respect for his Master," Mandeville wrote, "as soon as he has sense enough to find out that he serves a Fool."[19] What was needed were not servants who feigned respect, but masters who were not fools, and understood the limits of their own hypocrisy. The masters needed to be first-order, not second-order hypocrites.

So what we have here is a distinction between the class of persons among whom the different orders of hypocrisy are an issue—those people whom Mandeville tends to classify under the category of "Gentlemen"—and those for whom hypocrisy should be no issue at all—the "Vulgar," as Mandeville calls them. Gentlemen ought to play the game properly; if they do, the Vulgar ought to be gulled by it. But this doesn't answer the question of how gentlemen are to play the game properly— that is, how they are to be sure that their first-order hypocrisy is not second-order hypocrisy. "The well-bred Gentleman," Mandeville writes, "places his greatest Pride in the Skill he has of covering it with Dexterity, and some are so expert at concealing this Frailty, that when they are most guilty of it, the Vulgar think them the most exempt from it."[20] This is the most sophisticated version of the game—not merely concealing the vice, but concealing one's consciousness of the concealment, only to make it more perfect. Is it possible to retain genuine self-knowledge under these circumstances? Perhaps, but

Mandeville has also suggested that this sort of behaviour is a habit, learned at the cradle, and carefully regulated and shaped by skilful politicians, who must balance the need for self-awareness with the requirement that their performance of virtue be a convincing one. Moreover, the skilful politicians will by definition (in this pre-democratic age) be drawn from among the class of the well-bred gentlemen. They too have to play the game, even as they are attempting to regulate it. So the problem remains—how are we to draw the line between the people who are in control of their hypocrisy and the people who are not? More to the point, are there any guarantees that hypocritical politicians will be of the first-order and not the second-order kind?

Malicious versus fashionable hypocrisy

The best illustration of the difficulty of deciding what sort of hypocrisy one should expect of politicians comes in one of the books Mandeville wrote after *The Fable* had made him notorious throughout Europe. In *An Enquiry into the Origins of Honour* (1732), he offers a distinction between two different kinds of hypocrite that cuts across his earlier accounts. The book is a dialogue between two characters called Horatio and Cleomenes (it is Cleomenes who plays Mandeville's part in these exchanges[21]):

Cleomenes: There are two sorts of Hypocrites, that differ very much from one another. To distinguish them by Names, the one I would call the Malicious, and the Other the Fashionable. By Malicious Hypocrites, I mean such as pretend to a great deal of Religion, when they know their Pretensions to be false; who take pains to appear Pious and Devout, in order to be Villains, and in Hopes that they will be trusted to get an Opportunity of deceiving those, who believe them to be Sincere. Fashionable Hypocrites I call

those who, without any Motive of Religion, or Sense of
Duty, go to Church, in Imitation of their Neighbours; counterfeit Devotion, and without any Design upon others, comply occasionally with all the Rites and Ceremonies of
Publick Worship, from no other Principle than Aversion to
Singularity, and a Desire of being in the Fashion. The First
are, as you say, the Worst of them; but the other are rather
beneficial to society, and can only be injurious to themselves.

Horatio: Your distinction is very just, if these latter deserve
to be called Hypocrites at all.

Cleomenes: To make a Shew outwardly of what is not felt
within, and counterfeit what is not real, is certainly
Hypocrisy, whether it does Good or Hurt.

Horatio: Then, strictly speaking, good Manners and Politeness must come under the same Denomination.[22]

How does this distinction between fashionable and malicious hypocrisy compare to the one I have been drawing between first- and second-order hypocrisy? One might say that
fashionable hypocrisy, which on Mandeville's account includes good manners and politeness, is a kind of first-order
hypocrisy: it is the way we learn to behave in order to get by as
social animals. But what about malicious hypocrisy? In one
sense, it qualifies as second-order hypocrisy, in that it is an exploitation of the ubiquity of first-order hypocrisy in order to
conceal sinister motives. The malicious hypocrite doesn't simply hide behind the mask of piety but behind the fact that such
masks are readily available, and easy to hide behind. But
Mandeville draws the distinction in terms not just of motive
but of self-awareness: the malicious hypocrite knows what he
is about—knows indeed that he is a hypocrite—whereas the
fashionable hypocrite acts without design. Once the distinction is put in terms of self-awareness, then it becomes much
harder to map it onto the division between first-order and
second-order hypocrisy. Mandeville's point in the *Enquiry*

appears to be the conventional one that the worst sort of hypocrite is the person who is entirely aware of what he is doing: his wickedness lies in his self-possession. But if he knows what he is doing, then there is little danger that he will mistake what he is doing for genuine virtue. This danger is far greater for fashionable hypocrites than malicious ones.

The danger that fashionable hypocrisy will slip over into self-deception raises an important set of political questions. Do we really want to be governed or "policed" by individuals who lack the guile of the seasoned politician, and so are capable of being self-deceived? Would it not be better if our politicians were fully conscious of what they are doing, rather than simply being slaves to the fashions that they are endeavouring to regulate? But if they are fully conscious of what they are doing, does it not follow that their own hypocrisy, which is unavoidable in any social setting, will be of the malicious or designing kind? Mandeville says that malicious hypocrites are the ones who deliberately set out to injure others, whereas fashionable hypocrites can only be injurious to themselves. But politicians are quite capable of injuring others without meaning to, simply by dint of the way that they exercise, or fail to exercise, their power. Moreover, politicians who ape the fashions of the day, for the sake of a quiet life, might be said to have abdicated their responsibility to do something more than that (and it was precisely this—the abdication of political responsibility, the fashionably indolent sociability—that constituted the essence of Mandeville's attack on Shaftesbury). Can Mandeville therefore mean it when he suggests that malicious hypocrites are the only ones we should be worrying about?

I don't think he does mean it, and the fullest explanation of why not comes in Mandeville's lengthy discussion of the character of the politician who had become by the early eighteenth century, as he was to remain for the best part of two hundred years, a byword for the problem of hypocrisy in public life: Oliver Cromwell. In his attitude to Cromwell's perceived hypocrisy, Mandeville stands, as in so much else, interestingly placed somewhere between Hobbes and Rousseau. One of the most striking features of the story Hobbes tells in *Behemoth* regarding what he calls the "injustice, impudence and hypocrisy" of the parliamentary side in the English Civil War is that Cromwell gets off relatively lightly.[23] Hobbes treats his faults with much more circumspection than he does many of the other actors in the saga. This is in part because Cromwell arrived on the scene relatively late—he does not feature in Hobbes's account of the hypocrisy and scheming that preceded the war itself. But it is also because Cromwell was not the sort of hypocrite Hobbes most minded about—Cromwell's sympathies lay with the Independents, not the Presbyterians, which meant that there were limits to his piety about political power.[24] It does not follow from this that Hobbes much liked or admired Cromwell's character. He recognised that Cromwell was fickle, scheming, and sanctimonious—all the qualities that led others to view him as the worst hypocrite of all. But for Hobbes, what ultimately distinguished Cromwell was his adaptability in the cause of political supremacy, which is somewhat different from mere political hypocrisy. Hobbes captures the difference by arguing that Cromwell did not seek to colour political power as something it was not, but rather took his own colour from where the power lay: "He were nothing certain," Hobbes writes, "but applying himself always to the faction which was strongest, and was of a colour like it."[25] In other words, he was a kind of political chameleon, which is not necessarily the same as being a hypocrite, at least not for Hobbes.[26] Chameleons, though they may be hiding from their enemies, are nevertheless colouring, not cloaking, what lies beneath, because what lies beneath is essentially neutral: just their own skin, which, like everyone else, they are doing their best to save.

For Rousseau, in stark contrast, what lay beneath the surface in Cromwell's case was not neutral at all, but as bad as it gets. As a moral creature, Rousseau saw him not as a chameleon but as a corpse. In his first *Discourse*, Rousseau uses Cromwell to illustrate the anti-Rochefoucauldian claim that "to cover one's wickedness with the dangerous mantle of hypocrisy is not to honour virtue, but to offend it by profaning its standards."[27] He goes on:

> The vile and grovelling soul of the hypocrite is like a corpse, without fire, or warmth, or vitality left. I appeal to experience. Great villains have been known to return into themselves, end their lives wholesomely and die saved. But no one has ever known a hypocrite becoming a good man; one might reasonably have tried to convert Cartouche [a legendary eighteenth-century villain], never would a wise man have undertaken to convert Cromwell.[28]

Rousseau returns to the theme in *The Social Contract*, where he describes "the single self-seeker or hypocrite, such as a Catiline or a Cromwell," as "the scourge with which God punishes his children."[29] This is why a properly constituted state is so essential. Political theorists who "make great game of all the absurdities a clever rascal or insinuating speaker might get the people of Paris or London to believe . . . do not know that Cromwell would have been put to hard labour by the people of Berne."[30]

What is interesting about the position Mandeville stakes out with regard to Cromwell is that it manages to foreshadow something of Rousseau's later censoriousness while echoing much of Hobbes's earlier ambivalence. Cromwell, he tells us in the *Enquiry*, was "a vile, wicked Hypocrite, who, under the cloak of Sanctity broke through all Human and Divine laws to aggrandize himself."[31] In this sense, he exemplifies the malicious form of hypocrisy. But later in the book, Cleomenes paints a more complex picture.

Cleomenes: The chief motive of all [Cromwell's] actions was Ambition, and what he wanted was immortal Fame. This End he steadily pursued: All his Faculties were made subservient to it; and no Genius was ever more supple to his

Interest . . . In the most Treacherous Circumstance, to has-
ten the execution of his blackest Design, he could counterfeit enthusiasm and appear to be a Saint. But the most
enormous of his crimes proceeded from no more Principle,
than the best of his Achievements. In the Midst of his Vil-
lainies, he was a Slave to Business; and the most disinterested Patriot never watched over the Public Welfare, both at
Home and Abroad, with greater Care and Assiduity, or re-
trieved the fallen Credit of a Nation in less time than this
Usurper. But all for himself . . .

Horatio: I don't wonder you dwell so long upon Cromwell,
for Nothing can be more serviceable to your system, than
his life and actions.

Cleomenes: Able Politicians consult the Honour of the Age,
and the Conjuncture they live in, and Cromwell made the
most of his.[32]

What this suggests is that in addition to being a malicious
hypocrite, Cromwell was a kind of fashionable hypocrite as
well. This is not the innocently fashionable hypocrisy of the
occasional churchgoer—there was nothing innocent about
Cromwell in Mandeville's eyes. Nor was Cromwell keeping
up appearances out of an "aversion to singularity," but rather
in order to achieve the singularity of unrivalled political
power. Nevertheless Cromwell was, in Mandeville's own
words, "a slave to business," forced to play the part of the disinterested patriot, and assiduous in his cultivation of the public welfare. In this respect, his hypocrisy was unquestionably
beneficial to society, which according to Mandeville's earlier
distinction is the mark of fashionable hypocrisy. Moreover,
along with the intention to deceive, Cromwell's hypocrisy
contained an element, if not of self-deception, then at least of
selflessness, as he played his part to the full. Cromwell was
aware of what he was doing, but he was not fully in control of
the part he had to play. He was forced to adapt to what was
expected of him.

There is another sense too in which a politician like Cromwell mixed malicious and fashionable hypocrisy. This was in his readiness to consult the temper of his age. Being a designing hypocrite, Cromwell knew that he had to play on the passions of his audience. He was, Mandeville says, "a man of admirable good sense, and thoroughly well acquainted with human nature; he knew the force of Enthusiasm, and made use of it accordingly."[33] But he also recognised the limits of the ways in which it could be used. Horatio, second fiddle in the dialogue, puts it best:

> That his Pretences to Religion were no more than Hypocrisy, I have allowed; but it does not appear, that he desired others to be Hypocrites too: On the contrary, he took Pains, or at least made use of all possible means, to promote Christianity among his men, and to make them sincerely religious.[34]

It is important to understand what Mandeville is suggesting here. He is not arguing that politicians should encourage their followers to be sincerely virtuous. Rather, he means that the successful politician will never require the public to play a role they are incapable of sustaining. That demand would be second-order hypocrisy, and it would make a mockery of the business of political obedience: the entire performance would collapse.

Mandeville's central point, indeed his primary polemical purpose in writing about Cromwell in the *Enquiry*, is to insist that times have changed. "In Oliver's Days," he writes, "what was intended by a Mask of Religion, and a Shew of Sanctity, is now arrived at by the Height of Politeness, and a perpetual attachment to the principles of modern Honour."[35] Cromwell's genius as a politician was to understand, as a hypocrite himself, that he should not try to turn his supporters into hypocrites, because in the 1640s and 1650s the way to encourage virtuous-seeming behaviour was to foster it sincerely. But in the 1720s and 1730s, the way to encourage virtuous-seeming behaviour was to emphasise simply the outward show. To treat army officers in an age of politeness as Cromwell treated his officers in an age of enthusiasm would simply turn them into what Mandeville calls "Bigots," and allow hypocrisy to run riot. Much better to take the eighteenth-century man for what he was—to have an army of what Mandeville calls "dancing masters," or persons of fashion. If Cromwell had treated his army as though it were made up of dancing masters, he would have lost his ability to control them.

What Cromwell's political mastery suggests, then, is this: that the mask of virtue must suit what Mandeville calls the conjuncture of the age, and in some ages it may be best to suggest that it is not a mask. Second-order hypocrisy arises when this contingency is lost sight of. Thus it is possible to say that even a moralist like Shaftesbury is not necessarily wrong about virtue, because there may be circumstances when it is socially useful to encourage people in the pursuit of virtue. It is just that for Mandeville, an increasingly prosperous commercial society was not one of them. But Mandeville's clinical dissection of Cromwell's political character points to an additional, if somewhat more complicated lesson about political hypocrisy: that in order to prevent first-order hypocrisy from sliding into second-order hypocrisy, the politician should be a mixture of the malicious and the fashionable hypocrite. Malicious hypocrisy ensures politicians know what they are doing; fashionable hypocrisy ensures that they are in step with the spirit of the times. Malice without the desire to conform produces a dangerous detachment; fashionableness without designing motives produces a perilous lack of self-awareness. Either was disastrous in a politician aspiring to play his part to the full. What was needed was to combine the two.

Thus the Mandevillian politician has to have a kind of split personality, which means Mandeville is much more modern than his crude association with Machiavelli as one of the devils of political thought would allow. The genuinely Machiavellian politician leads a double life but is not a split person: he has abandoned Christian virtue for political virtue, which means Christian virtue is something he is content merely to ape. If anything, Mandeville's split political personality has more in common with the ethically divided soul of a Weberian politician, as described in Max Weber's classic 1919 lecture *Politik als Beruf* (a text that is, incidentally, awash with diabolical imagery).[36] Weber believed that political leaders had to combine detachment and involvement. Detachment without involvement reduced politics to a sterile game (mere malice); involvement without detachment turned politics into an absurd parade of convictions (mere fashion). The politician who was simultaneously involved and detached was a kind of contradiction in terms, but a necessary one. The same could be said of Mandeville's doubly hypocritical politician—fashionable enough so that his hypocrisy is not pure malice, malicious enough so that it is not just the fashion.

HYPOCRISY AND GOOD INTENTIONS

One thing is practically certain, though: the Mandevillian politician is going to look like a hypocrite to those whose lives he is policing. There is therefore a further question that needs to be considered here: how are the wider public meant to be satisfied with politicians who are divided between these two—and on their own, equally unpalatable—forms of hypocrisy? The short answer is: they won't be. In his most overtly political book, *Free Thoughts on Religion, the Church and National Happiness* (1720), Mandeville makes it clear that politicians are bound to appear to be hypocrites to the wider public, because all politicians are scheming men of fashion. This is what makes them suited to their role, but it is also what makes them so hard to take: "The envy, strife and all the feuds and jealousies of courts are so many safeguards to the liberty of the people," Mandeville writes, "[yet] they never fail to produce severe censure of those at the helm."[37] The safeguards come from the fact that the scheming of politicians is fashioned by the political and legal conventions of the age, "which even the boldest as well as the craftiest stand in awe of, and is a better security for the people than all the virtues ministers can be possessed of."[38] Mandeville wishes observers of the charade of political life to be sanguine about its hypocrisies, as a sign of its good health, while also being willing to accept that the entire charade of our own social existence is somehow under the politicians' control. The fact that they are all making a spectacle of themselves is meant to reassure us that they know what they are doing. This takes quite a lot of swallowing.

And what makes it even harder to swallow is that as well as being a book about politics, *Free Thoughts* is also a highly political book, with its own partisan purposes. Mandeville was seeking to defend the Whig ministries of the period (in the run-up to the South Sea Bubble of 1720) against their political opponents, particularly those high Tories whose readiness to censure the obvious corruption of public life Mandeville understood as a transparent attempt to restore their own political fortunes. Tory moralists were moralising scaremongers, which made them second-order hypocrites, in so far as their awareness of what they were doing served to undermine the very basis of the public performance in which they were engaged. As a doctor, Mandeville preferred to put the matter in medical terms:

> No woman in the height of vapours is more whimsical in her complaints . . . and melancholy madmen have not more dismal apprehension of things in the blackest fits of spleen, than our state hypochondriacs are daily buzzing in our ears.[39]

The only thing worse than hysterics in public life were people playing the part of such hysterics, which meant that there was nothing worse than an hysterical Tory.

What, though, was the correct attitude to corruption and hypocrisy in public life? For all the brilliance of his polemics, Mandeville cannot hide the essential weakness of his own position. He wants his readers to think about hypocrisy in two distinct and not easily reconcilable lights. On the one hand, everyone who knows anything about politics needs to recognise that moralising about it is absurd. If we moralise about it, we will simply reveal ourselves to be hypocrites and fools. Indeed, Mandeville suggests, it is best to presume the worst, for fear of being exposed. We should not attack a prince we oppose "for being immodest in his amours," lest the prince we prefer turns out to have conducted his "whole life as an entire scene of unlawful love."[40] (Mandeville is thinking of the King and the Pretender, but contemporary parallels are not hard to find—one just has to think of Bill Clinton and some of his Republican critics). Likewise, we should not talk up the probity of our favoured candidates for public office. In a warning that seems as fresh today as when it was written, Mandeville points out:

> Men have had their heads broke for defending the honesty of a courtier, who at the same time was abed with another man's wife, or bribing, over a bottle of Champagne, another minister who was to audit his accounts.[41]

Better in these circumstances not to pass judgment at all.

Yet at the same time, Mandeville also wants the public to accept that some politicians are not nearly as bad as the moralisers make them appear. Our understanding of the hypocrisy of public life should lead us to recognise that things are not so grim as the politicians paint them, because the politicians who bleat the loudest are the worst sorts of hypocrites. "He that knows how courtiers throw their faults upon others," Mandeville warns, "will have but little faith in what is rumoured about public ministers."[42] A large part of Mandeville's purpose here is to remind his readers that his preferred candidates for public office are much better people than their diehard Tory opponents would have the public believe. The immediate context is the brief and relatively inconsequential 1718 war with Spain, which many Whigs supported, as did Mandeville, and many Tories opposed, believing it to have been engineered as a distraction from domestic difficulties. Mandeville's defence of the war, coming from the author of *The Fable of the Bees*, is quite staggeringly moralistic (unless of course it is ironic, but in this political context it is hard to see how it can be). "We should not complain when the intentions of men are manifestly good, and they act for the interests of the nation," he writes. "An Englishman who loves his country, and complains of this conduct, must be an arch politician." So, he concludes: "That we should not misconstrue the intentions of princes and politicians, another criterion is requisite, which is, to avoid reaching out beyond the sphere of our understanding."[43]

There is an obvious double standard at work here: we should not pass judgment on the virtues of politicians for fear of discovering that they are worse than we thought them; equally, we should not pass judgment because they will often turn out to be far better than we imagined. Can this line be maintained? One way of doing so might be to distinguish between two different types of politician: the true leaders of men, and the rest, all the hangers-on and fawners and placemen who make up the bulk of the political class. The hangers-on will indeed be as bad as it is possible to imagine, since they will almost all by definition be either too obsessively malicious or too much creatures of fashion to make it to the top. By contrast, somewhere at the heart of political affairs will be the men who, like Cromwell, combine the various elements of political hypocrisy, and therefore manage to rise above it all. Again, there is a Weberian way of putting this. Weber understood that most people involved in politics were not fit for political leadership because they were either too idealistic or too bureaucratic—either too involved or too detached—whereas only a few, a very, very few, managed to see both sides of political life, and therefore succumb to neither. But this argument cannot work for Mandeville, because he couches his defence of the war with Spain solely in terms of the good intentions of its perpetrators: he does not say that they should be trusted because, like all good politicians, they are a mixture of malice and a desire to please; he says they should be trusted because their motives are beyond reproach. Moreover, Weber at least had a reason for thinking that the best qualified politicians would rise to the top, which is the democratic competition for power. Mandeville is talking about literal princes and their courts, and the idea that kings and their preferred ministers will always by definition possess the rare combination of qualities required of the successful politician would stretch anyone's faith in the benign workings of politics. It also hardly seems a suitable vehicle for anti-Tory polemics. Coming from Mandeville, it would be rank hypocrisy.

Any suggestion that Mandeville does think like this—that politicians who make it to the top are there because uniquely qualified to be so—is dispelled by the account he offers in the second volume of *The Fable of the Bees* of the qualities needed to become prime minister. "There are always fifty Men in the Kingdom," he writes, "that, if employ'd, would be fit for this Post, and after a little Practice shine in it."[44] The reason is simple: prime ministers derive much of their merit from the merit that is automatically assumed to attach to the office of prime minister. "A Prime Minister has a vast, an unspeakable Advantage, barely by being so, and by everybody's knowing him to be, and treating him as such."[45] How then can a writer who is happy to argue this—or the stronger claim "that any man of middling Capacity and Reputation may be fit for any of the highest posts"[46]—also think that certain politicians having made it to the highest positions of preferment are therefore beyond reproach, and acting only with the nation's best interests at heart? The most straightforward answer is that Mandeville, like any good hypocrite, was adapting his principles according to his personal taste or distaste for the politicians in question. At the end of the second volume of the *Fable*, he remarks, in standard Hobbesian fashion, "how differently men judge of Actions, according as they like or dislike the Persons that performed them."[47] In 1729 the prime minister was Robert

Walpole, and Mandeville did not like him, for what appear to have been entirely personal reasons (Mandeville's friend and patron Lord Macclesfield had been the subject of an earlier investigation for corruption instigated by Walpole that resulted in a £30,000 fine).[48] But in 1720, before Walpole had arrived to dominate the political scene, Mandeville was happy to defend the Whig ministry of the day, against its Tory and internal Whig opponents, with the aid of whatever tools were available. The central weapon to hand was the label of patriotism—the contest to pass one's own party off as "patriots" was the primary political struggle of the period—and Mandeville used it in order to prevent it from being used by the other side.[49] He was simply playing the game of politics as he understood it.

But there is another possible explanation of Mandeville's position that goes slightly deeper than this. He is not just distinguishing between his side and the other side on grounds of personal preference alone. There is a real difference between the two sides in Mandeville's eyes: the politicians of whom he disapproves are second-order hypocrites, whereas the Whigs he prefers are not. This is what makes certain sorts of Whigs—the ones who were sometimes known as "independent Whigs" in the political language of the period—trustworthy in Mandeville's eyes: they know how perilous it is to moralise in politics, which is why when they do make a virtue of their good intentions they should be taken seriously. Mandeville does not state this explicitly, but it is implicit in much of what he says—the only politicians who can be trusted with the language of virtue are the ones who know how little it is usually worth. Meanwhile, Walpole's cynicism, as Mandeville saw it, had become so all-embracing that he had lost the ability to make even this judgment.

The basic assumption that underlies this line of thought is by no means unique to Mandeville, nor to his age. It can also be found, for example, in the words of Oliver Cromwell, who defended his overseas adventures and his restrictions on civil

liberties in similar terms. His actions, he said in a speech before Parliament in 1655, were absolutely necessary, yet he acknowledged: "It is an easy thing to talk of necessities when
men make necessities. Would not the Lord Protector make
himself great, and his family great? Doth he not make these
necessities? And then he will come upon the people with his
argument of necessity!"[50] But what Cromwell is really asking
his audience is this: Do you think I would invoke necessity,
knowing what an arch-politician it must make me look? No—
you can be sure that I will only invoke necessity when it is
truly needed. Anything else would be "blasphemy," or, as we
might put it, the ultimate hypocrisy.

But if it is an argument of this kind that lies behind
Mandeville's defence of the sincere politicians of his own age,
it is hard to fit in with the rest of what he has to say about political hypocrisy. The problem is that it looks too much like just
another form of hypocrisy about hypocrisy. Politicians who
cite the ubiquity of hypocrisy in order to carve out an exception for themselves are still wearing a mask—they are like
stage actors who speak in asides to the audience to explain
what they are doing, despite the fact that this is all still part
of the act. In the politicians' case, they are adding an act
about hypocrisy to what might otherwise be simply an act of
hypocrisy. In so doing, they move from the first-order
hypocrisy of faking virtue to the second-order hypocrisy of
trying to find a way to make that fake virtue appear real. This
is not the same as the second-order hypocrisy of someone like
Shaftesbury in Mandeville's eyes: Shaftesbury was using his
apparent faith in the possibility of genuine virtue as a kind of
cover for his own selfish interests. But it is also possible to use
an apparent lack of faith in the possibility of genuine virtue as
a kind of cover. The politician does this whenever he lets his
audience know that they should not be fooled by what they
see—with a nod, and a wink, the politician allows the public a
glimpse behind the charade of political life, and in so doing

seeks to offer the public some reassurance that he knows what he is up to.

What makes this second-order hypocrisy is that it is an exploitation of the fact of hypocrisy for political purposes, and as such it has no limits—it is, in Mandeville's terms, effectively unconfined. Once politicians start to use their knowledge of hypocrisy in order to distance themselves from the game of politics as it is played by others, then hypocrisy has spread to the ranks of the people who are meant to be in control of it. Politicians who genuinely believe that their knowledge of the ubiquity of hypocrisy in political life makes them immune from it are self-deceived, since no one is immune from it, because it is ubiquitous. On the other hand, if politicians know they are not immune from it, then the claim that their knowledge grants them a kind of exception is itself just an act. Knowingness about political hypocrisy is no more an escape from it than any other kind of inside knowledge, because it too can be deployed as a mask.

If Mandeville shows us anything, therefore, it is that the line between first-order and second-order hypocrisy is extremely difficult to hold in any political context, and that it was as hard for him as it was for his contemporaries. In principle, it is possible to distinguish between these two types of hypocrisy. But in practice it is almost impossible to tell which is which. Even those rare politicians who appear to stay on the right side of the line between them will be vulnerable to the charge that they are exploiting their skill in the management of hypocrisy to mask what they are really up to. To hold out for the politician who is invulnerable to the charge of second-order hypocrisy will mean a very long wait, and, as Mandeville himself says of the problem of waiting for the right sorts of politicians to come along, "in the meantime the Places can't stand open, and the Offices must be filled with such as you can get."[51] We must not expect too much, but even not expecting too much is no guarantee against the most corrosive forms of hypocrisy, because the most hypocritical politicians will exploit our low expectations to convince us that their hypocrisy does not matter. Mandeville found no way out of this dilemma, and his own political writing serves to illustrate it. So perhaps the real lesson is that it is a mistake to expect any definitive answers from the ideas of a political thinker like Mandeville, for all his insights into the nature of political hypocrisy. In truth, hypocrisy was not his central concern anyway. His thoughts on hypocrisy were a vehicle for his critique of wishful moral and economic thinking, rather than the other way around.[52] Equally, he was not a political philosopher, but a polemicist and satirist of genius. It is dangerous to take what he has to say too literally, or expect too much overall coherence from it.

Yet despite what this suggests about the apparent futility of trying get from Mandeville a generalised understanding of the limits to political hypocrisy, there is another principle running through his body of thought that might serve as a practical guide to modern politics, including the politics of today. Mandeville was writing about a society in which hypocrisy was ubiquitous, which is one of the reasons that it is a society we can recognise. He wanted to prevent a ubiquitous feature of his society from becoming a self-defeating one. Attempting to do this by distinguishing between straightforward hypocrisy and hypocrisy about hypocrisy leads into some of the difficulties I have highlighted in this chapter, particularly in politics. But there is an alternative way of doing it. That is to argue that the worst hypocrisy arises when people pass off difficult things as though they were easy, and easy things as though they were difficult. Genuine self-denial is difficult to achieve— no one, least of all politicians, should pretend that it is easy. Equally, the appearance of self-denial is easily achieved; no one, least of all politicians, should pretend that putting it on is hard. These insights, which derive from Mandeville's work, apply to it as well. Mandeville's struggles show how difficult the line between first-order and second-order hypocrisy is to hold. This is one more thing that no one, neither Mandeville, nor Oliver Cromwell, nor anyone else engaged in the great game of politics, should pretend is easy. Nor, having made it easy for themselves, should they then pretend it is hard. It is second-order hypocrisy to pass off tough political decisions as foregone moral conclusions. Equally, it is second-order hypocrisy to pass off foregone political decisions as the result of much tough personal agonising. That seems as true now as it was then.

⊷ 3 ⊶

THE AMERICAN REVOLUTION AND
THE ART OF SINCERITY

BRITISH HYPOCRISY AND AMERICAN HYPOCRISY

No event in modern political history has been so marked by the problem of hypocrisy as the American Revolution. The most elementary reason for this can be summarised in a single word: slavery. The champions of American liberty made universal claims regarding the freedoms that belonged to all human beings which they nonetheless readily denied to the hundreds of thousands of human beings enslaved on their own continent. Some of our sense of the grotesqueness of this double standard is hindsight, and therefore anachronistic, but by no means all of it is hindsight. As Simon Schama has recently shown, the participants on both sides of the Revolution were acutely conscious of the hypocrisies involved, well in advance of the real battle being joined. The spectacle of Americans moralising about tyranny and oppression while indulging in the worst kind of oppression themselves was hard for many to stomach, and not only among those who were to remain loyal to the Crown. As Abigail Adams wrote to her husband John, the future president, in 1774: "It always appeared to me to be a most iniquitous scheme . . . to fight ourselves for what we are daily robbing and plundering from those who have as good a right to freedom as we have."[1]

74

Yet American freedom fighters were also aware that whatever their own hypocrisy, it was more than matched by the hypocrisy of their critics on the British side. Indeed, to be accused of hypocrisy for perpetuating slavery by a British political establishment that had repeatedly refused to outlaw the trade on which the practice depended was not difficult to depict as the ultimate double standard. But worse was to come when the Crown invited American slaves to seek their freedom by taking up arms against their colonial masters. Thomas Jefferson, in his original draft of the Declaration of Independence, spelled out exactly how far British hypocrisy went. Not only had the king refused to grant American requests to ban or limit the import of slaves to the colonies, thereby "prostituting his negative [i.e., his veto]" to the West Indian sugar lobby, "he is now exciting those very people to rise in arms against us, and to purchase that liberty of which he has deprived them, by murdering the people on whom he has obtruded them."[2]

This passage, the culmination of Jefferson's list of charges against the British Crown that made a declaration of independence inevitable, was cut by Congress from the final version of the document, to its author's lifelong chagrin. The reasons for its exclusion are politically complex—slavery was never an easy matter on which to secure any kind of political consensus—but also straightforward. The charge of hypocrisy was in 1776, as it has remained, a weapon to be handled carefully, because for all its rhetorical force it exposes those who wield it to an inevitable scrutiny of their own inconsistencies (as Garry Wills has put it, "Congress had good reason to believe that Jefferson's morally convoluted charge would just open it to ridicule").[3] Jefferson believed the Declaration of Independence was a weaker document for sidestepping the King's duplicity on the question of slavery, but it was unquestionably a stronger document for avoiding a direct attack on the King's hypocrisy on this matter, given the vulnerability of those who were to sign it on that score. In this respect, the issue of hypocrisy in relation to slavery was a "political" as much as it was a "moral" one—and it is in our tendency to see it as a moral issue that we run the risk of misunderstanding the concerns of those involved.

We tend to be preoccupied with the personal hypocrisy of the slaveholding class to which Jefferson belonged, and to be repelled by it. For that reason, slavery has provided the focus for later investigations into whether the American political thought of this period can be "redeemed."[4] But for Jefferson and the other members of the class who rebelled against the King, slavery was simply one of a number of areas where the problem of hypocrisy had become politically acute. Indeed, it was not slavery that made political hypocrisy an issue in this context; rather, it was political hypocrisy that made slavery an issue, because the slave question was symptomatic of the ways in which the double standards of empire had made it impossible for the colonists to control their own destiny. But for all their criticism of these double standards, the Americans had to be careful that they did not simply replicate them. The American revolutionaries were, after all, subjects of the Crown, and the entire revolutionary process was shaped by their need to repudiate that subjection in its own terms—they did not wish to be seen as traitors, but as patriots, driven to extreme measures by the altogether more extreme treatment to which they had been subjected. The thrust of the American case against the British state was that the King had been hiding behind an empty language of constitutionality and "right" in order to conceal his mistreatment of his American subjects. Independence was needed to give that language real substance again. But inevitably, to the King's supporters, it was the Americans who were hiding behind a fake language of constitutionality, because their own deployment of it was impossible to reconcile with their traitorous behaviour.

The challenge for the defenders of the American revolution was to explain why the fact that they too were British subjects made it impossible for them to remain British subjects. This was a delicate task, requiring an acute sensitivity to the politics of hypocrisy (a sensitivity that deserted Jefferson on the question of slavery, but on very little else). Too close an identification with the power they were seeking to repudiate would render them hypocrites, but so would too much distance, given that so much of what they wished to say had to be couched in their opponents' terms. The problem faced by the champions of American independence was the one faced by all revolutionaries—how to overthrow an entire political order without undercutting their ability to construct a new order in its place. But in the American case the difficulties were acute for two reasons. First, the language of American political thought in the pre-revolutionary period was almost entirely borrowed from British sources—there did not yet exist a home-grown tradition on which to draw (though that was to change rapidly in the period leading up to the ratification of the Constitution in 1787–1788), nor were there any obvious foreign examples to follow (though again that was to change with the French Revolution). It is true that many American thinkers of the period were well versed in the classical literature of republicanism, but again this tended to be refracted through British sources. There now exists a vast and contentious historical literature exploring the ways in which American revolutionary thought borrowed, adapted, or moved away from ideas that had their roots across the Atlantic, in law, theology, and moral and political philosophy.[5] I am not going to attempt to add to these controversies here. Instead, I want to focus on a more specific aspect of the tradition of what is sometimes called "Atlantic" political thought, which is the role within it of arguments about the limits of sincerity in politics.

This constitutes the second complicating aspect of American revolutionary attitudes to hypocrisy: the fact that many of the insights into the nature of political dissembling were drawn from a body of ideas that the Americans shared with their adversaries. The question of when, why, and how it might be acceptable to conceal one's true political principles and hide behind a mask of piety and virtue had become one of the major themes of eighteenth-century political argument, in part because of the deep impact of Bernard Mandeville's *Fable of the Bees* on the way people thought about these questions. The impact of these ideas extended to North America, where they became central to the discourse of revolutionary politics. In this chapter, I want to explore how three of the most prominent American thinkers of the period—Benjamin Franklin, John Adams, and Thomas Jefferson—adapted and developed prevailing British ideas about what it might mean to act sincerely in a political setting. (Though many of these ideas were explicitly English, it is important to retain the epithet of Britishness at this point because some of them were drawn from Scotland as well.) In doing so, I hope to address the wider and more enduring problem, exemplified by the American Revolution but by no means exclusive to it, of how politicians can counter political hypocrisy without becoming hypocrites themselves.

Nonetheless, for all the impact Mandeville had on the thought of the period, the one thing I cannot claim here is that the American response to the problem of political hypocrisy was an explicitly Mandevillian one. American revolutionary thought is in some ways an amalgam of the ideas that Mandeville most distrusted, or would have distrusted had he lived to see them. Among the thinkers who had the largest direct influence on the theorists of American independence were Shaftesbury, the great exponent of natural human sociability, along more significantly with Shaftesbury's mentor, John Locke; Bolingbroke (1678–1751), the arch-critic of Whig corruption in the 1720s and 1730s, who contrasted this corruption with an ideal of patriotic virtue; and Scottish Enlightenment authors such as Francis Hutcheson (1694–1746), Lord Kames (1692–1786), and Adam Smith (1723–1790), all of whom championed a conception of innate moral sense that was deliberately designed to rescue moral philosophy from Mandeville's impossible paradoxes. From writers like Locke, Bolingbroke, and Hutcheson came the quintessential American understanding of "right," "virtue," and "sentiment," just the notions that Mandeville thought were most likely to allow hypocrisy to run riot in a political setting, and precisely the ideas that did most to drive the American revolution forward. In this respect, Mandeville looks like an isolated rock around whom the streams of high-minded eighteenth-century political thought flowed until they reached America, at which point they washed him away altogether.

But the American political thought of this period cannot simply be reduced to anti-Mandevillian ideas such as these. In part this is because the Anglophone tradition on which the Americans drew itself had much deeper roots than that would suggest, stretching back from Smith and Locke to Hobbes and Francis Bacon (1561–1626), and back from there to the great names of classical and early modern republican and post-republican thought (including Tacitus and Machiavelli).[6] It is true that many Americans of the period—including Jefferson—were at pains to make explicit their rejection of what they understood as the Hobbesian view of human nature, but that is not true of all of them. John Adams, for example, was considerably more circumspect. Moreover, the political ideas of the American revolution stretch forward as well as back, towards the controversies of the early years of the republic, and the bitter party disputes in which both Adams and Jefferson took a prominent part. Political arguments like this—fractious, moralising, often deeply hypocritical—belong squarely in Mandeville's view of the world.

The other way in which American revolutionary thought can be connected to the themes I have discussed in the previous two chapters lies in its preoccupation with some of the problems that Hobbes and Mandeville pose for any rational conception of politics. The influence of Scottish Enlightenment conceptions of human moral sentiment is a testimony to this: these ideas were gratefully seized on because they offered a means of responding to the likes of Hobbes and Mandeville, who could not simply be ignored. In taking Hobbes and Mandeville seriously, the Americans also took seriously many of the puzzles concerning the problem of political hypocrisy that provide the central strands of the story I am attempting to tell in this book. The three authors that I will be discussing in this chapter were all, in their different ways, anti-hypocrites. But they were also, in their equally different ways, aware of the perils of anti-hypocrisy, and determined not to fall into the trap of overstating its significance.

The American revolution does provide the example of one significant political thinker who was as pure an anti-hypocrite as it is possible to meet in the history of modern political thought, at least the equal of Rousseau in this respect, and in some ways well beyond him, because a much less complicated figure. That man was Thomas Paine, who was well known to all three of the subjects of this chapter. Franklin helped to discover Paine (it was Franklin who provided Paine with his initial letters of recommendation before his first trip to America); Jefferson cultivated him once in America, and exploited the connection; Adams, by contrast, loathed and mistrusted him. It was Paine's *The Rights of Man* that provided the catalyst for the first great falling-out between Jefferson and Adams, thereby initiating one of the dominant story lines of American political history. But even Jefferson could not fully embrace Paine's particular brand of political sincerity. Indeed, Jefferson was only able to exploit his connection with Paine because he was a very different kind of political operator, much more subtle, much more shrewd, much more "cunning," to use one of the terms that was central to the political discourse of the period. Jefferson was as aware as anyone that sincerity had its limits.

This side of his character, coupled with the prodigious diversity of his accomplishments, has produced one of the enduring motifs of Jefferson studies: the view that he was a man of many masks, almost impossible for anyone to know fully. The same idea is also frequently applied to Franklin, a man of equally diverse talents, and equally hard to fathom. "So who was the real Benjamin Franklin?," as one recent commentator has framed it:

> First American and father of pragmatism? republican patriot and public servant? ambitious Tory imperialist? natural scientist? utilitarian hero of plodding and middling folk? devotee of the moral sublime? selfish opportunist? Francophile Deist? debauched aristocratic wannabe?[7]

By contrast, John Adams is not quite so complicated nor as hard to know, and in this if nothing else he has something in common with Paine, another man who found it extremely difficult to dissemble. But unlike Paine, Adams agonised about this side of his character—his natural sincerity—which he understood as an obvious failing in the way of life he had chosen for himself (and unlike Jefferson he did not pretend that his public prominence had somehow been chosen for him, against his own wishes). First as a lawyer, then as a revolutionary, then, like both Franklin and Jefferson, as a diplomat to the courts of Europe, and finally, like his great rival Jefferson, by whom he was eventually eclipsed, as the president of the United States, Adams discovered how inextricably bound up with hypocrisy are all the parts of public life. It became a preoccupation with him, but also a challenge, as he sought to identify which among this morass of hypocrisies were the ones that really mattered, and therefore where a place might still be found for the politics of sincerity.

The conclusions Adams reached on this question were strongly opposed to the views of Jefferson, and would have alienated Franklin too, had he lived to hear the worst of them. But the question itself is one whose salience all three recognised: how to prevent political sincerity from becoming its own kind of hypocrisy. The almost overwhelming historical significance of the long lives of these men, each crammed with incident, marked throughout by dramatic shifts of fortune, and encompassing by their end monumental political changes, means that there is a great deal to be said about how their own biographies encapsulate the difficulty of reducing a politician's character to its moral essence. Much of it has already been said, in the many biographies that have been written. In this chapter I want to explore what they themselves had to say about this difficulty, not simply in relation to their own lives, but also in relation to that body of modern political thought in which the problem of political sincerity loomed largest, and to which Hobbes and Mandeville also belong.

FRANKLIN AND THE HABIT OF SINCERITY

In his *Autobiography*, written towards the end of his life, Benjamin Franklin describes his first visit to London as a very young man (he was only eighteen when he arrived in 1724), in pursuit of printing business and intellectual adventure. At that time, he believed himself to be a free-thinking Deist, and it was in this capacity that he produced his first piece of philosophical writing, "a little metaphysical Piece . . . entitled *A Dissertation on Liberty & Necessity, Pleasure and pain.*" Franklin was later to consider this production to have been an "erratum" of his early years, a typical young man's mistake. However, he also notes that it made a small name for him in London, and was the means of bringing him to the attention of some interesting people. One of these was a surgeon called Lyons, author of *The Infallibility of Human Judgment*, who in turn "carried me to the Horns, a pale Ale-House in ——Lane, Cheapside, and introduc'd me to Dr Mandeville, Author of the Fable of the Bees, who had a Club there, of which he was the Soul, being a most facetious entertaining companion."[8]

It would be wonderful to know what Franklin and Mandeville talked about, and what lessons the young man took away from this encounter. Unfortunately, we can only speculate. What is clear, though, is that it did nothing to convert Franklin to Mandeville's side in the great moral philosophical disputes of the day. If anything, the reverse seems to have happened—when he returned from London, Franklin renounced his earlier Deism and embraced a philosophical position that was more consonant with traditional conceptions of Christian virtue. In 1735, he published another pamphlet that made this shift crystal-clear—as he describes it in the *Autobiography*, this was "A Discourse on Self denial, showing that Virtue was not secure, till its Practice became a Habitude, & was free from the Opposition of contrary Inclinations."[9] By identifying virtue as an inclination or habit that could with practise be made secure, Franklin was explicitly rejecting Mandeville's view that virtue had to be understood as a form of self-denial that could only exist in opposition to all our natural inclinations or habits of mind. In other words, Franklin had come down on Shaftesbury's side, having decided that virtue was consistent with the run of human sociability. Hence the pamphlet's deliberately anti-Mandevillian title: "Self-denial not the Essence of Virtue."

However, Franklin's own explanation for his move away from the view that human beings are naturally selfish emphasises not the philosophical but the practical demerits of that thesis. In the *Autobiography*, he describes his awakening to the problems posed by the Deist insistence on taking human beings for what they are—exemplified by the line "Whatever is, is right" that Franklin recalls as having been the motto for his London pamphlet—in the following terms: "I began to suspect that this Doctrine, tho' it might be true, was not very useful."[10] Indeed, the assumption that individuals were designed to pursue their own selfish desires, whatever these might be, could be considered self-defeating, because Franklin noticed that the behaviour of individuals who acted in this way tended to be undesirable, both for themselves and for others. It was therefore a question of utility: the traditional Christian virtues, including "truth, sincerity & integrity," were useful because they worked to the benefit of the people who practiced them. Franklin's personal experiences as recounted in the *Autobiography* were confirmation of this. Both his own youthful behaviour and that of his friends, "perverted" as he says by free-thinking ideas, caused them "great Trouble" (particularly in matters of the heart). By contrast, whenever Franklin made an effort to be open and honest with people, and to cultivate a reputation for hard work and reliability, then he found that his fortunes began rapidly to improve.

Yet once the matter is put in such pragmatic terms, then we are immediately back in Mandeville territory. The obvious question that arises, if virtue is to be pursued because of its benefits, and not because of its inherent value, is why individuals should not simply pretend to be virtuous, and reap the benefits that way. Franklin's own account of his progress through life emphasises the role of his truthfulness and sincerity in making a good impression on people. But if it is simply a matter of making a good impression, then what has genuine virtue got to do with it? Indeed, it is not difficult to make a utilitarian case for fake virtue over real virtue, because the individual who merely cultivates the outward appearance of truthfulness retains the capacity to lie and cheat when necessary, whereas the individual who is committed to being honest in all circumstances may sometimes find his honesty being used against him by those less scrupulous than himself. Franklin was well aware of this problem. His most explicit attempt to address it was given in a short essay he wrote in 1732 entitled "On Simplicity," which was published in the *Pennsylvania Gazette*. Here, he makes clear two things. First, that it is a mistake to think about the rewards of virtue in relation to isolated instances: this is simply fool's gold. What matters are not the one-off benefits to be gained in individual cases, but the more durable benefits that follow from acquiring a particular habit of mind. Second, that the main source for this insight long predates the argument between Shaftesbury and Mandeville. It comes a century earlier, in the writings of Francis Bacon.

Franklin's argument is an amalgam of two of Bacon's most influential essays: "Of Cunning" and "Of Simulation and

Dissimulation." These essays (first published in 1625) had gained a very wide currency in seventeenth- and early-eighteenth-century political thought, and were among the best known of all post-Machiavellian attempts to grapple with the problem of political deception.[11] Franklin's starting point is the essay on cunning. "Cunning," for Bacon, meant the kind of trickery that exploits the blind spots of one's rivals—it is the tactic of the cardsharp. To seek to deceive and trick others in this way can be useful in particular cases, but in the long run the habit of mind that promotes cunning becomes a handicap, because it constitutes a limited perspective on human affairs. It precludes an understanding of those circumstances when honesty really is the best policy, and therefore mistakes what Bacon calls "the real part of business."[12] Cunning men are to be distinguished from the genuinely wise by their inflexibility. Franklin endorses this view, and borrows an image directly from Bacon to capture its essence: "There is a great difference between a cunning Man and a wise One, not only in point of Honesty but in point of Ability; as there are those that can pack the Cards, who cannot play the Game well."[13]

Franklin wishes to go further than this, however. He also wants to show why wisdom itself should be equated with honesty, rather than simply with flexibility. For these purposes, the argument of Bacon's that matters is the one contained in "Of Simulation and Dissimulation," an essay that relates specifically to the question of when it makes sense to conceal or deliberately lie about one's true intentions or beliefs. This is a more subtle and complex problem than simply knowing how to avoid excessive cunning. To understand the choices involved, Bacon insists that it is necessary to separate out mere concealment from conscious deception. The latter is what he calls "Simulation," which occurs "when a man industriously and expressly feigns and pretends to be that which he is not"; the former is only "Dissimulation," as "when a man lets fall signs and arguments, that he is not that he is."[14]

Conceptually, this can be a difficult distinction to maintain—pretending not to be what you are is not always so different from pretending to be what you are not—but in practical terms, Bacon is clear that the difference is a significant one. Dissimulation means concealment, or holding something back. Simulation requires going out of your way to put something in the public domain that you know to be false. Both fall short of the whole truth, but only simulation is a deliberate policy of deception. Dissimulation, by contrast, may sometimes be the best option available in the treacherous circumstances of public life, where full disclosure can be extremely hazardous (and we should remember that public life for Bacon meant the deeply hazardous circumstances of late Elizabethan and Jacobean court politics). So the dissimulator can be said to hold things back because he has no choice; but the persistent simulator will find it much harder to offer this excuse, because to simulate is to lie "industriously."

Because of this difference between them, Bacon argues that simulation is "the more culpable, and less politic" form of behaviour, and he concludes that "a general custom of simulation . . . is a vice." This does not mean, however, that simulation is a bad thing in itself—the key term here is "custom." It is wrong to become habituated to lying, since it may leave one trapped in a pattern of mendacity that will be hard to escape and easy for others to dislike.[15] But so long as the lying is not habitual, then even simulation can have its advantages, particularly when it comes with the added element of surprise. Something similar is true of dissimulation, notwithstanding the fact that it is a less culpable activity in itself. "The habit of dissimulation," Bacon says, "is a hindrance and a poorness," because it is inconsistent with the true openness of mind that is the mark of the most successful men. On the other hand, those men whose minds are truly open will be open to the idea that dissimulation is often the best course of action, and they will be able to discern "what things are to be laid [bare], and what to be secreted, and what to be shewed at half lights."[16] Likewise, Bacon distinguishes between secrecy understood as mere silence and the sort of dissimulation that involves leaving a false trail. Habitual reticence is valuable, because it draws confidences, and teaches restraint. It is also consistent with that reputation for trustworthiness without which it is very hard to prosper. So, Bacon says, "an habit of secrecy is both politic, and moral."[17] Vocal dissimulation sometimes, and active simulation much more rarely, are necessary to supplement this habit only because it is not always possible to hold one's tongue without arousing suspicion.

Bacon summarises the intricate argument of the essay as follows: "The best composition and temperature is to have openness in fame and opinion; secrecy in habit; dissimulation in seasonable use; and a power to feign, if there be no remedy."[18] Franklin takes the core of this argument, and drops the qualifications. He does not distinguish either between dissimulation and simulation on the one hand, or between dissimulation and secrecy on the other. Instead, he equates them all with cunning, and he runs together Bacon's views about cunning with his views about concealment:

> Cunning, says my Lord *Bacon*, is a sinister or crooked Wisdom, and Dissimulation but a faint kind of Policy; for it asks a strong Wit and a strong Heart, to know when to tell the truth and to do it; therefore they are the weaker sort of Politicians that are the greatest Dissemblers.[19]

Having linked dissimulation with cunning, Franklin then goes on to identify honesty with wisdom, even though that is not how Bacon sees it.[20] For Bacon, wisdom lies in getting the balance between honesty and deception right, so that a reputation for honesty is preserved while a capacity for deception is retained. For Franklin, the only way to avoid the risks of becoming habituated to deception is to accustom oneself to honesty, with the result that the flexibility that Bacon prized is abandoned in favour of a deliberate abdication of personal discretion on matters relating to the truth. Franklin goes so far as to say that "wise Men cannot help being honest." He argues that any form of concealment will provide an obstacle to "true Wisdom," because the man who has something to hide will be unable to rely on the discretion and judgment of others. For Franklin, honesty really is the best policy.

Where Franklin also parts company with Bacon is in his embrace of the quintessentially eighteenth-century virtue of "simplicity," which is not what Bacon means by wisdom at all. "Simplicity of Speech and Manners is the highest Happiness as well as the Ornament of Life," Franklin writes, "whereas nothing is so tiresome to one's self, as well as odious to others, as Disguise and Affectation." This, apparently, is not just a question of policy but also of pure pleasure: "Even the most cunning Man will be obliged to own, the high and sincere Pleasure there is in conversing from the Heart, and without Design. What Relief do we find in the simple and unaffected Dialogues of uncorrupted Peasants, after the tiresome Grimaces of the Town!"[21] If we are a long way from Bacon here, we are also clearly a long way from Mandeville, who would suspect, with some reason, that all this was the rankest hypocrisy. Indeed, it is hard to reconcile what Franklin has to say about the natural virtue of simplicity with his apparent readiness to embrace the Baconian idea that life is like a game of cards, to be played with skill, not just skulduggery. So we are entitled to ask: what is Franklin thinking of here?

To help answer this question, it is worth comparing the use Franklin makes of Bacon's arguments with their deployment in a very different text that dates from the same decade as "On Simplicity," and was to have just as significant an impact on the subsequent development of American revolutionary thought. This is Bolingbroke's "The Idea of a Patriot King," which was written in late 1738. Bolingbroke's is an extended, highly polished, and deeply polemical assault on the corruption of the Walpole years. It attempts to recast Tory patriotism in the terms of classical (as opposed to Christian) virtue, by annexing it to the ideal of a monarch who stands above faction. Franklin's provincial journalism is far removed from all this high politics. But the link between them is Bacon on simulation and dissimulation.

Bolingbroke uses Bacon to argue that while political life may be impossible without some dissimulation, it nevertheless remains wrong to confuse this with overt lying.

> Simulation is a stiletto, not only an offensive, but an unlawful weapon; and the use of it may rarely, very rarely be excused, but never justified. Dissimulation is a shield, as secrecy is armour; and it is no more possible to preserve secrecy in the administration of public affairs without some degree of dissimulation, than it is to succeed without secrecy.[22]

By distinguishing between simulation and dissimulation, Bolingbroke sticks much closer to Bacon's original account than Franklin does. He also goes further in exploring some of its wider implications. Bolingbroke makes clear that while simulation and dissimulation both entail a form of concealment, only simulation involves the construction of a deliberate disguise. Keeping secrets is not the same as hiding behind a mask. Moreover, wearing a mask can make it much harder to keep secrets, because it reveals that one has something to hide. Bolingbroke insists that a virtuous ruler should not attempt to hide or conceal his private vices behind a public façade of probity, because such behaviour will eventually be found out, at which point it will be impossible to conceal anything. If a king wishes to appear virtuous he must act virtuously at all times, which means no drunkenness, no debauchery, no petty cruelties taking place behind the scenes. This is clearly an assault on the idea of private vices/public benefits, just as it is an obvious attack on the corruption of court life under Walpole. What it is not, however, is an argument in favour of inherent virtue over the mere appearance of virtue. Quite the opposite, in fact—Bolingbroke is saying that the only way to keep up appearances is to repudiate the idea that vices can be successfully disguised. Moreover, the neglect of appearances is a certain recipe for disaster, no matter how virtuous a king might be in other respects. "For want of a sufficient regard to appearances," Bolingbroke writes, "even their virtues may betray them into failings, their failings into vices, and their vices into habits unworthy of princes and of men."[23]

There is a paradoxical aspect to this argument. The best way to hide what one is up to is to avoid having to disguise it as something it is not—and the best way to avoid such disguises is to concentrate on maintaining appearances. Bolingbroke is championing what he calls "private decency," without which no public reputation of virtue will be secure. This decency cannot simply be an occasional performance, it must become a habit, because only if it is regular will it serve its purpose of closing the gap between reputation and reality. Yet once that gap is closed, then it becomes much easier to avoid prying eyes and constant speculation about one's motives. There is for Bolingbroke a freedom in the apparent constraint of having to reconcile private with public behaviour, and this freedom extends to the possibility of being able to conceal what one is really up to. This is the lesson he took from Bacon: the avoidance of routine simulation is the only secure means of ensuring that some things can be kept beyond the reach of one's enemies.

Franklin looks to be saying something very different. First, unlike Bolingbroke, his conception of virtue includes the Christian ideals of truthfulness and sincerity as well as the classical ones of honesty and probity, which makes it harder for him to put so much emphasis on appearances. Second, he has nothing to say about the importance of keeping secrets. Third, his bucolic ideal of simplicity seems starkly opposed to the sophistication of Bolingbroke's account. But behind all this, Franklin is making a case that is not so far from Bolingbroke's. For example, Franklin does not imply that simplicity has got nothing to do with appearances. Indeed, he pointedly describes simplicity as a form of dress—it is "the homespun

Dress of Honesty, and Chicanery and Craft are the Tinsel Habits and the false Elegance which are worn to cover the Deformity of Vice and Knavery."[24] Simplicity is a "habit" (in both senses of that word) but it is not a mask, because it is the form of dress worn by those wise enough to appreciate that a deliberate disguise merely advertises the unreliability of its wearer. "Who was ever cunning enough to conceal his being so?" Franklin asks. "No Mask ever hid itself."[25] Bacon and Bolingbroke share this view—the only habits worth acquiring are the ones that do not draw attention to themselves.

Where Franklin really differs is in the scope he gives to this lesson. Bolingbroke treats the problem of simulation and dissimulation as primarily a political one, and politics as primarily an activity conducted at court. He is arguing that the gap between public and private must be closed because the potential for its opening up is so great, in a world dominated by ceremony on the one hand and intrigue on the other. The setting for Franklin's account is nothing like this, and he does not limit himself to the environs of power. In fact, he does not limit himself at all. His view is that these are life lessons in the fullest sense, not just for princes, or courtiers, or men of business, but for everyone.

Another way to put this is that Franklin's is the democratic version of this argument, because it does not rely on any prior assumptions about who is a public man. We are all public men and women, which means that the distinction between the public and private looks increasingly obsolete. Bolingbroke believed that those who are serious about power should live as though their private lives were public, because that is the only way to ensure that some aspects of the public domain remained private. Franklin abandons such distinctions, and with them the idea of there being a place for secrecy, or for intrigue. This is not, therefore, a democratic understanding of virtue in any classical political sense. In fact, it is not really a political conception at all, because it finds no separate place for politics. Instead, it is a social conception of virtue, and it treats all human encounters, from affairs of the heart to the everyday transactions in a printing press, as occasions to practice the lessons that Bolingbroke reserves for the few.

This helps to explain the immense impact that Franklin's writings—including not just the essays and the *Autobiography* but also the Poor Richard maxims, with their homespun versions of the insights of Baconian humanism—have had on almost all aspects of American life, apart from the world of high politics, where the legacy of Franklin's example has been more limited. Yet it is one of the ironies of this story that among the benefits Franklin derived personally from his attempt to cultivate the social habits of virtue were manifest political ones. This is not true of the bulk of Franklin's life—including that part of it covered by the *Autobiography*—when his business and scientific achievements were not matched by achievements in the political sphere. He struggled to adapt to the intrigues and betrayals of court politics that he encountered when serving as a colonial agent in London during the 1750s and 1760s. In this context, Franklin's faith in the virtues of sincerity appeared naive. But the Revolution changed all that. Franklin went swiftly from being an advocate of conciliation between the Crown and the colonies to being one of the staunchest defenders of American independence. For some, such a volte-face would have been hard to achieve without appearing hypocritical, but Franklin's reputation for sincerity preceded him, and he got away with it. That reputation also preceded him to France, where he was sent as one of the first American commissioners at the end of 1776.

Franklin's diplomatic mission to France was the great political triumph of his life, and one of the most significant successes of the entire revolutionary period. It was achieved because of, not despite, the apparently apolitical nature of his conception of personal integrity. Franklin's "simplicity" gained him enormous popularity across French society, from aristocrats to radical intellectuals, and from the court to the general public. More surprisingly, it also provided the secret of his success as a diplomat at a time of high political intrigue between America, France, and Britain. Franklin refused to conduct his ambassadorial affairs with the usual discretion—he left papers lying around, did not care who opened his letters, and happily gossiped and flirted with anyone who would listen. As Bernard Bailyn has put it, this appalling lack of secrecy turned out to be an "adroit manoeuvre," because it left those trying to spy on American intentions unable to believe that things could be as slapdash as they seemed, and convinced that Franklin's openness must be concealing a cunning plan.[26] They assumed his simplicity was a disguise. It was not, but it worked to that effect by confounding those who refused to accept that anyone could be so careless of his secrets. This, perhaps, is the ultimate extension of Bacon's original insight that the best way to keep things hidden is to act as though one has nothing to hide.

Yet it would be wrong to read too much into it. Franklin's diplomatic success was, in Bailyn's words, "half contrived, half lucky." What's more, the circumstances in which it was achieved were so unusual as to defy the thought that this provides a model for other sorts of political behaviour. Franklin's fame, his age, and his eccentricity led the French to indulge him in ways that no diplomat has been indulged since. He came to France as the representative of a new kind of simple virtue whose appeal lay in its absence of obvious politicking motives. No appeal of that kind can last for long in politics. It is hard to imagine how it could have been extended back into the fractious party politics of the new American republic. Certainly, Franklin's ability to get away with anything while in France was a source at least as much of bemusement as of pride back home. When he died in 1790, his passing was treated as a world historical event by the French, who were just beginning their own experiment with the politics of republican virtue. But his death received a more muted response from the political elite of the new United States, who were starting to be concerned with other things.[27]

Adams and the science of sincerity

Among those who refused to believe that Franklin could be all that he seemed during his time in France was his fellow commissioner there, John Adams, who did not get along with Franklin at all. Adams mistrusted Franklin's brand of sincerity, which he considered to be pure hypocrisy, and cover for his personal vanity. He was also frustrated by seeing Franklin, who seemed to make no effort to keep things to himself, flourish in the duplicitous world of European court politics, whereas Adams, who wished to keep secrets, seemed unable to do so. In large part, this was a matter of temperament. Adams was an ambitious, highly intelligent but thin-skinned man, and he lacked much of Franklin's sense of ease with himself. He also lacked his ability to convey the impression that he had nothing to hide, despite the fact that he gave more of himself away. In the words of his cousin Samuel Adams, John Adams "was equally fearless of men and of the consequences of a bold assertion of his opinion . . . He was a stranger to dissimulation."[28]

Yet Adams's inability to dissimulate successfully was not for want of trying, and nor did it reflect a lack of interest in the philosophical literature on the subject. In a diary entry for August 19, 1770, when he was still making his way as a lawyer in New England, Adams records his meeting with a Mr. Tyler, who assures him that "the Author of the Fable of the Bees understood Human Nature and Mankind, better than any Man that ever lived." This provokes a series of reflections on the nature of "worldly wisdom" that continue in his entry for the next day:

> There are Times when and Persons to whom, I am not obliged
> to tell what are my Principles and Opinions in Politicks or Reli-
> gion. There are Persons whom in my Heart I despize; others I
> abhor. Yet I am not obliged to inform the one of my Contempt,

nor the other of my Detestation. This kind of Dissimulation, which is no more than Concealment, Secrecy and Reserve, or in other Words, Prudence and Discretion, is a necessary Branch of Wisdom, and so far from being immoral and unlawfull, that [it] is a Duty and a Virtue.[29]

This is close to Bacon, though expressed rather more moralistically (and with considerably more personal feeling). But perhaps conscious of his own problems in holding to such advice, Adams did not think it wise to draw too many general conclusions on this basis. "It is difficult to establish any certain Rule, to determine what Things a Man may and what things he may not lawfully conceal."[30]

Adams preferred instead to consider the political implications that followed from the fact that human beings are difficult to read. His political writings, published during and in the aftermath of the Revolution, do not devote much attention to the question of when people should be permitted to hide the truth. Instead, Adams was interested in the constitutional arrangements that best suit a species that cannot be relied on to see past appearances. In this respect, Adams's approach to the problem of hypocrisy is the opposite of Franklin's. Where Franklin was interested in exploring how an individual could retain a reputation for sincerity in a world of disguises, Adams wanted to know how to govern a society in which everyone could be so easily duped.

Adams's sense that human beings could not be trusted to recognise genuine virtue did not simply follow from his observations of the success of men like Franklin. It was also the result of his extensive reading in the classics of political realism, which extended from Aristotle and Tacitus through to Bacon, Hobbes, Mandeville, and Bolingbroke. On this basis, Adams was able to construct his own science of the natural superficiality of man. He believed that the historical evidence, along with personal experience, showed: first, that all societies divided into the many and the few, and therefore must contain an aristocratic as well as a democratic element; second, that an ideal society would be one in which the few were made up of the naturally virtuous; but third, that what people valued above genuine virtue was simply the appearance of distinction in whatever form, and the more visible the better. So real, as opposed to ideal, aristocracies tended to be made up of the well-born, the handsome, and the rich. This was not simply a reflection of what human beings looked for in others; it was also what they sought for themselves, for Adams also believed that the most basic human desire was simply to be noticed. He called this the *"spectemur agendo"*—the motivation to act under observation—and he argued that no political society could survive for long unless it took this passion seriously.

Given this, it is not hard to see why Adams, like Hobbes and Mandeville before him, should have thought that it was a waste of time to worry too much about everyday hypocrisy. People can hardly help pretending to be better than they really are, given that this was one of the surest ways to attract widespread attention. What exercised Adams, instead, was the hypocrisy of those who sought to overlay the *spectemur agendo* with high-blown language about virtue, integrity, and public-spiritedness. The dangers of this sort of hypocrisy were most acute in a democratic or republican setting, where it might be tempting to indulge in fantasies about the prevalence of genuine virtue, whereas under a monarchical or aristocratic form of government the importance of superficial distinctions would be much more visible, and therefore harder to ignore. In the aftermath of the Revolution, as Americans debated the best constitutional arrangements for their new republic, Adams became increasingly insistent on due recognition being given to the aristocratic element in political life. This led to repeated accusations that he had been corrupted by his experiences among the aristocracies of Europe, or worse still, that he had become a closet monarchist. As Thomas Jefferson was to put it, many years later, "the glare of royalty and nobility, during his mission to England, had made him believe their fascination a necessary ingredient in government."[31] But Adams maintained that this was quite wrong. He was not arguing in favour of aristocratic or monarchical government. He was arguing against democratic hypocrisy.

There were many different strands to this argument. In his extensive constitutional writings—including his monumental *Defence of the Constitutions of the United States* (1786–1787)—Adams drew on classical political thought to insist that political stability required a balance of aristocratic and democratic orders. He wished to preserve a separate chamber of the legislature for the wealthy and the well-born, so that these superficial attributes might be on display where everyone could see them.[32] He was deeply suspicious of the vogue for a single popular assembly ("unicameralism") that seduced, among others, his great rival Benjamin Franklin. The flaw in this scheme was not that it excluded the aristocratic elite, since it was impossible to exclude such elites—the undeserving rich, in Adams's terms, are always with us. Rather, the problem with pure popular government was that it would provide a cover for aristocratic machinations, and conceal the extent to which accidental qualities were still a significant feature of all forms of politics. The only way to promote genuine merit in republican politics was not to make any assumptions about its inevitable triumph. What was needed instead was a constitutional arrangement that found space for virtue by separating it out from the mere appearance of distinction. This was the central lesson Adams took from history: "The virtues have been the effect of the well-ordered constitution, rather than the cause."[33]

Also needed were the right incentives. Adams was deeply opposed to the view that politicians should be expected to serve the republic out of the goodness of their hearts, which would simply open the door to more hypocrisy. As he put it in a letter he wrote to the radical English clergyman John Jebb in 1785: "Although there are enough disinterested men, they are not enough in any age or any country to fill all the necessary offices, and therefore the people may depend upon it, that the hypocritical pretence of disinterestedness will be set up to deceive them, much oftener than the virtue will be practised for their own good." Hence Adams believed that politicians should be paid for what they do. But as well as receiving remuneration, politicians should also be rewarded with signs and symbols of distinction—the titles and honours that traditionally attached to the holding of office. This would serve two purposes: first, it would work on the natural human appetite for popular attention, and thereby attract as many people as possible into politics; second, it would leave the appearance of virtue in the control of the republic, and take it out of the hands of the aristocracy. If a state chose to avoid public symbols of distinction on the grounds that they were spurious baubles, this would merely generate the kind of political scheming it was designed to forestall, because it would force people to dress up their baser motives in the language of republican virtue. Without due attention to the appearance of things, Adams believed, you would simply end up with "a universal system of Machiavellian hypocrisy."[34]

Adams came to these views in the years of turbulence and political uncertainty that preceded the ratification of the new federal constitution. But the event that really confirmed him in them was the French Revolution. It inspired him to write his most contentious work, the *Discourses on Davila* of 1790 (Davila was a seventeenth-century Italian historian of the French civil wars whose writings Adams had discovered through Bolingbroke).[35] The *Discourses* were composed with a number of audiences in mind, including the French themselves, whom Adams saw as likely to be tempted by their revolutionary adventures into the more absurd reaches of republican hypocrisy. "FRENCHMEN!," he wrote,

Act and think like yourselves! . . . Acknowledging and boasting yourselves to be men, avow the feelings of men. The affectation of being exempted from passions is inhuman. The grave pretension to such singularity is solemn hypocrisy . . . Consider that government is intended to set bounds to passions which nature has not limited.[36]

(A handwritten addition to Adams's own copy of the *Discourses* ruefully notes: "Frenchmen neither saw, heard, nor felt or understood any of this. J.A. 1813.") His main target, however, was his fellow Americans, whom he saw as increasingly stirred up by the imaginary vision of a new French dawn, and therefore liable to be tempted into some damaging new hypocrisies of their own. Adams reminded his readers that he had lived in France, and though he understood the appeal of French philosophical conceptions of natural virtue, he also knew something of the character of the men who had produced them. "Go to Paris," he wrote, witheringly. "How do you find the men of letters? united, friendly, harmonious, meek, humble, modest, charitable? prompt to mutual forbearance? unassuming? ready to acknowledge superior merit? zealous to encourage the first symptoms of genius? Ask Voltaire and Rousseau. . . ."[37] Instead of indulging in fantasies of French public-spiritedness, Americans would be better off returning to the example of Great Britain, the durability of whose constitutional arrangements testified to the importance of taking men as they are, and balancing their natural impulses against each other. "[As] the world grows more enlightened," Adams declared, "false inferences may be drawn from it, which may make mankind wish for the age of dragons, giants and fairies."[38] France was becoming a land of rationalist fairy tales; Britain, the traditional bogeyman of the American political imagination, was the place where a realistic conception of politics might still be found.

Unfortunately for Adams, this was the wrong lesson at the wrong time. Most Americans were in no mood to be told that they should be looking to the British past, rather than the French future, for their political inspiration. Equally, as Gordon S. Wood has argued, Adams's preoccupation with Europe and its history had perhaps blinded him to the genuine innovations contained in the new American federal constitution.[39] Post-1787, politics could not simply be reduced to a choice between classical mixed government and doomed experiments in the politics of democratic virtue. The U.S. Constitution offered another option, which was a government of separated powers but not separate ranks, founded on the idea of popular sovereignty but filtered through the mechanism of political representation.

Whether or not Adams understood the significance of these changes, he certainly turned out to have a tin ear for their political ramifications. The real problem with the *Discourses* was that their arguments came to be confused in the public mind with Adams's error of judgment on the question of the appropriate titles for the high offices of the new federal state. In 1789 Congress had to decide what to call the new president. The House of Representatives quickly came down on the side of the plainest possible appellation—"George Washington, President of the United States." But Adams, along with others in the Senate, favoured something more regal, and suggested "His Highness" or "His most benign Highness" or even "His Majesty, the President." Because titles played such an important part in Adams's political architecture, and because he suspected that those who favoured republican simplicity were invariably the worst hypocrites of all, he stuck to this position for longer than anyone else, and far longer than was wise, once it became clear that public opinion was decisively against him. The controversy tarnished his reputation, and made him a figure of fun (his portly appearance meant that he acquired the nickname in the press of "His Rotundity"). It also made it easier to portray his championing of the British conception of mixed government as not merely old-fashioned, but positively sinister.

Clearly Adams got himself on the wrong side of this question about titles, so far as his own political fortunes were concerned. But what about the wider question of where to set the limits of hypocrisy in politics? In many ways, Adams's obsession with dressing up power in the trappings of distinction was not so much evidence of his hypocrisy (as many believed) but of his anti-hypocrisy. He shared a view that we have encountered already in this book: that what mattered was to protect politics from the hypocrisy of those who refused to acknowledge the role that outward appearances played within it. In other words, Adams was opposed to the second-order hypocrisy of modern republicanism, and he contrasted it with the first-order hypocrisy of both classical republicanism and constitutional monarchy. This did not mean that he wanted a constitutional monarchy for the United States. Rather, it meant that he feared a republic caught up in its own rhetoric would lose control of the politics of superficial appearance, and thereby become prey to the far more dangerous hypocrisy of spurious aristocratic virtue dressed up in democratic clothes. No state could do without ceremony and show, but a state that believed it was above these things was liable to succumb to them in their most destructive forms.

Adams remained convinced that the subsequent history of the French Revolution showed he was right about this. He also came to suspect that the early history of the American republic also provided glimpses of worse to come. In the *Discourses on Davila* he wrote: "It is universally true, that in all the republics now remaining in Europe, there is ... a more constant and anxious attention to [the] forms and marks of distinction than there is in the monarchies." And in a handwritten note in the margin dating from 1812, he added: "Our mock funerals of Washington, Hamilton, Ames, our processions, escorts, public dinners, balls, &c., are more expensive, more troublesome, and infinitely less ingenious."[40] If it was just a question of dinners and balls, this would hardly seem to matter. But underlying all Adams's warnings was a fear that the inescapable aristocratic element in American life—meaning the fake aristocracy of birth, wealth, and looks rather than a true aristocracy of virtue, merit, and talent—would be concealed beneath the surface of a self-congratulatory democratic politics, where it could do more damage, and where it would remain less accountable. Do we really want to say that Adams was wrong about this?

Where I think we can say Adams went wrong, however, is in his failure to appreciate how hard it is to separate out first-order from second-order hypocrisy. If anything, it was not that he went too far in his desire to accommodate signs and symbols in the new democratic order—it was that he did not go far enough. Adams believed that it ought to be possible to preserve at least one part of political life from empty rhetoric and showmanship. This domain was the scientific study of politics, and Adams repeatedly complained that the most important political terms—like "monarchy," "aristocracy," and "democracy"—were too often bandied about for effect, with little or no attempt to take seriously their true meaning. Adams revealed his own brand of republican sincerity when he complained that the scientific language of politics was being "employed like paper money, to cheat the Widow and the fatherless and every honest man."[41] Much better, in Adams's terms, to call the president "Your Highness" than to use a term like "republic" without understanding what it really meant.

But just as paper was destined to become the currency of the United States, so words like "democracy" and "republic" could not be preserved from the inevitable human tendency to inflate the value of anything that has a surface appeal. It was not possible to tolerate the trivial hypocrisies of political performance, yet somehow to preserve the integrity of the language needed to put these hypocrisies in context. This was a classic academic's mistake (and Adams, for all his varied career out in the world, was in some ways a classic academic). In the politics of the new republic, everything was liable to superficial treatment, including "scientific" arguments showing how important it was to find some accommodation with superficiality. Adams failed to appreciate that nothing could be placed out of bounds so far as political hypocrisy was concerned. In order to deal with the threat posed by hypocrisy, one had to be prepared to encounter it everywhere, and from anyone.

JEFFERSON AND THE POLITICS OF SINCERITY

The politician who did most to exploit the weakness of Adams's position after the publication of the *Discourses on Davila* was Thomas Jefferson. The occasion he used was the appearance in the United States of a book that seemed to offer a rebuke to Adams's fixation on the old idea of a mixed constitution. That book was Thomas Paine's *The Rights of Man*, which Jefferson passed on to a Philadelphia printer with a note saying that it would serve as an answer to "the political heresies that have sprung up amongst us." When the volume was published in the spring of 1791 with Jefferson's endorsement prominent on the title page, most readers clearly understood that the heresies referred to were the ones contained in the *Discourses on Davila*. Adams found himself on the receiving end of violent denunciations in the press, where he was accused of being a monarchist, a friend of the British, and an enemy of republicanism everywhere. His son, John Quincy Adams, came to his defence by publishing a series of responses to Jefferson under the pseudonym "Publicola," but this only made things worst (not least because many assumed that "Publicola" was Adams senior). When Jefferson finally wrote to Adams to explain himself, he pleaded innocence. The endorsement of Paine, he said, had never been intended for publication, and he was "thunderstruck" when he discovered that it had been so used. Blame for the controversy rested with Publicola, who had stirred things up, and with the increasing trend for newspaper controversy more generally, from which Jefferson deliberately kept himself aloof.

This was dissimulation. What Jefferson did *not* say was that he knew perfectly well that Publicola was not Adams himself but his son; and nor did he admit that he had had Adams in mind when he wrote the original note. When Adams responded to this letter with some anger, Jefferson sent another in which he moved from dissimulation to simulation, or what we would now call lying. He told Adams that when he referred to "heresies," so "far from naming you, I had not even in view any writing which I might suppose to be yours."[42] Yet when Jefferson had written earlier to Washington to explain himself, he had acknowledged that Adams was his target (Washington was one of the people he most wished to be apprised of the unpopularity of Adams's views), blaming what followed on the printer for making public what should have remained private. There can be no doubt that it was Jefferson who behaved worst throughout this affair, but it was Adams who came out worst in the end. The damage done to his reputation did not prevent him from succeeding Washington as president in 1797, but the stigma of heretical monarchism clung to him, and was ruthlessly exploited by Jefferson's supporters in the presidential election of 1800, which Adams lost, and Jefferson eventually won.

For Bacon, the mark of the truly wise politician is to know not simply how to dissemble, but also when, in extremis, to embrace a lie. Jefferson got away with his lie, and once they were both retired from public life he even managed to repair his relationship with Adams as well. Yet Jefferson was something more than simply the model of a Baconian politician. Part of the reason for this is that the type of politics he had to embrace went beyond Bacon's distinction between simulation and dissimulation. The political battle between Adams and Jefferson, particularly during the virulently abusive campaign of 1800, was carried out in the newspaper press by proxies happy to peddle whatever dirt could do the most damage to the opposing camp. Jefferson liked to claim he was above all this, and that it was not his doing; nevertheless, he was aware of it, he benefitted from it, and he did nothing to stop it. Allowing falsehoods to gain currency while keeping one's own hands clean is something more than just dissimulating, and Jefferson's aloofness in this context looks a lot like hypocrisy—the hypocrisy of the politician who dissembles about his own reliance on the lies of others. Yet some hypocrisy is unavoidable here. Journalists, whatever they might tell themselves, have different habits from politicians, which means that the maintenance of a reputation for probity is less important for them than creating a splash. Politicians, meanwhile, whatever they might tell themselves, depend on journalists to do their dirty work. In an ideal world, we might wish politicians to do their own dirty work, but in the real world, that would simply leave them exposed to the hypocrisy of their rivals. To put it in Bacon's terms, once there exists a class of journalists for whom "the power to feign" has become the main weapon in their armoury, then politicians have less need of that power for themselves. Jefferson exploited this fact of modern political life, and he can hardly be blamed for doing so.

However, it is important to note that Jefferson would never dream of defending himself in such a "worldly-wise" fashion—in this respect, Bacon's terms were not Jefferson's. For all his worship of Bacon, it was the scientific Bacon Jefferson admired, not the purveyor of morally ambiguous snippets of political wisdom. Like Franklin, Jefferson made it clear that he rejected the subtlety of many of Bacon's distinctions when it came to personal sincerity, and believed instead in a more straightforward and consistent truthfulness. In a letter he wrote to his nephew in 1785 offering some advice about personal conduct, he stated:

> Nothing is so mistaken as the supposition that a person is to extricate himself from a difficulty, by intrigue, by chicanery, by dissimulation, by trimming, by an untruth, by an injustice. This increases the difficulties tenfold; and those who pursue

these methods get themselves so involved at length, that they can turn no way but their infamy becomes more exposed.[43]

These strictures are hard to reconcile with Jefferson's own subsequent behaviour. Then again, this is not advice for a career politician, but for a young man first making his way in the world—it is closer to the advice that Franklin believed should serve as the default position for everyday life.

Where Jefferson went further than Franklin was in his explicit rejection of a Hobbesian conception of human motivation. He described the principles of Hobbes's political philosophy as "humiliation to human nature," and he held fast throughout his life to the view that human beings were naturally sociable, and inclined towards virtue. He drew on the Scottish Enlightenment response to Mandeville to argue that virtue should not be opposed to our natural inclinations, but understood rather as a natural tendency distinct from pure selfishness. Doing good, Jefferson maintained, is consistent with the pursuit of pleasure, because "nature hath implanted in our breasts a love of others, a sense of duty to them, a moral instinct in short."[44] This instinct could be cultivated and enhanced with the aid of education. As a result, there was no need to see virtue as involving a necessary double standard: with due care and attention, it ought to be possible for human beings to do good without having to seem better than they really are. Jefferson's view of the world, more than Franklin's, and certainly more than Adams's, was a deliberate rejection of Mandeville's.

Nevertheless, for all this, Jefferson was never an apostle of personal integrity in the manner of Thomas Paine. Paine's own public career was eventually destroyed by the publication of *The Age of Reason* (1795), in which he made clear his belief that there ought to be no limits to the truth, and no excuses for concealing it, in private life, in politics, and above all in religion. Some of Paine's reasoning in favour of the imperative of sincerity was pragmatic—"so it is with pious fraud as with a bad action," he wrote at one point, "[that] it begets a calamitous necessity of going on"—and therefore not far from Jefferson's. But he goes further, and establishes a principle of "mental truthfulness" by which everything else must be judged:

> It is impossible to calculate the moral mischief . . . that mental lying has produced on society. When a man has so far prostituted and corrupted the chastity of his mind as to subscribe his professional belief to the things he does not believe, he has prepared himself for the commission of every other crime.[45]

Jefferson sympathised with this position, as he sympathised personally with Paine when Paine found himself effectively ruined for attempting to uphold it. But Jefferson never adopted this position himself. That is, he never suggested that individuals must always be true to what they really believe. Instead, he limited himself to saying that individuals who lose the habit of truthfulness in the end lose their ability to know what it is they believe. At the conclusion of his advice to his nephew, he says: "This falsehood of the tongue leads to that of the heart, and in time depraves all good dispositions."[46] Jefferson is working from the outer person to the inner person, whereas Paine goes from the inner to the outer—from a corrupted chastity to wider moral mischief.

Likewise, when it came to politics, Jefferson reasoned from the outside in, not from the inside out. He championed freedom of religion so that people might learn to be honest with themselves, rather than suggesting that they must be honest with themselves in order to have true freedom of religion. His faith in democracy—in letting the people choose whom they should be governed by, instead of seeking to protect them from those who might exploit them—followed the same logic. Only by providing the outward forms of democratic openness could the people learn to recognise what true fraudulence in politics consisted in. In a letter he wrote to John Adams in

1813, Jefferson claimed, somewhat disingenuously, that this had been the sole ground of difference between them:

> You think it best to put the pseudo-*aristoi* into a separate chamber of legislation, where they may be hindered from doing mischief . . . I think the best remedy is exactly that provided by all our institutions, to leave to the citizens the free election and separation of the *aristoi* from the pseudo-*aristoi*.[47]

By *aristoi* Jefferson meant the genuinely virtuous; by pseudo-*aristoi* he meant the holders of the empty titles of birth and rank. Later on in the same letter, he refers to the "tinsel-aristocracy," whose fake virtues only democracy can expose. The phrase is reminiscent of Franklin's use of the term "tinsel habits" to describe the superficial wisdom of the cunning. Democracy, for Jefferson, was the homespun dress of political honesty, by which the trappings of political privilege might be exposed.

The problem, though, was that democracy was more than this, as Jefferson was well aware. It was also a battle for power, between factions of people willing to deploy whatever weapons were to hand to secure their own advantage. In the early years of the republic, these factions took the form of parties who fought about most things, including the French Revolution, monarchism, democracy, money, and titles, as well as the personal characters of both Thomas Jefferson and John Adams. Jefferson, given his attachment to an ideal of democratic sincerity, was publicly committed to seeing all this factionalism and name-calling as essentially superficial. As he famously put it in his first inaugural address, having emerged victorious and relatively unscathed from the seething pit of American electoral politics: "We have called by different names brethren of the same principle. We are all republicans—we are all federalists."[48] But in his private letters he painted a somewhat different picture. There he suggested that the divisions between the parties corresponded to a deep division in human nature, between the "Honest men" on the one hand, and the "Rogues" on the other. Or as he put it in a letter he wrote in the early years of his presidency:

> The division between whig and tory is founded on the nature of men, the wealthy and nerveless, the rich and the corrupt seeing more safety and accessibility in a strong executive; the healthy, firm and virtuous feeling confidence in their physical and moral resources, and willing to part with only so much power as is necessary for their good government.[49]

Once the fight is put in these terms, there could only be one winner—the Whigs/Republicans would defeat the Tories/Federalists, because they had right, strength, and the people on their side. "I believe," Jefferson wrote in 1797, "and here, I am sure, that the great mass is republican."[50]

Jefferson wanted to believe that underneath the spurious acrimony of party politics there was a real divide between courage and cowardice that democracy would bring to the surface. But how then to explain the persistence of acrimonious party politics, with all its name-calling and chicanery, within American democracy? One answer was to suggest that this was in fact a reflection of the triumph of republicanism, and that the party divisions were simply a function of underlying agreement on principles. "I always expected," Jefferson wrote towards the end of his presidency, when the Federalists were in some disarray, "that whatever names the parties might bear, the real division would be into moderate or ardent republicanism."[51] As time went on, however, Jefferson started to believe that something else was happening beneath the surface. When the Federalists abandoned their original name and started to pass themselves off as Republicans, Jefferson warned that "the amalgamation is of name only . . . Hence new Republicans in Congress preaching the doctrines of the old Federalists."[52] In 1823, he wrote that the Federalists "have shrunk from the odium of their old appellation, taken to themselves a participation of ours . . . under the pseudo-republican mask."[53] And in one of his last letters from 1825, he declared:

> The common division of whig and tory, or according to our denominations of republican and federal . . . is the most salutary of all divisions, and right, therefore, to be fostered instead of being amalgamated. For take away this and some more dangerous principle of division will take its place.[54]

This is not so far removed from Adams, notwithstanding the fact that it is specifically designed to make the difference between Jefferson's party and Adams's party clear. Better, Jefferson is saying, as Adams had once said, to have the undeserving lined up where you can see them, rather than hiding behind the empty titles of republicanism.

Jefferson's shifts on the question of party politics—from seeing its divisions as integral to seeing them as superficial to seeing them as integral again—is a reflection of the inherent tension in his idea of democratic sincerity. One the one hand, the rise of democracy meant that the party of the pseudo-*aristoi*—the Federalists—should be defeated, as indeed they ultimately were. On the other hand, the persistence of party politics meant that the defeated party could hide behind the cover of false names. Another way to put this is as follows: if democracy worked in the way Jefferson hoped, then party divisions should become superficial, because under the surface republican principles will have triumphed; but if party divisions have become superficial, that would work to the advantage of the class of men who had previously been represented by the Federalists, and were happiest playing around with titles. Party disputes, according to Jefferson's view of the world, ought to be trivial, because people are naturally sociable and democratic virtue is unstoppable. But if we are to have such disputes, it is preferable in the end for them to be nontrivial, so that those who oppose the Jefferson view of the world should have nowhere to hide.

This tension caused Jefferson to shift on other questions too. A free press, for example, which formed a crucial part of Jefferson's faith in openness of popular opinion, also caused him deep misgivings when it failed to live up to its democratic billing. "Nothing now can be believed which is seen in a newspaper," he wrote to a friend in 1807. "Truth itself becomes suspicious by being put into that polluted vehicle."[55] Newspapers, like political parties, ought to be nonpartisan enough to be vehicles of truth, but also openly partisan enough not to serve as cover for falsehood. It is easy to portray this as having it both ways. Jefferson liked newspapers that supported his version of the truth and disliked those that did not, which meant, among other things, that he liked newspapers that rubbished the purported truths of his enemies. The Jefferson who complained about newspapers in 1807 was also the Jefferson who rose to the presidency on the back of them in 1800. Likewise, the Jefferson who wanted democracy to triumph over the party system was also the Jefferson who did most to ensure the victory of his own party in the rough and tumble of democratic politics.

This then leads us to the inevitable question: was Jefferson a hypocrite? All these seeming inconsistencies, coupled with Jefferson's obvious relish for power, and his readiness to use it while president in spite of his own view that a taste for a strong executive was the mark of a rogue, make it hard to resist seeing him in this light, and that's before we even get to the question of slavery. Certainly John Adams, from early on, thought he knew Jefferson's type. When, in 1793, Jefferson retired to Monticello, apparently sick of public life, Adams wrote to his son John Quincy:

Jefferson thinks he shall by this step get a reputation of a humble, honest, meek man, wholly without ambition or vanity. He may even have deceived himself into this belief. But if the prospect opens, the world will see . . . he is ambitious as Oliver Cromwell.[56]

Others have gone further. In one of the greatest of all novels about modern politics, Gore Vidal's *Burr* (written from the perspective of Jefferson's one-time vice president Aaron Burr, whom Jefferson eventually put on trial for treason), Jefferson is portrayed as the ultimate hypocrite: a man of limitless sanctimony, vain, preening, cold-hearted and ruthless, always willing to dress up his personal failings in the garb of republican sincerity—to the extent that he refused to deliver his presidential addresses to Congress in person because that would be "monarchical," and therefore had a clerk read them for him, when the truth was that his weak nerves and reedy voice simply made him dread public speaking. "Had Jefferson not been a hypocrite I might have admired him," Vidal has Burr say. "After all, was he not the most successful empire-builder of our century, succeeding where Bonaparte failed. But then Bonaparte was always candid when it came to motive, and Jefferson was always dishonest."[57]

Burr, however, is history written from the loser's point of view. The other unavoidable fact about Jefferson, as even Burr has to concede ("in the end, candour failed; dishonesty prevailed"), is just how successful Jefferson's brand of hypocrisy proved. This is the alternative view: that what its victims see as hypocrisy was from a different perspective simply masterful politics. Even one of John Adams's most recent admirers, C. Bradley Thompson, who has attempted to resurrect Adams's reputation as a political theorist, is forced to admit he was thoroughly outmanoeuvred by Jefferson the politician. "Unlike John Adams, who always put his cards on the table, Thomas Jefferson was a master at palming his ace. He may very well have been the greatest politician of his generation."[58] This palming of the ace is an image with strong echoes of Bacon, suggestive perhaps of great cunning but not great wisdom. But in Bacon's terms, the successful deployment of cunning is the mark of true wisdom, because it can only reward those who understand its limits. If this is political wisdom, Jefferson had it.

Jefferson also had his own understanding of politics as a game of cards. In a letter he wrote to a political supporter, John Taylor, in 1798, in the early days of the Adams presidency, he counselled patience:

> If the game sometimes runs against us at home, we must have patience till the luck turns, and then we shall have an opportunity of winning back the *principles* we have lost. For this is a game where principles are the stake.[59]

It is an arresting image, and a quintessentially Jeffersonian one. Politics is a game played with principles, and shot through with luck. How, one might ask, can these be genuine principles if one is willing to stake them? But it is an essential part of Jefferson's political outlook to suppose that these two things can be combined, and what is more, to imagine that in the great game of politics, those whose principles are the right ones will be better equipped to ride out the luck and win in the end. In this way, Jefferson's conception of politics could accommodate both high strategy and high principles. That, indeed, is what it was designed to do.

It does not make sense, therefore, to accuse Jefferson of the crude hypocrisy of the anti-hypocrite—to see him as someone who could not live up to his own standards of political integrity. His standards of integrity were intended to be flexible, and were not simply anti-hypocritical. He was more flexible than Franklin, because he was more political, and more flexible than Adams, because he was less rigid in his distinction between first-order and second-order hypocrisy. Even one of Jefferson's most famous early statements of political principle—his declaration, in his 1774 pamphlet *A Summary View of the Rights of British America*, that "the whole art of government consists in the art of being honest"—which is often taken to offer a rebuke to his later political behaviour when in office, is in fact nothing of the sort.[60] The key term here is not "honest" but "art." Politics, for Jefferson, was an artificial exercise in honesty, in which what mattered was preserving one's room for manoeuvre by preserving one's reputation for integrity. In this, he was simply following Bolingbroke, almost to the letter.

But Jefferson went beyond Bolingbroke in a number of respects. He was more successful by far (Bolingbroke's own career was marked by a conspicuous failure either to achieve his objectives or to reach high office). He also understood the democratic extension of the art of honesty, which brought in an element of playing to the gallery that Bolingbroke would have disdained. But perhaps most importantly, Jefferson had an extra element to his personality that Bolingbroke lacked, the one that Adams identified when he compared him to Cromwell: Jefferson was ready to take himself at face value—to believe in the best of himself—which can be crucial in maintaining a reputation for principled political action. He did not worry too much about whether his high principles could survive being staked in the low game of politics, and he did not think that they needed to be adapted accordingly. He simply trusted in his own ability to maintain his integrity. Whether this should qualify as a form of self-deception, as Adams suggests, is a very difficult question to answer.

What it does suggest, however, is that there is another model of the successful politician to which Jefferson conforms, and that is Mandeville's, for whom Cromwell also provided a template. Like Mandeville's Cromwell, Jefferson understood the conjuncture of the age in which he lived, and he sought to achieve a form of political sincerity that suited it. Equally, as with Mandeville's Cromwell, that form of sincerity was a mixture of knowingness and a certain lack of self-knowledge, or at least of self-scrutiny. This enabled him to negotiate the game of politics without succumbing either to excessive artifice or excessive innocence. Adams saw the political need for artifice but could not find a sufficient place for innocence; Franklin saw the political need for innocence but could not find a sufficient place for artifice. Jefferson found a place for both.

But it is easier to internalise the conflicting dynamics of political hypocrisy and political sincerity when the political tides are running your way. The tide started to turn against Jefferson towards the end of his life, at which point he became a man out of time, as John Adams had been for much of his political life. The issue that did it, ironically, was slavery. The Missouri Compromise of 1820, which divided the United States into slave and nonslave territories according to a geographical principle adopted by Congress, horrified Jefferson, who believed it spelled the "the knell of the Union."[61] It also spelled the end of the old party divisions, which became subsumed under new distinctions between "democratic" and "national" republicans. It was in the aftermath of this that Jefferson made his plea to go back to the old divisions between "whig" and "tory," and the old names, which at least had the merit of transparency. As it was, political principle had become attached to "a geographical line," and the line between the parties had been overlain with new names and confused identities. So Jefferson found himself in the position Adams had been a generation earlier, demanding that a limit be set to political hypocrisy, that "pseudo"-principles be lined up where one can see them, and that the words used to describe the essence of politics should not get mixed up with more superficial distinctions. The fact that Jefferson's warnings were worth heeding, just as Adams's had been, and were a mark of intellectual honesty that went beyond the "art" of honesty that Jefferson had displayed in government, should not blind us to another fact about his predicament: this kind of honesty can also be a sign of political weakness.

⟶┼∞ 4 ∞┼⟵

BENTHAM AND THE UTILITY OF FICTION

HYPOCRISY AND UTILITARIANISM

One way of thinking about hypocrisy, as we have seen, is as the wearing of masks, with the intention to conceal or deceive. Countering hypocrisy seems to require the removal of the mask. In the history of modern political thought, Jeremy Bentham (1748–1832) stands out as a thinker for whom the business of unmasking was integral to everything he did. H.L.A. Hart, the greatest twentieth-century commentator on Bentham's work, has described the central theme running through it as "demystification."[1] Bentham himself put it in these terms: his task was to join with those others "whose care it has been to pluck the mask of Mystery from the face of Jurisprudence."[2] And not only jurisprudence: throughout his career, Bentham sought to peel back the layers of obscurity and deliberate deception that had concealed the truth about politics, religion, private and public morality. What Bentham hated, more than anything, was the hypocritical concealment of the basic facts of social existence behind a mask of apparently superior wisdom. It seems to make sense, therefore, to place Bentham among those political theorists for whom hypocrisy and truth-telling stand in direct opposition to one another, and who take the side of openness against concealment. If anyone does, it is Bentham who appears to belong in the list of liberal rationalists who have no time for hypocrisy.

But it is not as simple as that. As always, it very much depends what sort of concealment we are talking about, and Bentham was well aware that not all hypocrisies are the same. Take, for example, his attitude to that great exemplar of the problem of hypocrisy in modern politics, Oliver Cromwell. In his *Introduction to the Principles of Morals and Legislation*, Bentham borrows an example from Hume's *History of England* to illustrate how easy it is for people to conceal their true feelings behind an outward show of emotion:

> A man may exhibit . . . the exterior appearances of grief, without really grieving at all, or at least in anything near the proportion in which he appears to grieve. Oliver Cromwell, whose conduct indicated a heart more than usually callous, was as remarkably profuse with tears . . . To have this kind of command over one's self, was the characteristic of the excellence of the orator of ancient times, and is still that of the player in our own.[3]

Even though Bentham hardly shared Hume's politics, this passage might suggest that he shared much of Hume's suspicion of political operators like Cromwell, who could put on an act as the occasion demanded. Far from it, however. Bentham adored Cromwell, tears and all. In a letter he wrote in 1817 to "The Citizens of the United States" (offering, with typical bravado, to codify their laws for them), Bentham described Cromwell as "that wonderful man," and lamented the absence of his reforming zeal from the world as he now found it: "The spirit which animated the English in those days is no more— we are content to be 'cheated', we are content to be 'abused'."[4] What Bentham loved about Cromwell was that he was not content to be cheated or abused, but sought instead to expose the hidden workings of power, particularly as concealed behind the mumbo-jumbo of law and established religion. In other words, Cromwell was himself an unmasker, and the fact that he might have had to put on a mask in order to perform that role was neither here nor there. Bentham saw clearly the distinction between being a hypocrite in the means of personal conduct and a truth-seeker in public ends.

But Cromwell's tears were not highlighted by Bentham in order to make a point about political power. Rather, Bentham was making a different but related point, that those who make the law should not fall into the trap of assuming that people are what they seem. Cromwell's behaviour shows that the visible manifestations of the human passions are not always to be trusted, and the legislator who seeks to regulate our affairs should not take everything at face value. A certain amount of dissembling is a fact of life. But Bentham goes further than this, particularly in his later writings—he does not simply think that dissembling is unavoidable; he also thinks it is socially useful. In his *Deontology* of 1829, in which he outlines his understanding of the virtues, Bentham argues in favour of the merits of the polite concealment of one's true feelings. For example: "Let a man be naturally ever so stupid, do not let him see, much less give him to understand, that you think him so."[5] Likewise, "if a man is doing or saying anything which is unpleasant to you, instead of directing him to cease, rather propose something else."[6] The *Deontology* is a surprising book in many ways. There is advice on how to behave in all sorts of tricky social situations, even including an extended passage on problem of how to behave when someone is suffering from wind at the dinner table. Like Hobbes, Bentham was very interested in the ways that smells bring out the unavoidable double standards of human behaviour: smells we don't mind when produced by ourselves are repugnant to us when produced by others. So we need to be very careful:

Solid, liquid or gaseous, the contents of one man's stomach are not agreeable to the sense of smell of another. As often as a portion of gas makes its way from your stomach, be careful therefore so to direct the course of it, that no person in the whole company shall be within range of it. By a turn of the head while at table, this may always be managed. But if, sitting with his face to company, a man stops the blast by keeping his lips closed, and then it suffers to escape without change of position, the consequence is that, by the tensed state of the lips, the whole company feel themselves threatened with the explosion, and whether the smell does or does not reach the organ so as to affect the sense, uneasiness is produced by the apprehension of it.[7]

Bentham being Bentham, this is somewhat complicated advice, and it is not always easy to see how it should be followed. But what is clear is that he believes that in these circumstances a certain amount of deliberate concealment of the truth is desirable.

Bentham is very aware in the *Deontology* that he is giving what his readers will recognise as eighteenth-century advice in a nineteenth-century setting. In a striking comparison, he admits that what he has to say about a whole range of questions of appropriate etiquette is not that different from the guidance available from Lord Chesterfield, whose *Letters to His Son* (first published in 1774) had by this point replaced Mandeville's *Fable of the Bees* as the wickedest social manual of them all.[8] Like Chesterfield, Bentham is advocating what many would regard as rank hypocrisy: the concealment of selfish motives behind a mask of civilised behaviour. Where he differs from Chesterfield, Bentham says, is not in the sorts of dissimulation he sanctions, but in the reasons he is able to give to justify this kind of behaviour: he, unlike Chesterfield, has a system that is able to reconcile selfishness with social benefits—it is called the system of utilitarianism. In utilitarian terms, it is absurd to think of publicly beneficial actions motivated by self-regarding interests as hypocrisy. Instead, such behaviour is the very definition of virtue. The other advantage of Bentham's system, he claims, is that it reveals the limits of politeness. "In the forms of politeness so-called," Bentham says, "there is much unnecessary lying."[9] One example he gives is the Spanish saying "This house is yours (*mi casa es su casa*)," which "is to tell a lie to no purpose whatever."[10] Here is the clearest possible indication that Bentham is not simply on the side of truth as against lies—he is also on the side of useful as against unnecessary lies.

In defining virtue in utilitarian terms, Bentham was clearly distancing himself from Mandeville, for whom socially beneficial selfishness is only ever, at best, the simulacrum of true virtue, and never the real thing. Nevertheless, Bentham strongly echoes Mandeville elsewhere in his writings when he makes clear what he does consider to be hypocrisy in moral matters. In his *Table of the Springs of Action* (1815), Bentham contrasts utilitarianism with what had come to be known as "sentimentalism," the late-eighteenth- and early-nineteenth-century doctrine that prized benevolence and fellow feeling as integral to human nature, whose roots can be traced all the way back to Shaftesbury and whose influence extended through to the political thought of the American Revolution and beyond. Bentham was a staunch anti-sentimentalist, and it is perhaps no coincidence that he struck up a personal friendship with Aaron Burr, the most anti-sentimental of all the American founders—John Adams notwithstanding—and the man who came to supplant Adams as Thomas Jefferson's archrival.[11]

We do not know what Bentham's view was of Jefferson—though if his main source of information was Burr, then we can be sure it would not have been favourable—but we do know that what he disliked about sentimentalism was the scope it offered for hypocrisy. The utilitarian, Bentham believed, can never dress up his self-denial as anything more than displaced self-interest; the sentimentalist, by contrast, may come to believe that he has genuinely put the interests of his fellow creatures first. This, says Bentham, is the philosophy of the hypocrite. "The utilitarian can never serve sinister interests by his doctrine," Bentham claims. "The sentimentalist, often [does]. He preaches the doctrine of self-denial, generosity etc., that others may practice it for his benefit."[12] Utilitarian self-denial, in Bentham's words, "confesses [its] selfishness," whereas sentimentalist self-denial tries to hide it.[13] Like Mandeville, and in some senses like Adams as well, Bentham believed that the worst sort of moral hypocrisy was hypocrisy *about* the self-serving roots of socially useful behaviour.

HYPOCRISY AND EMPTY WORDS

In all these respects, Bentham's attitude to hypocrisy sounds like an amalgam of ideas we have encountered already. But what it does not convey is Bentham's distinctive sense of the role language can play in disguising people's true motives for action. For Bentham, the real danger with hypocrisy was not that it allowed people to pretend to be what they were not, but that it left people unable to distinguish between meaningful discourse and mere babble. We might have to wear masks to hide our own feelings, Bentham accepted, but words themselves should not become a way of masking reality. The best way to capture the essence of Bentham's anxieties here is to look away from his moral philosophy and instead at what he has to say about the problem of hypocrisy in the context of a very specific controversy, one that combines his worries about the interplay between the languages of law, religion, and politics.

In 1813, Bentham delivered a pamphlet in Oxford entitled *Swear Not At All* ("Containing an Exposure of the Needlessness and Mischievousness as well as Anti-Christianity of the Ceremony of an Oath"). It is a typical Bentham production—overlong, hard to follow, endlessly discursive, excessively technical, but also very funny in places, and with a core of good sense running all the way through it like a sliver of steel. It contains Bentham's views about the absurdity of requiring people to swear oaths before taking up certain offices, binding them to uphold the terms of that office, and binding God to punish them if they should stray. Its particular target was the requirement that members of Oxford and Cambridge universities should have to promise by oath to abide by statutes that governed membership of those two institutions. The central thrust of his case is given in the pamphlet's extensive subtitle, which says, among other things, that it will contain "a Proof of the open and persevering contempt of moral and religious principle, perpetuated by [such oaths], and rendered universal in the two Church-of-England Universities, more especially in the University of Oxford."[14]

Now, the practice of requiring people to swear to be good in God's name before taking up some beneficial position looks like an obvious invitation to hypocrisy: it will inevitably encourage some people to say things they don't really believe, and to affect religious convictions they don't actually possess, in order to get on. Bentham's subtitle seems to promise an argument of this kind. But in fact, that is not his concern at all. What Bentham detests about oaths is that *no one* can possibly mean them, whatever the state of his own religious beliefs: they are absurd because the words are meaningless in themselves (in particular, Bentham thinks it is pointless to seek to bind God in some kind of pseudo-contractual arrangement to punish malefactors—"so help me God," etc.—since if God is God, he will punish whom he likes). So the hypocrisy Bentham is warning against is not the hypocrisy of the people who take these oaths without meaning them, but the hypocrisy of the people who continue to insist on their necessity. "This instrument of priestcraft," Bentham writes, "has been made an instrument of deceit, hypocrisy and mischief in the hands of lawyercraft."[15] It is the people who draw up oaths who are the real hypocrites.

Bentham's essential unconcern with first-order hypocrisy is made clear by the distinction he draws between Oxford and Cambridge universities in the pamphlet. Every member of

Oxford University, he says, is a perjurer, because at Oxford it is a requirement to swear to obey the statutes of the university. Given that these statutes included such rules as pledging "not to walk about in an idle manner in the city or its suburbs," no one can possibly mean it when he swears to abide by them, since walking about in an idle manner is more or less the point of going to university. In Cambridge, by contrast, no one has ever had to perjure himself, because there the oath only requires that members of the university should agree to *submit to punishment* if they do break the rules. This is a difference Bentham traces back to the civil war: Oxford pledges obedience because it was an essentially Royalist university; Cambridge pledges mere submission because it was a hotbed of Presbyterianism. But as far as Bentham is concerned, the pledge of submission is a pointless one: everyone submits to punishment in the act of being punished, so all the Cambridge oath means is that anyone who provokes the university authorities to take punitive action will indeed have provoked them to take punitive action. In the "purpose of sincerity," Bentham concludes, Oxford and Cambridge might be considered very different places: Oxford is full of hypocrites, and Cambridge is not.[16] But in point of what Bentham calls "the impropriety of the ceremony," the two places are just the same. This is because in both universities people are required to utter meaningless pledges under oath, and the pledges are equally meaningless whether they can't be upheld (as in Oxford), or they can't not be upheld (as in Cambridge). Hence the title of the pamphlet, which is taken from the New Testament—the injunction there, as Bentham points out, is not *"Ye shall not swear falsely,"* but *"Swear Not At All."*[17]

The hypocrisy Bentham hates is the hypocrisy of empty words masking real power. In the case of Oxford and Cambridge, what is being hidden is a mixture of laziness and something more sinister: it is the laziness of those who endlessly put off reforming the governance of their universities on a rational basis, coupled with their sense that were they to do so, other irrational aspects of university life (what is taught, who is admitted, who enjoys the privileges) would be exposed. Bentham's overriding conviction is that words that lack meaning are only insisted on by people with something to hide. Equally, however, he is happy to accept that words that do mean something can serve their purpose even when people do not mean them when they say them. What he calls "imposture" may be a necessary evil, particularly in circumstances of political oppression—priests, for example, may have to perform ceremonies in which they do not believe in order to curb the power of military rulers (the example he gives in the pamphlet is that of Jephthah, forced by an oath to sacrifice his own daughter following a victory in battle, not because the priests genuinely believed such sacrifices were divinely ordained, but because they were a means to establish unequivocally the limits of his power).[18] Bentham distinguishes between empty words and fake beliefs: the former can only ever serve sinister interests, but the latter may be a useful weapon in the hands of those who genuinely seek the public good. After all, as Bentham says, "if fraud could never be employed but to the promotion of happiness, fraud would not be vice, but virtue."[19]

This line of argument comes at the end of *Swear Not At All*, in an extended historical discussion that is designed to teach an explicitly anti-Hobbesian lesson: that fraud may be needed to counter despotism, or arbitrary power. Bentham was adamantly opposed to the Hobbesian idea that rulers should not be subject to constraint by those over whom they rule. Hence the need sometimes for priests to dissemble in order to bring tyrants to heel. But despite these political differences between them, Bentham's central concerns with the problems of hypocritical language echo Hobbes in a number of important respects. Above all, they echo Hobbes's treatment of the relationship between deceptive language and deceptions about power. This makes Bentham a kind of anti-Hobbesian Hobbesian, which is not an easy or comfortable thing to be. It leaves him open to the charge of inconsistency, and perhaps even of hypocrisy. But it is one of the themes of this book that just because you are open to the charge of hypocrisy, that does not mean you are wrong. There is a lot to be said for Bentham's attempt to circumscribe a Hobbesian view of power with arguments that have their own roots in Hobbes's ideas about political language and how it should be deployed. I want to go back to Hobbes briefly to explore what he has to say about the misuse of language, before returning to Bentham, to see where he differs from Hobbes, and where therefore his distinctive contribution to the understanding of political hypocrisy lies.

INCONSTANT AND INSIGNIFICANT LANGUAGE

In chapter 4 of *Leviathan* ("Of Speech"), Hobbes highlights two particular ways in which language can fail to communicate properly. One consists of what he calls "words insignificant": these are words that don't mean anything, that are simply empty sounds. The other is what he calls "inconstant" names. These are the names of qualities that mean different things to different people, "because all men are not like affected with the same thing," so that we give things different labels depending on whether they please us or not.[20] This is the problem I discussed in the first chapter, which Hobbes specifically relates to the names of the virtues—the fact that "one man calleth Wisdome, what another feare," and so on. But the point I want to make here is that inconstant and insignificant terms pose different kinds of problems from each other. Insignificant terms are inconstant by definition—they can mean whatever you want them to mean—but inconstant terms are not always insignificant. That is the problem.

To borrow one example from Hobbes's own list of inconstant names: "stupidity" is not a word that fails to signify anything meaningful (Hobbes pointedly says that words of this kind are of "*inconstant* signification" rather than of "*insignification*"). We all pretty much know what "stupid" means—it means slow-witted or otherwise unable to think clearly. The difficulty is that we can't agree who has this defect, because if we like what someone says and does, we won't want to call it stupid—we will call it something else (the antonym Hobbes suggests is "grave"). Take someone like George W. Bush, whose entire political career has been dogged by an ongoing disagreement about whether or not he is in fact stupid. The problem here is not that we don't know what it means to be stupid; the problem is that for people who dislike what Bush says, the stumbling manner in which he says it is a sign of his stupidity, but for people who like what he says, that selfsame manner is evidence of his gravity, or even, for many, of his sincerity, which is precisely another such inconstant term. (There is, of course, a further possible view, which is that Bush is merely pretending to be stupid in order to pose as a man of the people, and mask what he is really up to; but this possibility is hardly likely to resolve the disagreement as to what counts as stupidity.) In a sense, the difficulty with inconstant terms like these is not that they signify too little, but too much—not only the perceived nature of the entity referred to, but also, as Hobbes puts it, "the nature, disposition and interest" of the person who does the perceiving.[21]

For Hobbes, both inconstant and insignificant terms are potentially very dangerous—they stand in the way of true ratiocination. The major difference between them, however, is that the dangers of inconstant language are manageable. Indeed, the management of these terms is a large part of what Hobbes's civil science is about.[22] They can be managed in two ways. First, the dangers of inconstancy can be neutralised by political authority, which provides a framework of authorised meanings within which linguistic differences can be contained. In a civil society, it is the sovereign's job to make sure that arguments about what counts as courage, say, don't get out of hand. The other way inconstancy can be rendered relatively harmless is through metaphor. This is because metaphors, in Hobbes's terms, can "profess their inconstancy."[23]

And this explains why Hobbes, the champion of clear and open language, was not being hypocritical in resorting as he did in *Leviathan* to metaphors in order to communicate his vision of politics (the book is replete with them, from its title on).[24] Metaphors can be useful in communicating ideas without unravelling the sense of the terms being used, because they are not trying to hide anything.

Insignificant terms, by contrast, are never useful, and never manageable (and also, by implication, never properly metaphorical). No one should use them, not even—*especially* not even—sovereigns. Because they fail to signify anything meaningful, they can only ever be an attempt to obscure the truth. For instance, it is not clear how an insignificant term could profess its insignificance (as an inconstant term can profess its inconstancy). If I make it clear to you that in talking gibberish I am talking gibberish, all I give you is a reason to stop listening. That is why insignificant language always has to pretend to be something it is not, which is what makes it, in the term we still use about it today, "pretentious."

Hobbes distinguishes between two kinds of insignificance: first, new words that don't mean anything, such as the empty technical language of "the Schoolmen" (i.e., the Aristotelians who dominated university life in the first half of the seventeenth century) and all other such academic jargon; and second, familiar words that can mean something on their own, but can't mean anything when used in conjunction with each other, because they are contradictory, as in the phrase "incorporeal body," or, more pointedly for Hobbes, "free subject." People who talk like this must have something to hide, because there is never a good reason to deploy language in this way. Inconstant terms, on the other hand, are an important part of language, and cannot simply be avoided—they need to be handled carefully. So deploying inconstant terms, as I tried to show in the first chapter, does not make one a hypocrite in Hobbes's eyes, except when they are used to hide the truth about political power (by redescribing disobedience in the terms of justice, and so on). But making language insignificant is always a form of the worst kind of hypocrisy, because it seeks to conceal the basis of political order, which is meaningful communication.

Bentham shares more or less entirely Hobbes's view about the dangers of meaningless language, though he expresses it in slightly different terms. Like Hobbes, he thinks that all meaningful words are the names of things, but that some words only pretend to be the names of things, when in fact they don't refer to anything at all. Some such words are not in themselves meaningless on Bentham's account, but nevertheless refer to things that cannot exist, as for example with a term like "unicorn," which means something relatively unambiguous (a white horse-like creature with a horn on its head) but doesn't refer to anything real. Bentham called such things "non-entities." But other words Bentham believed were empty by definition. Bentham brings these abuses of language under the broad heading of fictions, and it was against the influence of what he called "nugatory and dangerous" fictions that he fought throughout his intellectual life. These fictions were dangerous for Bentham precisely because they were nugatory: their emptiness was a cover for a multitude of sins. The other word Bentham used to describe them was "nonsense." And the greatest purveyors of such dangerous nonsense, he believed, were lawyers.

As with Hobbes, it is possible to distinguish between two separate kinds of nonsense here. One way of speaking nonsensically for Bentham was to use meaningful words in a way that contradicted their own meaning. This is what happened in most technical legal fictions, which required people to use language in a manner that must be false—for example, when treating corporations as though they were persons in their own right (like Hobbes, Bentham was very suspicious of "incorporeal bodies," though in Bentham's case this may have had something to do with his lifelong fear of ghosts). Bentham calls these legal fictions "wilful falsehoods." The same phenomenon occurred whenever jurists brought words together that only made sense apart, as for example when they talked about "natural rights"—these words are not nonsensical in themselves, but they are nonsensical in conjunction with each other, because for Bentham rights are non-natural (that is, man-made) by definition. Moreover, when the word "imprescriptible" is added to the phrase "natural rights," what you get, famously, is "nonsense upon stilts," because a right that is not prescribed by force is just one more word piled on top of another.[25] The other kind of nonsense is the meaningless jabber of professional jargon, all the technical terms and obscure phrases that lawyers use to hide what they are up to from the public. Such words are not falsehoods as such, because their obscurity makes it impossible for the outside world to judge them by such standards. What they are is simply noise.

The term that is sometimes used for the latter kind of nonsense is cant—the singsong of words without meaning (the word itself comes from the old French *canter* meaning "to chant" and was originally used to describe "the whining of beggars").[26] The term that covers the first kind of nonsense—wilful falsehoods—is lies. Both cant and lies, for Bentham as for Hobbes, are the marks of hypocrisy, and of the same kind of hypocrisy—the worst kind—despite the differences between them. A clear illustration of this is provided by Bentham's argument in *Swear Not At All*. Broadly speaking, oaths are in Bentham's terms empty fictions, which is what makes them so dangerous. The oath that is sworn in Oxford happens to be a lie (hence everyone in Oxford is a perjurer); the oath sworn in Cambridge happens not to be a lie (hence no one in Cambridge is). But the Cambridge oath is purest cant—it is just noise, because no one who utters it is in fact saying anything at all.

Now it is important to emphasise here that not all cant is necessarily hypocrisy, though the two words are often used interchangeably, just as not all lies are necessarily hypocritical.

Some writers, indeed, have been at pains to draw quite a sharp distinction between cant and hypocrisy. One such was Bentham's friend William Hazlitt, whose targets in making this distinction included the man often seen as the anti-Bentham, Samuel Taylor Coleridge. Hazlitt spells this out in his essay "On Cant and Hypocrisy":

> Mr Coleridge is made up of *cant*, that is of mawkish affectation and sensibility; but he has not sincerity enough to be a *hypocrite*, that is, he has not hearty dislike or contempt enough for anything, to give the lie to his puling professions of admiration and esteem for it.[27]

Here, cant is viewed as an absence of the deliberate and scheming forms of deception that are taken to be the mark of the true hypocrite (this sort of cant is closer to what Mandeville might call fashionable hypocrisy than the truly malicious kind). Like fashionable hypocrisy, cant may not be a bad thing—there may be times when the singsong of platitudinous chitchat does not really matter, when it is a mark of harmless social conformity (though it has to be said that for someone like Coleridge, as an arbiter of taste, it's hard to see when those times would be, and that of course is Hazlitt's point). But in the law it always is a very bad thing to cant, because it always gives the lie to a pretended commitment, which is the commitment of anyone involved in the law to take the terms in which it is expressed seriously. Canting lawyers are therefore hypocrites.

So it is with lying. I may tell you a lie without necessarily being a hypocrite, because I am not necessarily giving the lie to some other aspect of myself (this is especially likely to be true if lying on a routine basis is just the kind of thing you expect from me). But if I say things that *cannot* be true, in a context in which I have some prior commitment to upholding meaningful discourse (in a work of philosophy, say), then the "falsehood" (as Hobbes calls it) is also an act of hypocrisy. Bentham, like Hobbes, believes we have a prior commitment to uphold meaningful discourse in matters of law, religion, philosophy, and, by extension from all these, politics.

Useful fictions

However, Bentham's account differs from Hobbes in two important respects, and it is on these that I now wish to concentrate. First, with regard to inconstant terms. Like Hobbes, Bentham believed that people use terms of approval and disapproval according to whether or not they are personally attracted or repulsed by the thing being described. Hobbes's solution to this problem was to superimpose political authority on inconstant language. But Bentham's solution is to concentrate on the two terms that lie at the root of this inconstancy but that are not inconstant themselves: "pleasure" and "pain." Of course, one person's pleasure may be another person's pain (which is why we need politics, to sort out the resulting disputes). But it does not follow from this that we are bound to use the words pleasure and pain to refer to different things. If the heat pains me but pleases you, that does not mean that you cannot accept my description of what I am feeling as pain, or at least distress. This is different from a term like stupid—if George Bush pains me but pleases you, you will not be able to accept my description of him as stupid. Bentham relies on the fact that pleasure and pain are terms that refer to what he calls "real homogenous entities."[28] And he does so, in part, because he does not want to be Hobbes: that is, he does not want to have to rely on arbitrary power to deal with the problem of inconstancy. He believes consensus can follow from the fact that we all know what pleasure and pain are, and can therefore agree on the need to maximise utility.

The second difference between Bentham and Hobbes relates to the broad category of terms that Bentham calls fictions. Bentham is not opposed to the use of all fictions, particularly when writing about politics. In addition to nugatory and

dangerous fictions, there are what he calls "useful and necessary" fictions, which he defines as "those innoxious ones
which in the state of imperfection to which language stands
forever condemned are necessary to the giving of communication of ideas from mind to mind."[29] The fiction to which he ap-
pends this unwieldy definition, and the one to which he most
often resorts in his own discussions of politics, is what he calls
"the fictitious judiciary . . . of a sort of imaginary tribunal that
the force of public opinion must be spoken of as bringing itself
into action."[30] In other words, this is the fiction of "the tribunal [or court] of public opinion," a phrase that remains more
or less familiar to this day—we still sometimes talk about people having been convicted or acquitted in the court of public
opinion. This is not a metaphor for Bentham. It is a fiction because it describes something that does not in fact exist—there
is no actual court of public opinion—but it is not a contradiction in terms. There *could* be a court of public opinion, were
the public capable of passing judgment in some decisive and
authoritative way (whereas there could never be any such
thing as a natural right). Moreover, when public opinion does
prove decisive in some political controversy, it must be assumed that the public has passed a judgment of this kind,
through some form of intermediary. So what we have here is
something that doesn't exist, but whose meaning can be reduced to entities that do exist (like intermediaries and their
decisive judgments). It is a kind of shorthand, or shortcut to
the truth.

Why does Bentham need these sorts of useful fictions? This
is a complicated question, with a range of possible philosophical and linguistic answers that have been much discussed in
the literature on Bentham.[31] But I want to focus on the political
motivations here. Bentham's primary political use for fictions
of this kind is to establish limits to what governments can expect to get away with, even if that means stretching the limits
of what language can be allowed to do. So it is with "the court
of public opinion"—it is a fiction that serves to capture the

thought that even governing powers can be made to heed the public interest. Nothing could be clearer from one of the examples Bentham gives of how the court (or as he calls it, "tribunal") of public opinion actually works in practice. If the public is to pass judgment, it needs a kind of committee willing to give that judgement voice. "In this strain for example," Bentham says, "thought and acted the Members of that Section of the Public Opinion Tribunal by whose warrant, under the denomination of a warrant by the Members of the High Court of Justice, the life of Charles the First of England was extinguished at Westminster in the year 1649."[32] The court of public opinion authorised the cutting off of the king's head. That is why it is not a metaphor.

But this raises an obvious difficulty: isn't there something fundamentally hypocritical about Bentham, the scourge of fictions, being willing to sanction fictions when he deems them politically necessary? Of course, as a utilitarian, Bentham cannot be expected to rule out fictions in absolute terms: nothing is absolutely right or wrong except in so far as it is or is not useful. If fictions, like frauds, were always useful, they would not be vices but virtues. But Bentham here does not simply say that some fictions are useful; he also says they are necessary. And the difficulty arises from what Bentham has to say elsewhere about the idea of necessity: first, that the term is itself a fiction (necessity in this sense is a "non-entity," so that although we might know what necessity means, there is no more such a thing as necessity out in the world as there is such a thing as unicorns); and second, that pleas of necessity are precisely what make legal fictions mendacious. "Behold one of the artifices of lawyers," Bentham writes in his *Book of Fictions*, "they refuse to administer justice to you unless you join with them in their fictions: and then their cry is see how necessary fiction is to justice! Necessary indeed; too necessary; but how came it so, and who made it so?"[33] Nor is it any sort of mitigation for lawyers to point out that their fictions often have an element of truth in them. Indeed, this is just further evidence of how manipulative their pleas of necessity really are. "The spice or two of truth," Bentham writes, "buried here and there amidst the heaps of falsehood, serve to make the compost the richer, and the better adapted to deception and misconception."[34]

Necessary fictions, then, look like a large part of the problem in the corruption of public life, which makes it hard to see how they can be part of the solution as well. But in this diatribe against the legal profession, Bentham implies that there is a distinction between fictions that are necessary and those that are "too" necessary. This distinction is important to make sense of what Bentham means when he talks about necessity. Fictions are unacceptable for Bentham when they are used as instruments of power to mask partial (or as he calls them, "sinister") interests. So a fiction can be considered "too necessary" if the removal of the fiction reveals nothing there but the partial interests of those who deploy it, rather than the reality for which the fiction is a shorthand. Bentham shares the essence of Cromwell's view that "men make necessities." But he extends this view to ask an earlier variant of Lenin's famous question, "Who, Whom?" If you can tell whose particular interests the fiction serves, and at whose broader expense, then you can see why it is not simply necessary, but too necessary to serve its ostensible purpose.

Is this distinction enough to rescue Bentham from the charge of violating his own standards of truth-telling when it comes to the fiction of the court of public opinion? Let us look again at the example Bentham gives of the workings of this tribunal—the execution of the king under the double denomination of a warrant from the High Court of Justice, itself warranted by the Tribunal of Public Opinion. Now compare this to what Bentham says about legal fictions: they are uttered, he says, "for the purpose of giving injustice the colour of justice."[35] The execution of Charles was an act of power of which Bentham evidently approved. So by colouring it with the justice of warrant from the tribunal of public opinion, isn't he doing just what he accuses the abusers of legal fictions of doing? How is this different from the revolutionary tribunals in France, which Bentham abhorred, dressing up what they did in the language of natural rights? After all, it is not as if the public actually approved of the execution of the king (all the evidence suggests that most of them did not), nor sanctioned it in any meaningful sense. There wasn't a vote, and the public didn't sign the death warrant—the best one can say is that it was sanctioned by various pamphleteers on their behalf. Moreover, the execution was the act of a particular interest group within the government (it was Cromwell and the army against the Presbyterians in their new alliance with the king). Why isn't bringing in a fiction of public sanction here just more special pleading, and therefore more hypocrisy on Bentham's own part and in Bentham's own terms?

In order to see why not, it is first necessary to be clear what Bentham is saying when he talks about colouring things with the language of justice. Unlike Hobbes, Bentham did not believe justice was an inconstant term—it is a fiction, or a kind of shorthand, that can be cashed out in the terms of utility as well as power (thus it is unjust in Bentham's terms to use political power for purposes that militate against the greatest happiness of the greatest number). Lawyers who colour injustice as justice are lying about what they are up to, and hence their colouring is also a kind of cloaking—words are being used to hide the truth. What lawyers are hiding is the fact that they are not in the business of maximising overall utility; they are merely in the business of maximising their own utility. Dressing up injustice as justice for Bentham is like dressing up disobedience as patriotism for Hobbes (disobedience for Hobbes being an equivalently constant term, one that can be cashed out in a way that everyone should be capable of understanding). So the real question is, why can't Bentham simply say that the execution of Charles was just (which he clearly believed it was), as Hobbes could say that it was disobedient (which he also clearly believed that it was)? Why does Bentham need to embellish an act of utilitarian justice with the fake sanction of public opinion?

The answer has to do with the workings of power as Bentham understood them, and gets to the heart of what he has to say about political hypocrisy. Bentham believed that one of the tests of the justice of a political act was whether public opinion would stand for it, because public opinion was expressive of the widest possible set of interests. The revolutionary tribunals in France did not pass this test because they were clearly engaged in acts designed to coerce the public. But the killing of the king in 1649 could pass such a test, because it confronted arbitrary power with the wider interests of the public at large. The difficulty with public opinion is that the public cannot give direct voice to its interests, because the public is not a person. It needs a real person or group of real persons to act for it (hence the need for a committee). And hence the need for a fiction: the fiction that the public is acting in its own right, even though in fact it is the public that is being acted *for* (in this case, by the members of the High Court of Justice).

The really useful fictions in politics for Bentham are the ones that give people on the receiving end of power the power to act. It is a theme that recurs throughout his writings. It is the reason, for example, why Bentham was willing to allow that even the fiction of a "social contract," though nonsensical (there never was nor could be such a contract), might once have been useful; it was a fraud on a par with priestly ceremonies that demanded sacrifices of the king, because the idea of a social contract made kings aware that they were not free to do what they pleased. In circumstances of absolute rule, Bentham believed, it is hard to see how political progress could have been achieved without the aid of such fictions. But those days are now over—"what formerly might have been tolerated or countenanced under that name would, if now attempted to be set on foot, be censured and stigmatized under the harsher appellations of *incroachment* or *imposture.*"[36] There is no longer any need for such crude fictions as that of the social contract, any more than there is for such crude superstitions as human sacrifice (and perhaps even for such crude politics as the human sacrifice of the king). But that does not mean there is no more need for fictions—what remain, even under more enlightened conditions, are the fictions of democracy.

DEMOCRATIC FICTIONS

Bentham gives an example of such a democratic fiction in his *Political Tactics*: "Recognising the fallibility of the people," he says, "it is proper to act as though it were infallible; and we ought never, under pretence of this fallibility, to establish a system which would withdraw the representatives of the public from its influence."[37] There are two ways of making sense of this sort of fiction. One is that we must pretend the people are always right, even though we know that the people sometimes make mistakes, and misjudge what is in their best interests. But another way to put it is that the people are fallible because the entirety of public opinion can never be captured in a single judgment—even majority voting is only ever a partial representation of what the people as a whole think. The truly infallible voice of the people—the sum total of their wants and interests—is always mediated through the preferences of particular individuals or groups of individuals, which must be taken to stand in for the whole. The same applies to the concept of popular sovereignty. We treat the people as sovereign, although the people as a whole cannot be sovereign, since sovereignty only attaches to specific persons, who act on the people's behalf. We treat the people as sovereign so that their representatives do not forget that theirs is only ever a partial view of the people's interests.

It is this line of thought that most obviously sets Bentham in opposition to Hobbes, but it too has its roots in Hobbes, for whom "the people" is also a kind of fiction, requiring representation in order to be able to act in the first place. The difference is that Hobbes did not want to allow room for any real persons to claim to represent the people but the sovereign. So the fiction of the people's collective identity does no work in Hobbes's theory, except to emphasise the absolute dependence of the people on their sovereign representative. Bentham, by contrast, wanted to make sure that no one could claim to be the sole representative of the people, which is why the fiction of popular rule came to carry so much weight in his theory. In this respect, Bentham and Hobbes are really opposite sides of the same coin. For Hobbes, the truly useful fiction of modern politics is, as he puts it in *De Cive*, that "the king *is* the people"; the point of this fiction is to establish that the people can have no personality apart from that of their sovereign. For Bentham, the one truly useful fiction is that "the people *is* king" (or as he himself liked to put it, "the People is my Caesar"); it establishes that no single person can claim to represent the people's views or wishes. So the difference between Hobbes and Bentham is essentially this: Bentham was a democrat and Hobbes was not. But Bentham's democracy is still just an inversion of the fiction that lies at the heart of Hobbes's theory of the state.

It is important to emphasise that Bentham was not always a democrat. In his early career he thought that it was enough to expose the hypocrisy of those who used legal fictions to hide the truth about their power, without bringing in the people to pass judgment. But what he discovered was that exposing the workings of power is not the same as countering it—when you pull aside the mask to reveal what lurks there, you discover, as Bentham did, just how entrenched sinister interests can be.[38] Power had to be confronted with power, which meant confronting sinister interests with the wider interest of the general public, under the guise of the tribunal of public opinion. There are thus two ways of dealing with fictions: one is to expose them, which may well leave the power that lies behind them in place; the other is to confront them, which may well require deploying some fictions of one's own.

Bentham was never entirely happy with this latter course. Ostensibly, he put the need for his own use of fictions down, as he said, to the "imperfections of language" rather than the imperfections of democratic politics. But in the case of the fiction of the court of public opinion, there is more than just linguistic shorthand at work; there is also a kind of sleight of hand, since the judgment of the court always resides with particular individuals or groups of individuals representing the public, and never with the public as a whole. And this is just as true of the representatives whose judgment Bentham is most often willing to substitute for the judgment of the public, the free press: the critical opinion of newspapers, as he admits, in the end boils down to the judgment of their editors. Indeed, in a representative democracy, Bentham believed that the editors of newspapers were second in importance only to prime ministers.[39] Newspapers were needed to give voice to the social sanction of public opinion, just as politicians were needed to give voice to its political sanction. But what was true of one was true of the other: whenever one looks for the court of public opinion in operation, one will always find particular persons there instead.

Bentham did what he could to circumvent this fact of political life: that arbitrary power needs to be confronted with public opinion, but public opinion can only be expressed by something that takes on the appearance of arbitrary power. The struggle involved explains why his later career is marked by two contradictory trends: on the one hand, he became more and more democratic, keener on exposing the workings of power to public opinion wherever possible; on the other, his writing became more and more technical, neologistic, precise, long-winded, as he tried to pin down the operations of the people's representatives in nonfictitious terms. He wanted more democracy, which entailed a kind of fiction, but he also wanted the language of democracy—both the language used to describe it and the language used by its practitioners—to minimise its reliance on fiction, deception, and rhetorical dissimulation.

So Bentham tried to devise a means of providing public opinion with something like a real court of its own. He advocated the use of citizens' juries to scrutinise government representatives, and to subject them to censure when necessary.[40] But citizens' juries, for all their ability to monitor the people's representatives, are simply representatives of the people themselves, and require monitoring, which Bentham attempted to do with his own lengthy stipulations about how they should operate and under what conditions. Moreover, towards the end of his life Bentham became increasingly dubious about the use of the word "representative" itself, unlike his friend James Mill, who embraced it.[41] Bentham feared it was just more cant, an empty word that can mean whatever you want it to mean. He thought it ought to be possible to describe the role of these so-called representatives in the more precise terms of their official functions and aptitudes. But linguistic precision as a means to pin down the workings of popular politics is self-defeating—the more precise one is about the functions of the people's various representatives, the further one is removed from the necessary fiction of the court of public opinion that underlies their role. That is why we have never been able to dispense with the idea of "popular representation," even though the phrase is something of a contradiction in terms, as Bentham recognised. It has become our enduring shorthand for one of the necessary fictions at the heart of democratic politics.

To his many critics, Bentham's increasing technicality, long-windedness, and neologistic precision were simply their own kinds of cant. Thomas Macaulay, in his demolition of James Mill's essay "On Government" in the *Edinburgh Review* of 1829—the demolition consisting in pointing out that Mill's literal-minded, interest-based utilitarianism could not cope with the fictions at the heart of the concept of representation—spares some time to lay into Bentham as well: "It is one of the principal tenets of the Utilitarians," Macaulay writes, "that sentiment and eloquence serve only to impede the pursuit of truth. They therefore affect a quakerly plainness, or rather cynical negligence and impurity of style. The strongest arguments, when clothed in brilliant language, seem to them so much wordy nonsense. In the meantime, they surrender their understandings, with a facility found in no other party, to the meanest and most abject sophisms, provided those sophisms come before them disguised with the externals of demonstration. They do not seem to know that logic has its illusions as well as rhetoric—that a fallacy may lurk in a syllogism as well as a metaphor."[42] Macaulay just about stops short of calling this hypocrisy, and settles for self-deception instead.

I do not think Bentham was much of a hypocrite, nor was he particularly self-deceived. He knew that not all political truths could be reduced to a syllogism, and, like Hobbes, he understood the value of metaphor. But he struggled with his conflicting impulses about power: he wanted to expose its deceptions by his precise use of language, but he also wanted to confront its deceptions with some necessary deceptions of his own. Bentham's struggles suggest an important truth about democracy: that it has some necessary fictions at its heart, and if we try too hard to circumvent them we will start talking cant, as Bentham himself did, the cant of an artificially precise language of politics—we will become lost in a world of jargon, and end up consoling ourselves with the mere sound of well-meaning words. We see this all the time in contemporary politics, and we see it in contemporary political science as well. However, if we become too comfortable with these fictions, and ignore the fact that they are fictions, then we will start lying, not only to others but to ourselves—these are the lies of an uncritical faith in democracy. We see this in contemporary politics, and in much contemporary political theory too. The temptations of cant and lies are ever present in democratic politics, because democracy is itself a kind of useful fiction. This was Bentham's insight, and also, in a sense, his curse.

⟶⊷ 5 ⊶⟵

VICTORIAN DEMOCRACY AND
VICTORIAN HYPOCRISY

Novelists, journalists, and politicians

In this chapter I want to explore the fraught territory of Victorian hypocrisy and Victorian anti-hypocrisy, and their relationship to the unstoppable rise of democratic politics. I want to do so by looking at three eminent Victorians for whose political and intellectual concerns the question of hypocrisy was central. The three are Anthony Trollope (1815–1882), John Morley (1838–1923), and Henry Sidgwick (1838–1900). Of course, the phrase "eminent Victorians" is itself redolent of hypocrisy, because of its indelible association with Lytton Strachey's volume of debunking biographies under that title. The last two of the three authors I am going to discuss were eminent Victorians in the Strachey sense, in that they both stand somewhere in the immediate background to his book. Morley was, among many other things, the biographer of William Gladstone, and it was Morley's sort of biography—reverential, sequential, remorselessly public in its emphasis—that provided the pattern that Strachey wished to undo. Sidgwick was one of the characters whom Strachey had considered for inclusion in *Eminent Victorians*, but eventually decided against, perhaps because too much of what he wanted to

142

say about him was overtly sexual in nature. Strachey believed that Sidgwick belonged among that group of Victorian intellectuals whom he considered to be literally as well as metaphorically impotent: they shared, he said, "an innate incapacity for penetration—for getting either out of themselves or into anything or anybody else."[1]

Trollope was a very different sort of Victorian, from an earlier generation and full of bluff and hearty worldliness (indeed, many of his contemporaries wondered how so crass a man could write such psychologically astute novels). I want to connect Trollope to these others for two reasons. First, the book of Trollope's I wish to discuss—*Phineas Redux*, the second of his Phineas Finn novels and the fourth novel in the Palliser sequence about high Victorian politics—appeared in 1874, the same year that saw the publication of Morley's *On Compromise* and Sidgwick's *The Methods of Ethics*, which I take to be two of the central texts for understanding liberal Victorian attitudes to political and moral hypocrisy.[2] The year 1874 was important politically in its own right—it was the year that Benjamin Disraeli reaped the electoral rewards for the most brazen act of political opportunism in modern parliamentary history, the Tory passage of the 1867 Reform Act. Disraeli's victory in the 1874 election marks the beginning of the Conservative Party's dominance as a modern election-winning machine (before 1874, the Tories were out of office more years than they were in; since 1874, notwithstanding Tony Blair's recent hegemony, they have been in office more years than they have been out). Disraeli's rise to power provides the backdrop to the political events described in *Phineas Redux*. The second reason I want to talk about Trollope's book is that it contains, not least in its treatment of Disraeli (lightly concealed behind the character of Mr. Daubeny, who takes on the formidable Liberal leader Mr. Gresham, who is of course Gladstone), perhaps the clearest-eyed account of the workings of political hypocrisy of the entire Victorian period.

As we have seen, it is not unusual to look to nineteenth-century novels for insights into the great dance of hypocrisy and anti-hypocrisy: Judith Shklar makes use of Hawthorne and Dickens; other novelists who get drawn into these discussions include Jane Austen (particularly her most "theatrical" novel, *Mansfield Park*), and George Eliot, whose *Middlemarch* is one of the holy texts of hypocrisy studies. But what all these writers have in common is that they tend to be much more sensitive to the nuances of private hypocrisy than the public or political kind. George Eliot, for example, while fully comprehending the difficulties and compromises that the pursuit of virtue demands of us in the private sphere, tends to see virtue as its own reward in politics, which is one of the reasons why her "political" novels, such as *Felix Holt*, are among her least successful. As one commentator puts it, George Eliot's political narratives "punish egoism and reward virtue, and therefore refuse to admit that calculating political players sometimes win."[3] In *Phineas Redux*, the reverse is true. Trollope is more sensitive to, and about, the hypocrisies and deceptions of politicians than he is to the deceptions and dissimulations that can exist, say, between husbands and wives, or parents and children, where his approach tends to be more melodramatic. In the private sphere, Trollope likes to see virtue triumph, and if it won't, to see its defeat as evidence of the wickedness of the world; whereas in politics, at least in this novel, he understands that things are not so simple. This is why, even if he is not a great novelist *per se*, he is a great political novelist.

Phineas Redux is also far more sensitive to the problems of political hypocrisy than Trollope himself was in an earlier incarnation as a social critic in the mould of Thomas Carlyle. In 1855, Trollope wrote a book called *The New Zealander* (the title is a reference to Macaulay's celebrated vision of the demise of England in the face of the enduring strength of Roman Catholicism, and of the day when "some traveller from New Zealand shall, in the midst of a vast solitude, take his stand on a broken arch of London Bridge to sketch the ruins of

St. Paul's"—an image of doom that became one of the great clichés of the age).[4] In *The New Zealander*, Trollope set out many of the ideas that lay behind his later political novels. The book was never published in Trollope's lifetime (the reader at Longman's to whom he submitted it rejected the book as a "feeble imitation of Carlyle," which is unfair, but not all that unfair).[5] Its interest lies in what it has to say about the problem of political hypocrisy, and what it says about the difficulty of taking a stand against it.

The central theme of Trollope's criticism in *The New Zealander* is the corrosive hypocrisy of the English political establishment. Public life in England, in Parliament and in the press, had become a battleground of inflated demands for purity, in which no one really believed, and behind which the worst sort of impurity could flourish. "It is the trade of the opponent to attack," Trollope wrote, "it is the trade of the newspaper to be indignant, it is the trade of the minister to defend; and the world looks on believing none of them."[6] In these circumstances, it might be expected that Trollope would take the Judith Shklar line, and argue for a greater understanding of the unavoidability of hypocrisy in politics, in order to prevent the inflation of hypocritical claims generated by the prevalence of anti-hypocrisy. But in fact Trollope takes the opposite, inflationary route. If all this talk of purity is merely hypocrisy, he says, then what is needed is not a greater acceptance of insincerity, but a greater intolerance for it. People in public life, particularly members of Parliament, need to start saying what they mean and meaning what they say; above all, they need to start voting in accordance with what they know to be true. "Each honourable member," Trollope declares, "who is induced by any circumstances to vote that Black is White does whatever in him lies to destroy the honour of England."[7]

The political background to this outpouring of indignation lay in the parliamentary hearings that had been taking place at the beginning of 1855 into the adulteration of food and drugs. What emerged from these hearings was that most of what was on sale in London was fake: padded, substituted, tricked up, and fraudulent. What was more, the worst of these adulterations often coincided with the brazen advertising of their purity: coffee sellers who promised that their products were not mixed with chicory turned out to be the ones whose coffee was nothing but chicory.[8] Throughout *The New Zealander*, Trollope harks back to this theme: England had become a country of self-advertised purity, full of hyperbole, sanctimony, and hypocrisy, in which retailers, newspapers, politicians were all outdoing each other to prove they were whiter than white, whereas it was becoming increasingly clear that what they called white was in fact black—colouring, in Trollope's terms, is unequivocally a form of cloaking, in all walks of life. Trollope demands a return to a reliable standard of public integrity, in which fraudulent concealment is exposed for what it is. But this demand is incoherent, which is the main reason why *The New Zealander* is such an unsatisfactory book. After all, it was thanks to Parliament that the coffee merchants were getting their comeuppance, and thanks also to the star witness of the parliamentary hearings, a scientist called Arthur Hill Hassall, who had literally put coffee under the microscope. But Trollope has no answer to the question of who can expose Parliament. There are no microscopes for detecting fraudulent political behaviour; there are only other politicians, and the newspaper press. Yet to demand Parliament be exposed by its own members is to demand that politicians question each other's integrity, which is merely to inflate the conditions of anti-hypocrisy—opponents will attack, ministers will defend, newspapers will become indignant, and the whole round will carry on as before.

Phineas Redux returns to some of these themes, particularly the hypocrisy of members of Parliament when it came to corrupt electioneering, which they all condemned and from which they all stood to benefit. "The House was bound to let the outside world know that all corrupt practices at elections were held to be abominable by the House," Trollope writes.

"But Members of the House, as individuals, knew very well what had taken place at their own elections."[9] Nonetheless, *Phineas Redux* is a far better book than *The New Zealander*, for two reasons. First, it is a novel, so it does not need to suggest solutions; it is content merely to paint the picture for what it is. Second, the political circumstances had changed, both for Trollope, and for the country. The 1867 Reform Act had promised to close the gap between political rhetoric and political reality, by cleaning up some of the lingering scandals of the electoral system; but of course, it succeeded merely in opening up a new gap between rhetoric and reality, as Trollope well understood—both a gap between democratic purity and the impure motives of politicians needing to get elected, and a gap between parliamentary purity and the impure motives of the politicians who schemed to get the bill passed. What's more, Trollope had his own personal experience of post-1867 politics: he stood for Parliament as Liberal candidate in the Yorkshire constituency of Beverley in 1868, and though Gladstone's Liberals swept the election, Trollope lost to an unscrupulous Tory opponent who was willing to bribe his constituents. Eventually the result was overturned following the complaints of disgruntled local Liberals, but Trollope did not get the seat as a result; instead, the constituency of Beverley was abolished. The first *Phineas Finn* novel, written in 1867, is quite a sunny book, but also quite a moralising one; *Phineas Redux* is much darker, but also much more resigned—it is the book of someone who has seen a bit of politics as it is, and understands that cleaning it up once and for all is fool's gold.

But by 1874, Trollope had also witnessed what was perhaps the most remarkable feature of post-1867 politics, the ongoing progress of Benjamin Disraeli to the very pinnacle of English public life, and subsequently of European public life as well— as Bismarck was later famously to remark of Disraeli at the Congress of Berlin in 1878, "*Der alte Jude, das ist der Mann.*" One of the nauseating sub-Carlyle features of *The New Zealander* had been its treatment of Disraeli: all Trollope will say of him there is that "the English people cannot suddenly be made great and good by the wisdom of a Jew."[10] *Phineas Redux* offers a much more complex picture. Disraeli's Jewishness (in the character of Daubeny) is not emphasised; instead, what is emphasised are his magical qualities. He is Cagliostro, the magician, the man who can make something out of nothing, and turn any situation to his own advantage (in the book, in what is a double satire both of the 1867 Reform Act and of the subsequent disestablishment of the Irish Church, Daubeny is shown persuading the Tory party to vote for disestablishment of the Church of England, in order to outflank Gresham by forcing him either to go against his political interests by backing a Tory government or to go against his moral principles by opposing a "Liberal" measure; the result is a sequence of political cross-dressing that would put Tony Blair and David Cameron to shame). Many contemporaries (including, it has to be said, the man himself) understood Disraeli's political inspiration to be primarily Machiavellian; but for Trollope, Daubeny is both more artful and more artless than this, a man who has no principles and no ends in view.[11] He simply enjoys the game for what it is, and revels in his own ability to conjure something unexpected out of it.

What this means, among other things, is that for Trollope, Disraeli is not a hypocrite, which was the other most common characterisation of the time. Instead, the hypocrite is Gladstone, who in the book, after much conspicuous agonising, chooses to bring down the government and oppose disestablishment, in the cause of the higher good of capital-L Liberalism. Gladstone is a hypocrite because he *has* principles that he chooses to subvert in practice. Disraeli has no principles; all he has are words.[12] This has echoes of Hazlitt's earlier distinction between hypocrisy and cant, though Disraeli in Trollope's eyes is not so much canting as incanting, making words do magical things. The perils of the Disraeli approach to political life is that while he remains in control of himself, he has little or no ultimate control over the politics he creates, because it is conjured out of thin air. This is an image of political mischief that has long roots in the tradition I have been discussing: it is there in Hobbes, in his preface to D'Avenant's *Gondibert*, where he describes the foibles of "conjurers, that mistaking the rites and ceremonious parts of their art, call up such spirits, as they cannot at their pleasure allay again; by whom storms are raised, that overthrow buildings, and are the cause of miserable wracks at sea."[13] Hobbes's analogy is of course political, and it relates to the politics of his time (he is writing in 1650, a year before he published *Leviathan*). Nevertheless, this could easily be Trollope on Disraeli. But not Trollope on Gladstone. For by contrast, the perils of the Gladstone approach is that in order to retain political control, and to avoid such miserable wracks, he loses control of his own moral identity. Trollope does not take sides in *Phineas Redux* between the incautious magician and the wary hypocrite (his account of both men is in some ways remarkably sympathetic, and he does a good job of capturing the hold they each have on their respective parties). Instead, he paints the two as locked together in a giant charade, part of what Shklar would call the "discrete system of hypocrisy and anti-hypocrisy," of sanctimony and cant, that is democratic politics.

Where Trollope does take sides is in the endless struggle between the political class itself and those who are goading the politicians on from the outside. In the *New Zealander*, Trollope had portrayed the hypocrisy of the House of Commons as the apex of a pyramid of public sanctimony. In *Phineas Redux*, the worst hypocrites of all are not in the Commons, but outside it, in the press, particularly in the form of the odious popular journalist Quintus Slide, editor of *The People's Banner*. Slide hides behind the sanctity of "public opinion"—the idea that the people must scrutinise, the people must know, the people must judge their representatives—in order to pursue an entirely personal agenda of malice, jealousy, and destruction. In a way, this looks like a satire of Benthamism, with its blind faith in public opinion in general and the scrutinising role of newspapers in particular; and if so, the effect was deliberate. Trollope was, in *Phineas Redux*, as he remained throughout his life, appalled by what he understood as crude utilitarianism, with its selfish virtues and its fake public morality. In the book, Phineas himself becomes the victim of a selfish society that cannot accommodate his gentlemanly virtues and comes close to hanging him for a murder he did not commit. In the earlier novel, *Phineas Finn*, it is politics that has no room for its hero's scruples, and ultimately Phineas chooses to abandon political life altogether; it is a mark of how much darker the second book is in general that it is society as a whole that now has no room for Phineas, and nearly destroys him, not as a politician but as a man. In the end, he has a kind of nervous breakdown. This is the melodrama I referred to earlier. But the melodrama stops short of politics: no one in the upper reaches of political life as described by Trollope has a breakdown (though in a later book Plantagenet Palliser, another gentleman and also by this point prime minister, comes close). Certainly Gladstone and Disraeli do not contemplate retreat from the scene; they just keep on going.

Yet it is one of the ironies of Trollope's book, and one of the reasons why I am interested in it here, that although so up-to-date in its politics, it was rather out of date in its conception of utilitarianism. By 1874, the dominant strands of utilitarianism, as Trollope would have been increasingly aware, did not mean Benthamism, certainly not so far as that implied a benign faith in the "censorial" workings of public opinion.[14] John Stuart Mill had seen to that, under the influence of, among others, Coleridge and Carlyle. In truth, the leading utilitarians of the age were worried about precisely the same things that Trollope was worried about, and if anything, more so; in some respects, their anxieties about the impurities of public life, the readiness of politicians to pretend that black is white, and the delight of the newspapers in cheering them on, were more like the super-censorious Trollope of *The New Zealander* than the beady-eyed novelist of *Phineas Redux*. This was true both at the practical end of the utilitarian movement in the mid-to-late Victorian period, as exemplified by Morley's *On Compromise*, and the philosophical end, as exemplified by Sidgwick's *The Methods of Ethics*. It is to these writers, and their conceptions of political hypocrisy, that I now wish to turn.

COMPROMISE AND THE POLITICAL SPIRIT

John Morley was at this point in his career—1874—the editor of the *Fortnightly Review*, a journal that Trollope had helped to found twenty years earlier. It was a career that would eventually take him into the Commons, and then into the Cabinet, and finally into the India Office as its secretary of state. *On Compromise* itself, however, is a fairly uncompromising book about the nature of political ambition, and in it Morley gives full rein to his anxieties about what he calls "the triumph of the political spirit," by which he means the abandonment of principle and the readiness of politicians of every stripe to dissimulate and compromise in the cause of party. The background, as for *Phineas Redux*, lay in the parliamentary debates about disestablishment in Ireland, and particularly surrounding its consequences for university education, over which both parties twisted and turned for party advantage. In his later biography of Gladstone, Morley described the contortions involved in the defeat of Gladstone's Irish University Bill (which had itself been heavily watered down to appease Irish opinion in the Commons) by a coalition of Irish members and Disraeli's Conservatives: "The measure that had been much reviled as a dark concordat between Mr. Gladstone and the pope," he wrote, "was now rejected by a concordat between the pope's men and Mr. Disraeli."[15] At the time, he put it more bluntly: "It is hard to decide which is the more discreditable and demoralising sight. The education of chiefs by followers, or followers by chiefs, into the abandonment in a month of the traditions of centuries or the principles of a lifetime, merely to induce the rapid and easy workings of the [party] machine."[16] Many of Morley's targets in *On Compromise* are familiar from Trollope, and they include the daily newspaper press (though Morley was himself to try his hand as editor of the *Pall Mall Gazette* in due course), which he described as "that huge engine for keeping discussion on a low level, and making the political test final."[17] Like Trollope, Morley feared that the press and the politicians would feed off each other, and off each other's sanctimony and hypocrisy, until the line between truth and convenience became impossible to draw.

Nevertheless, unlike Trollope, Morley was a follower not only of Carlyle, but of John Stuart Mill as well. As such he needed to do more than rail against things and demand something better. He needed to find a rational and workable solution. The one he came up with was relatively clear-cut (though it has been missed by some commentators, who have seen him as a kind of mirror of Carlyle, all condemnation and no compromise).[18] Morley accepted that compromising on the truth was unavoidable in politics, but he argued that it was unacceptable in other areas of life, where it was corrosive and stultifying—compromise was what he called "the House of Commons view," which he described as "a view excellent in its place, but apt to be blighting and dwarfing out of it."[19] He did not believe the House of Commons view to be hypocrisy *per se*, and when it was, he accepted that the hypocrisy was often well-meaning. But in a line that could have come straight from Mill, he wrote that "a well-meaning hypocrisy in individuals [could result] in a profound stagnation in societies."[20]

So how was the line to be drawn between the unavoidable compromises of political life and the intolerable hypocrisies to which they could lead? Morley offers two distinctions to serve as a guide. First he distinguishes between words and actions: between the "expression of an opinion" and what he called "the positive endeavour to realise that opinion."[21] In undertaking the first, no compromise should be allowed: one should always speak the truth about one's convictions. But in attempting the second, trying to make what one believes come to pass, compromise is unavoidable, and some concealment may be necessary; these are the necessary compromises of politics. The other distinction Morley drew was between words and silence, echoing a thought that goes back at least as far as Bacon: no one, Morley claimed, should pretend to hold to opinions that were knowingly false, but it was certainly permissible to remain silent on questions over which speaking out would result is speaking falsehoods. So he distinguished between what he called "wise reserve," which was allowable in some circumstances, and "voluntary dissimulation," which was not. You could conceal the truth about yourself by your silence, and you could compromise with the truth in order to improve your chances of realising it in practice; but you should never lie about what you fundamentally believe.

In political terms, this line of argument led to the sharpening of two dividing lines, and the blurring of a third. One line that Morley sharpened up was between religion and politics. Essentially his book is saying that the House of Commons spirit should never be allowed to infect questions of religion, where speaking the truth was all-important; those who had doubts about their faith should not compromise on those doubts (in particular, they should not sign up to the creed of the Anglican Church for the sake of convenience). Morley, like Sidgwick, who had famously resigned his fellowship at Trinity College, Cambridge in 1869, was one of those members of Oxford and Cambridge universities who had found themselves unable to subscribe to the Thirty-Nine Articles, and had had to leave as a result. In Morley's case this decision also led to a painful and permanent breach with his own father. *On Compromise* is a defence of this form of religious sincerity—sincerity about one's doubts—and it spoke to a generation who had shared these experiences.

The other line that Morley's argument served to sharpen was between Liberals and Tories. Unlike Trollope, Morley thought that Tories were the worst of the hypocrites in public life, and they certainly come off worst in his book. To be a Tory, he believed, was to subscribe to certain principles, including a faith in the timeless mysteries of the constitution. Tories who play political games with the constitution are therefore going against their own beliefs, and handing their party over to "aristocratic adventurers and plutocratic parasites" (and this is a line that could have come from the earlier Trollope).[22] Liberals, by contrast, have among their principles an openness to practical considerations—they believe, in Morley's words, that "the conditions of social union are *not* a mystery, but the result of explicable causes, and susceptible to constant modification."[23] So the necessary compromises of political life are less of a compromise for Liberals. (Though this did not mean that Liberals could afford to get wholly consumed by the art of compromise—"If those who are the watchwords of Liberalism were to return upon its principles, instead of dwelling *exclusively* on practical compromises, the tone of public life would be immeasurably raised," Morley said.[24]) This is a variation on an argument we have seen before: when principled Liberals compromise, you can trust to their compromises precisely because they take compromise so seriously; just as Mandeville had suggested that when Whigs take the moral high ground, you can trust them, because they know just how treacherous the moral high ground is. As I said before, I do not think this is a good argument: it is too transparently self-serving. But it is an argument that has consistent appeal, at least for Liberals.

The line Morley's book serves to blur is within the realm of political activity itself, between speech and action, or ideas and practice. After all, in politics it is not at all easy to distinguish words from actions—to put your ideas into practice, you have to persuade people, among other things, of their truth. Words are weapons, so it is not clear how much help it is for politicians, or for those observing them, to discover that you should never compromise in the expression of your opinions, only in the attempt to realise them in practice. Equally, it is not easy to distinguish political reserve from political deception—politics is an adversarial business, and questions demand answers. Not answering the question is of course a time-honoured way for politicians to avoid an outright lie. But politicians can't avoid answering the question by saying nothing; if they do, they make it too easy for journalists to expose them to ridicule. As Bacon put it, in a slightly different context: "They will so beset a man with questions, and draw him on, and pick it out of him, that, without an absurd silence, he must shew an inclination one way; or if he do not, they will gather as much by his silence as his speech."[25] Politicians have to say something. So their reticence will be a voluble sort of reticence, and if it is to avoid the unacceptable forms of hypocrisy, it will only be by ascending to the status of cant.

Out of this sharpening of two distinctions, and muddying of a third, three practical political lessons emerge from Morley's account that explain the wide impact that his book had on his contemporaries. The first lesson is that one should stick to the beliefs one brings to politics from the outside—particularly one's beliefs about the most appropriate forms of religious expression—without compromise; somewhere in the hinterland of any politician there should be a person of principle. Second, once in politics, it will be much harder to say where compromise should cease; words and actions will tend to get jumbled up, which means that compromise may be quite widespread. But third, if one is a Liberal, one can at least be confident that one's compromises are less morally objectionable than those of the other side, and that Liberal cant is preferable to Tory hypocrisy. This was a hugely attractive message for a generation of Liberal politicians who came into politics wishing to do good, having broken with conventional religion but seeking a more appropriate outlet for their religious impulses, unwilling to compromise on their beliefs but aware of the compromises that politics would require of them, and confident only that their party was likely to be on the right side of any compromises that might be made, and the Tories on the wrong side. These were the "new" Liberals who eventually emerged from under Gladstone's shadow, and whose legacy runs through to British politics today, all the way to "New Labour." It is a truism of political history that this generation of politicians fell under the intellectual spell of T. H. Green (1836–1882). But it is also true that many of them fell under the spell of Morley's *On Compromise* as well (including Asquith, Haldane, and Grey—prime minister, lord chancellor, and foreign secretary respectively in 1914, when Britain went to war—all of whom cited the profound influence of Morley's book on their moral and political outlooks), making it one of the most influential political books of its era. Morley's biographer calls *On Compromise* a "*Prince* [i.e., Machiavelli's *The Prince*] for Victorian liberalism."[26] But this doesn't seem right, or fair. For its intended audience, it had a far deeper resonance than that.

POLITICIANS, PRIESTS, AND LAWYERS

Certainly it was much more politically influential than Sidgwick's *Methods of Ethics*, published the same year. Nevertheless, Sidgwick's book is the one that has lasted—it is the one that is still studied in universities today. This is because Sidgwick, who was exercised by many of the same concerns that exercised both Morley and Trollope, attempted to provide something that was not on offer from these others: an account of the deep philosophical roots of the double standards of public life. I cannot possibly do justice here to the subtlety of Sidgwick's argument in *Methods of Ethics*, nor to the intensity of his lifelong engagement with the question of hypocrisy, which forms the subject of Bart Schulz's massive biography of Sidgwick, *Eye of the Universe* (and in which the focus is on the relationship between this preoccupation and Sidgwick's deeply sublimated sexuality). Instead, I will try to pick out some related themes.

The first is that Sidgwick clarified perhaps more completely than anyone had before or has since just why the dilemmas of when and where to compromise are ubiquitous in moral, social, and political life: they have their origins in the basic dilemma of morality itself, which is how to reconcile the competing demands of self-interest and the general good. Sidgwick set out to show how these demands could be reconciled and concluded that in the end they could not, except in the case of a few, rare individuals blessed with a peculiarly selfless temperament (and that was an accident of psychology, not a result of philosophy). Utilitarianism was true for Sidgwick, but it was a deeply divided philosophy, offering a justification both for the pursuit of one's own interests and for the sacrifice of one's own interests for the sake of the greater good. This meant that there were no easy answers, either in ethics or in politics, to the question of where to draw the line between personal and public integrity. It also meant that Sidgwick was highly suspicious of attempts to impose one-size-fits-all political solutions on the ongoing struggle between self-interest and collective interest, including those of earlier utilitarians. In an essay on "Bentham and Benthamism" that Sidgwick wrote in 1878 for the *Fortnightly Review*, in response to a personal commission from its editor John Morley, he stated: "The difficulty that Hobbes vainly tried to settle summarily by absolute despotism is hardly to be overcome by the democratic artifices of his more inventive successor."[27] Benthamism, for Sidgwick, was no great advance on Hobbism in this respect; and a blind faith in the workings of democracy and public opinion was no advance at all on a blind faith in absolute power.

The *Methods of Ethics* itself does not have much to say about politics. The testing ground that Sidgwick was most interested in, throughout his life, for the puzzles of when and where to compromise with the truth was religion, from his 1870 essay on "The Ethics and Conformity of Subscription," written in the aftermath of his decision to resign his Cambridge fellowship on grounds of conscience, through to his articles on "The

Ethics of Religious Conformity" written in the late 1890s, shortly before his death. Overall, Sidgwick's approach to the problem of when a person may conceal the truth about his own religious beliefs can appear (particularly in retrospect) absurdly casuistical, as he endlessly slices and dices the dilemmas in the search of ever finer distinctions. But it is also openly casuistical: Sidgwick uses the word himself to convey his sense that nothing can ever be truly decided here except on a case by case basis.

Nevertheless, he is able to offer some general guidelines for the cases as they arise. First, like Morley, Sidgwick distinguishes between dissimulation and silence: it is generally wrong to say things that one does not believe, even to lay a false scent, but it may often be right to refuse to say anything at all. Sidgwick practiced this principle himself with regard to his own religious doubts: having resigned his fellowship because he could not openly pledge himself to the Thirty-Nine Articles, he then kept silent on questions of faith for utilitarian reasons—"The reason why I keep strict silence now for many years," he later wrote in a letter, "with regard to theology is that while I cannot myself discover adequate rational basis for the Christian hope of happy immortality, it seems to me that the general loss of such a hope, from the minds of average human beings as now constituted, would be an evil of which I cannot pretend to measure the extent."[28] Second, Sidgwick distinguishes between membership and leadership within a religious community: it may be permissible for members of a congregation to say things they do not strictly believe when reciting the creed that it would be wrong for an officiating minister to say, given the extra burdens of responsibility of that office. Third, Sidgwick distinguishes between metaphors and non-metaphors (and this is where he can appear at his most casuistical): it may be possible to express faith in Christ's having "ascended" into heaven without literally believing it, because "ascension" can be a metaphor for some kind of spiritual uplift, but no one can take the virgin birth to be a metaphor—

virginity has what Sidgwick calls "a perfectly simple and definite negative meaning."[29] So any cleric who doubts that Christ was born of a virgin should resign his office.

However, Sidgwick also thinks that it is crucially important that some doubters remain within the church, or else religion will never "progress." So when ministers find themselves forced to utter as statements of faith things about which they have doubts, but do not consider those doubts sufficiently serious to require them to quit their office, they must make their doubts known. That is, they must publicise their own compromises with the truth. Otherwise there is a danger that the morality of religious conformity will become esoteric, and to the mildness of the original deception will be added a more serious deception about the standards of truth itself. Equally, there is a danger that Protestant clerics who are not open about their own doubts will lose sight of what is distinctive about the faith to which they belong. Sidgwick, like Hobbes and Mandeville before him, takes it for granted that Catholics are inveterate hypocrites, in the sense that play-acting is of the essence of the Catholic faith. But the reason all these writers nevertheless worry more about Protestant than Catholic hypocrisy is precisely because in the Catholic case it is unavoidable, whereas Protestants have the capacity to exercise discretion and personal judgment. Moreover, concealment on the part of Protestant clergy will leave them not merely compromised on their own account, but also in a far weaker position to criticise Catholic hypocrisy when they would wish to.

Overall, this is complicated advice, allowing for considerable flexibility within fairly strict limits. It is advice that one can easily imagine having some political analogies: if one replaces creed by party program, then it could be said that some "doubters" must remain in the party if it is to progress, that manifesto commitments need not always be read entirely literally, but that politicians who wish to be in a position to castigate the obvious hypocrisy of their opponents must be careful about their own compromises with the truth, and so on.

However, the important point is that Sidgwick himself did not see this general advice as naturally translatable into other spheres of human activity. He believed that in different areas of social existence the guiding principles also had to differ about the necessary deceptions. What is most striking about Sidgwick's overall position, certainly in comparison to Morley's, is that he does not consider party politics, or the House of Commons, to be among those places where one could afford to be *more* lax about dissimulation and false statements of faith than in matters of religion, or, as Morley might have put it, more "political." If anything, the reverse is true. Sidgwick came to loathe how "political" politics had become. Certainly in his later writings—and above all in his major work on politics, *The Elements of Politics* (1891)—Sidgwick is more censorious about dissembling politicians than he is about dissembling priests, for whom he appears to have much more obvious sympathy.

He is also more censorious about dissembling politicians than he is in *The Methods of Ethics* about two other categories of potential dissimulators: lawyers and philosophers. Lawyers, Sidgwick accepts, must have their own professional code of ethics, which will allow them to protest their clients to be innocent even when they have the gravest suspicions that this is not true. Philosophers, as laid out in a notorious passage from *The Methods of Ethics*, may have to embrace not just esotericism, but esotericism about their esotericism, because free-spoken utilitarianism can be "dangerous" to certain useful social practices, including religion. This is what has come to be known as "government house" utilitarianism. "The Utilitarian conclusion, carefully stated," Sidgwick says, "would seem to be this: that the opinion that secrecy might render an action right which would not otherwise be so should itself be kept comparatively secret; and similarly it seems expedient that the doctrine that esoteric morality is expedient should itself be kept esoteric."[30] This, as has often been noted, seems to allow philosophers to say almost anything.[31] So philosophy, like law, can have its own code of morality when it comes to telling the truth. Why not politics?

In order to see why not, let us take the comparison between politics and law first. Lawyers, for Sidgwick, have two advantages over other dissemblers. First, everyone understands that the legal profession is built on a certain amount of play-acting. In that sense, unlike clergymen, lawyers do not have to advertise their doubts about the veracity of what they are saying. But Sidgwick is aware it is not as simple as this, because to be an effective advocate, one must go out of one's way to stifle the doubts of one's audience. "Though jurymen are perfectly aware," Sidgwick writes in *The Methods of Ethics*, "that it is considered the duty of an advocate to state as plausibly as possible whatever he has been instructed to say on behalf of any criminal he may defend, still a skilful pleader may often produce an impression that he sincerely believes his client to be innocent; and it remains a question of casuistry how far this kind of hypocrisy is justifiable."[32] It is in these testing circumstances that the second advantage kicks in: courts of law don't just have juries, they have judges as well, able to rein in the histrionics.[33] This is what Sidgwick most mistrusted about democratic politics—as he says in *The Elements of Politics*, it is like playing to the jury without a judge. He makes the point by way of an extended analogy:

Every plain man knows that a lawyer in court is exempt from the ordinary rule that binds an honest man only to use arguments which he believes to be sound; and that it is the duty of every member of a jury to consider only the value of the advocate's arguments, and disregard, as far as possible, the air of conviction with which they are uttered. The political advocate or party leader tends to acquire a similar professional habit of using bad arguments with an air of conviction when he cannot get good ones, or when bad ones are more likely to be popularly effective; but, unlike the forensic advocate, he is understood, in so doing, to imply his personal belief in the validity of

his argument and the truth of the conclusions to which he desires to lead up. And the case is made worse by the fact that political advocacy is not controlled by expert and responsible
judges, whose business is to sift out and scatter to the winds
whatever chaff the pleader may mingle with such grains of
sound argument as his belief affords; the position of the political advocate is like what that of the forensic advocate would be,
if it was his business to address a jury not presided over by a
judge, and largely composed of persons who only heard the
pleadings of the other side in an imperfect and partial way.[34]

On a case by case basis, there may perhaps be times when
politicians, like lawyers, need to fake sincere belief. But because politics does not operate on a case by case basis (the
cases all run into each other), there is nothing and no one to
hold the line between acceptable dissimulation and unacceptable hypocrisy. As a result, Sidgwick believed, hypocrisy in
democratic politics was out of control. If the politicians won't
control it, the jury of public opinion certainly can't. The court
of public opinion is, as even Bentham recognised, nothing
more than a fiction.

Sidgwick's solution was to encourage his readers to cultivate within themselves a judicial capacity—indeed, he writes,
"it might be regarded as the duty of educated persons generally to aim at a judicial frame of mind on questions of current
politics."[35] He would also prefer better educated people to
stay out of party politics altogether. In other words, he wanted
to supplement democratic politics with an aristocratic compo-
nent, made up of individuals able to sift out the truth from the
chaff of political rhetoric. One advantage of this would be to
escape the endless hypocrisy of democratic politics. But another advantage would be to create a political class who would
be in a position to dissemble or conceal where necessary,
though always in a controlled way. Sidgwick has two different
understandings of what it means to be a "politician." One is to

be a party political huckster, the kind that caused him to despair about democratic politics. The other is to be what he called "a sincere utilitarian," which is by definition not to be a party political huckster, but also by definition to be someone who will understand the limits of sincerity in judging what is for the best; someone, that is, who may need to engage in some concealment, or double standards, of his own.[36]

Notoriously, the place where this esoteric utilitarian morality tended to play itself out was in the international sphere, and particularly within the politics of empire. Sidgwick's view of international politics was one that has obvious resonance today. He was a federalist, who believed in fostering semi-formal ties between developed nation-states (particularly within Europe) and wished to encourage all states to see themselves as subject to international law. But he also accepted that in some circumstances it was necessary to fight wars for the sake of the greater good, and that in such circumstances the highest standards of international morality could not be met. Equally, he recognised that within the civilising mission of imperial politics, uniform standards of truth-telling could hardly be expected to hold, and in some special cases pious frauds might even be necessary. What was distinctive about the sphere of international politics for Sidgwick, as opposed to domestic politics, was that it ought to be possible to remain in control of any necessary deceptions or double standards, because they would not be subject to the vicissitudes of public opinion.

This did not mean that public opinion had no part to play in shoring up political morality. In a late essay on "Public Morality" (1896), Sidgwick criticises what he sees as the crude prevalence of "neo-Machiavellianism" in late nineteenth-century international politics, by which he means the view that political morality is distinct from personal morality. Sidgwick believed that this was a false distinction, because in both cases the moral agent is torn between self-interest and the greater good. Both for individuals and for states it is hard to say for sure when self-sacrifice is the morally right thing to do. But in the case of states, there is at least the advantage that when politicians believe that some higher cause trumps the national interest, they can put it to the test of the wider public: "The government may legitimately judge that it is right to run a risk with the support of public opinion that it would be wrong to run without it."[37] In this way, democratic politics provides a kind of safeguard against the risks of quixotic behaviour in international relations, because its tempering effects can be brought in when needed; whereas in domestic politics, public opinion is what creates the dangerous illusions in the first place, precisely because it is itself untempered by anything.

What is striking about Sidgwick's views concerning international politics is that they are so similar in tone to Sidgwick's views about truth-telling in religion: sensitive to the endless compromises that may be necessary, alive to the case by case differences, conscious of the tensions between the individual and the general view. The essay on "Public Morality" is of a piece with Sidgwick's writings on morality in general— it is recognisably the work of the author of *The Methods of Ethics*. But it is not of a piece with his views about party politics, which are very far from being so nuanced. When it came to the working of public opinion in domestic politics, Sidgwick was generally dismayed and much more sweepingly censorious. And he was particularly dismayed and censorious when domestic party politics got mixed up with international moral obligations. He was, at the end of his life, disgusted by the Boer War and particularly by the ghastly Tory jingoism that accompanied it. Sidgwick was a liberal imperialist, which meant that he liked his imperialism to be progressive, sensitive to circumstances, and accompanied with a certain amount of hand-wringing when necessary (though not when not). Above all, he liked it to be detached from the miserable "black-is-white" world of the party political machines.

This leads me to two observations by way of conclusion to this account. Sidgwick's approach to the problem of when it is permissible to compromise with the truth is in some ways the opposite of Morley's. Sidgwick was prepared to countenance all sorts of compromises in all sorts of areas of human existence, so long as it was possible to remain in control of any compromises that had to be made. This was true in law (thanks to the wisdom of the judge), in religion (thanks to the scruples of the minister), even in international politics (thanks to the philosophical detachment of the liberal imperialist). But he could not see how it was possible within the ghastly posturing of party politics. Hence he sought to escape from the unacceptable hypocrisies of party democracy by focussing his attention on those areas of moral existence in which compromise could be rendered acceptable by remaining bounded by philosophical judgment and casuistry. Morley took the opposite view. He saw that political compromise was unavoidable, and felt it could only be rendered safe by being accompanied by an uncompromising approach to the truth in all other areas of social existence. Morley believed that the uncompromising truth-teller could only survive in the compromised world of the House of Commons by recognising that the Commons was a place apart. Sidgwick believed that because the Commons was a place apart, and truth had become thoroughly compromised there, meaningful compromise was only possible outside. So Sidgwick, as a follower of John Stuart Mill, remained apart as far as possible from the messy world of party politics, whereas John Morley, who was also a follower of John Stuart Mill, plunged right in.

Yet it is one of the ironies of this story that Morley, though arriving there by quite a different route from Sidgwick, ended up in something like the same place: trapped in an imperial refuge from the messiness of domestic politics. Morley, unlike Sidgwick, was an anti-imperialist; also, unlike Sidgwick, he was a supporter of Home Rule (Sidgwick saw it as a fateful compromise on liberal principles—"a pusillanimous surrender of those whom we are bound to protect, and posterity," he called it).[38] Both were horrified by the Boer War, Sidgwick because it confirmed his suspicions of democracy, Morley because it undermined his faith in it. In the shake-up of British politics that followed the war, Morley returned to the Cabinet, and from 1905 to 1910 was Secretary of State for India. In that role, he suffered many agonies of conscience about the things he was required to do politically that did not sit well with his principles. The government had hoped to use him as a kind of cover, to "colour" their actions: if the author of *On Compromise* was at the India Office, then it was hoped that no one would mistake the government's policy for an unacceptable compromise. But of course, precisely because Morley's appointment looked like cover, that's what many people did, accusing him, as he reported it in a letter, of " 'shelving the principles of a lifetime' [and] 'violently unsaying all that he has been saying for thirty or forty years.' "[39]

Morley himself turned for comfort to thoughts of what strong men of the past would have done in his circumstances, particularly Oliver Cromwell (whose biography Morley had also written). When confronted with the necessity of repressive measures that sat ill with his liberal conscience, he longed for some of Cromwell's certainty. He also hankered after some of Cromwell's short way with advisers who displeased him. He felt that the only way he could keep his integrity in the position he occupied was to remain apart from the rest of the business of government, and out of the Commons as much as possible. He wished to be simply an "official," making administrative judgments, and not swept along by the needs of the party machine. In the end, Morley's approach to politics became positively Sidgwickian. And as with Sidgwick, it seems to have made him miserable and left him politically unfulfilled. In the end, there is no escape from the messy and unmanageable hypocrisies of domestic democratic politics in the seemingly cleaner and crisper compromises of liberal imperialism. In fact, there is no escape at all. Trollope, who was an arch-imperialist, and no philosopher, and a failed and embittered politician, unlike Sidgwick, who didn't even try, and Morley, who succeeded better than he can have wished, saw this more clearly than either.

6

ORWELL AND THE HYPOCRISY
OF IDEOLOGY

ANTI-INTELLECTUAL INTELLECTUALISM

Of the thinkers I have looked at so far in this book, perhaps none had such an abiding fixation with the problem of hypocrisy as the person I will be discussing in this chapter, George Orwell. It was, in many ways, the central theme of his work (this is a view I will attempt to defend in what follows). The only one similarly obsessed by hypocrisy was Sidgwick, who was haunted by its spectre throughout his life. But Sidgwick was a philosopher, and philosophy provided him with a way to think through and around his concerns, even if it provided him with no ultimate escape from them. Orwell was not a philosopher; he was a writer. Moreover, for most of his working life, he was not simply a writer; he was a book reviewer (that was how he earned his living, and he carried on reviewing up until almost the end of his life), which meant that hypocrisy was not simply an intellectual concern for Orwell—it was also the calling card of his profession. In this respect, the authors I have discussed whom he most resembles are Mandeville and Trollope. Mandeville was not a philosopher and he wasn't just a writer; he was also a doctor, which he considered, with good reason, to be among the most hypocritical of all vocations (as he pointed out, it is a very short step from

Hippocratic to hypocritic principles), and it was from the medical profession that Mandeville drew much of his own understanding of the double standards that animate all human endeavours, even—especially even—the noblest-seeming ones.[1] There are not many professions, or callings, that can claim to rival medicine for the range and varieties of hypocrisy that they place on display. But book reviewing is certainly one of them.

When it comes to hypocrisy, book reviewing has it all. It has the common-or-garden hypocrisy of being able to dish it out but not being able to take it: the reviewers who dole out criticism with abandon but squeal like stuck pigs when someone dares to misunderstand or misrepresent one of their own books. It has the classic hypocrisy of pretended knowledge or wisdom: the reviewers who pass magisterial judgment on a book they only got half-way through, or were not equipped to understand, or, most likely, both. And of course, it has the ubiquitous hypocrisy of private score-settling routinely passed off as impersonal truth-telling: all book reviewers (and as an occasional book reviewer, I would of course include myself in this description) have been kinder—or crueller—about a book than they might have been, for reasons that they felt were best excluded from the review itself. It is no coincidence that the British satirical magazine *Private Eye* devotes almost as much space to the double standards of the book-publishing and book-puffing world as it does to politics (and slightly more than it does to medicine). The world of books is kept afloat on an ocean of hypocrisy.

This was Orwell's world, as it had been Trollope's before him, and both men understood its foibles very well. Trollope, if anything, was the more censorious, and the shallow hypocrisy of literary London disgusted him throughout his life, even as he moved effortlessly within it. The novel that he wrote immediately after *Phineas Redux* was originally intended to be a satire of this aspect of Victorian commercialism, though it turned into a larger and more biting satire of financial speculation as well. The book is *The Way We Live Now,* and its first chapter ("Three Editors") remains one of the great mocking accounts of the moral economy of the literary world. Orwell's celebrated short essay "Confessions of a Book Reviewer" is more sympathetic towards the reviewer's plight, as befits a man who was less reviewed against than reviewing. Nevertheless, it makes clear that much of a writer's existence is taken up with what is "in essence humbug. He is pouring his immortal spirit down the drain, half-pint at a time."[2] Orwell was also perfectly clear about why writers nevertheless keep going, despite all the moral hazards of their vocation—in "Why I Write" he lists as the primary motive for all literary enterprises "sheer egoism . . . it is humbug to pretend that [it] is not."[3] So humbug played a big role in Orwell's sense of what it meant to be a writer, and he felt it was crucially important not to be a humbug about that.

How does Orwell's own literary career fare, judged by these standards? In the magnificent new edition of Orwell's *Collected Writings,* in which everything he wrote—occasional journalism, letters, diary entries—is reproduced in chronological order day by day, it is possible to see the little moral crises of the book reviewer's life approaching, and how Orwell dealt with them. So, for example, in 1936 Orwell starts to allude in various letters to the imminent prospect of having to review Cyril Connolly's novel *The Rock Pool.* He even writes to Connolly telling him how eager he is to get hold of a review copy. Connolly was a contemporary of Orwell's from Eton, and a friend; more importantly, he was a patron for Orwell, who was still struggling to make his way as a writer, and who therefore depended on Connolly's good opinion. So it is with a mild sense of dread and embarrassment that one awaits the reproduction of the review itself. And it is with something like shock that one discovers that despite all his motives to the contrary, Orwell was wonderfully dismissive of *The Rock Pool,* with even the token praise ("The book looks like it has been worked at over a period of years . . . I criticise Mr. Connolly's subject matter because I think he could write a better novel if he concerned himself with ordinary people") hardly designed to sooth the author's feelings.[4] It is a fantastically patronising review considering he was discussing the work of his own patron. Clearly, in George Orwell, the sheer egoism of the writer and the impulse to tell the truth stood in an unusual relation to one another. Or so it appears. But the *Collected Works* have been supplemented by a final volume, called *The Lost Orwell*, which draws together newly discovered material missed out in the earlier volumes. In it, there is a letter Orwell wrote on May 2, 1936, two months before his Connolly review appeared. Orwell's third novel *Keep the Aspidistra Flying* had just been published, and Orwell describes it as having received "the most awful (critical) slating . . . Even Cyril Connolly has deserted me."[5] His treatment of Connolly in return is therefore not so unusual after all.

Does any of this really matter? For some people, it does, and is symptomatic of a deeper malaise: the malaise of the hypocritical anti-hypocrite. On this account, Orwell's much vaunted "honesty" is seen as a cover for, rather than a confession of, his own authorial egotism. Stefan Collini, in a notably critical essay in his book *Absent Minds: Intellectuals in Britain*, complains that Orwell's book reviewing habits were artificially designed to preserve his integrity in the face of personal temptations. He cites as evidence Orwell's refusal to have anything to do with Auden, Isherwood, and Spender, whom Orwell christened the "pansy poets," for fear that he might actually like them in person and so feel unable to lay into them in print. When he did finally meet Spender, who visited Orwell in hospital in 1938, he found he did indeed like him, and he did then stop attacking him. This sort of double standard is not unheard of among book reviewers, and some professional reviewers will make a point of spurning the company of authors in order to avoid falling into this kind of trap (though it is not clear what you can do when you are stuck in hospital). Nevertheless, it remains true that it is a recognisable form of hypocrisy to behave in this way, and one that is consistent with a certain kind of artificially induced sincerity, which can manifest itself in a variety of different guises.

For example, in his book about *Truth*, the philosopher Simon Blackburn addresses the problem of the false sincerity of those who deliberately insulate themselves from reasonable doubts in order to maintain the convictions they know they need to prosper. Among the examples Blackburn gives are those of mid-to-late-nineteenth-century clerics who possessed a sincere faith but suspected that they would lose it if they were to read the latest scientific research throwing doubt on the Bible story. So they chose not to read it, and remained relatively, but also artificially, serene in their sincerity.[6] There is a political analogy here too. If, say, one were a democratic politician sincerely believing that another regime posed a threat to national security because of its weapons programme, and also recognising that maintaining the sincerity of one's convictions was crucial to persuading the public of this threat, then one might seek to insulate that sincerity from reasonable doubts, by deliberately avoiding any evidence that might raise such doubts. In this way, the politician remains sincere, and is able to act in "good faith." But the politician is still a hypocrite. The old adage says: "If you can fake sincerity, you've got it made." This is usually treated as a paradox or simply a joke, but the truth is that it is in fact quite easy to fake sincerity in philosophy or in politics, though it certainly doesn't mean that you have got it made. All you have to do is wrap your sincerely held beliefs in epistemic cotton wool.

Orwell's book reviewing habits resemble these forms of fake sincerity, though the resemblance is only a faint one—it is unlikely that meeting Spender made Orwell think more highly of his poetry, only that it made him less comfortable saying what he really thought about it. Certainly they seem to belong very much at the mild end of the spectrum. Not for Collini though, who sees all this as symptomatic of a wider problem in Orwell's thought, which turns out to be a wider hypocrisy. Collini convicts Orwell of the hypocrisy of the anti-intellectual intellectual, which he calls "that most unlovely and least defensible of inner contradictions."[7] It may well be true that Orwell, in his desire to castigate fellow leftists for the slipperiness and sloppiness of their thought, for the fraudulence of their values, and for the simple-mindedness of their judgments, overlooks the extent to which he is himself guilty of some simple-mindedness, and some fraudulence, of his own. But the question I am interested in here, as elsewhere in this book, is not whether this is hypocrisy, but whether it is the kind of hypocrisy that matters. Why is anti-intellectual intellectualism the least defensible hypocrisy of all? Collini gives as an example of this vice Orwell's attitude to Jean-Paul Sartre, whom Orwell dismissed on the grounds that he couldn't make head or tail of the philosophy, and didn't want to try, but whose books he nevertheless felt qualified to pass judgment on. Clearly this is not ideal in a book reviewer. But if the corollary of this hypocrisy was that Orwell saw through totalitarianism in ways that Sartre did not, isn't it a price worth paying?

Part of the problem here is that the question of Orwell's hypocrisy is still a raw political one. How to understand the hypocrisy (or otherwise) of Hobbes, Mandeville, Bentham, and Sidgwick now seems like a series of historical problems lacking any enduring political heat (Jefferson, because of slavery, is different). But that was not how it was in their lifetimes, nor for a generation or two after their deaths. We are sufficiently close to Orwell that we can still feel the heat, and Orwell is still cited in anger as part of the most acrimonious of contemporary political debates. What someone like Collini is doing in insisting on a warts-and-all account of Orwell's hypocrisy is not just getting at Orwell, but getting at those like Christopher Hitchens who have turned Orwell into a secular saint, and then mobilised him in that capacity on their own side in the ongoing controversy about the Iraq War. Hitchens has recently published his own intellectual biography of

Orwell, in which he says that having read through the entire collected writings, he finds almost nothing of which Orwell admirers need to be ashamed.[8] (Collini's review of this book was published under the self-explanatory title " 'No Bullshit' Bullshit.") More to the point, Hitchens also believes that Orwell still serves to remind left-wing intellectuals of what *they* ought to feel ashamed of. Orwell loathed the hypocrisy of leftists who would happily criticise Churchill and Roosevelt, but would not say a word against Stalin. Replace Churchill and Roosevelt with Blair and Bush, and Stalin with Saddam (or bin Laden, depending on your preference), and Hitchens believes you have history repeating itself. Hitchens, like a number of other supporters of the Iraq War among the British journalist class, was himself once on the far left, but the arrival of war has turned him into a scourge of his former allies.[9] It is not hard therefore to see why he wants Orwell to have been right about everything. And it is not hard to see why others might want to suggest that Orwell was not all he has been painted as being.

The one thing that tends to get lost sight of in these contemporary arguments is what Orwell himself actually had to say about the role of hypocrisy in political life. Orwell has become a kind of talisman for different sides of a ferocious battle for the banner of political integrity. Yet what is immediately apparent from his own writing is that the problem of hypocrisy for Orwell, as for the other authors I have discussed, was not a simple one, and certainly goes well beyond his view of the intolerably facile moralising of various left-wing intellectuals. For Orwell, political hypocrisy, and indeed political integrity, constituted an area of human existence where a series of finer distinctions were needed, not just right or left, never mind right or wrong. Orwell does not directly connect to the tradition I have been discussing so far (in fact, there does not appear to be a single reference to Hobbes, Mandeville, Bentham, or Sidgwick anywhere in his collected writings, though unsurprisingly as a lover of "good bad" fiction, he does have quite a lot to say about Trollope), but nevertheless he shares a good deal in common with these other authors. He was an anti-hypocrite who sharply distinguished between different kinds of hypocrisy, who accepted that some forms of hypocrisy were inevitable, and who ended up celebrating aspects of the hypocrisies that he felt democratic politics could not avoid, while eviscerating those hypocrisies by which he believed democratic politics might be destroyed.

He shares other characteristics with the wider English liberal rationalist tradition as well. Orwell was not remotely impressed by Machiavellianism ("this shallow piece of naughtiness" as he called it).[10] Equally, like Hobbes and Bentham, he was deeply suspicious of obscure, clichéd, or fatuous language. In a sense, he was more like Hobbes than like Bentham, in his loathing of neologism, technical elaboration, and intellectual pretension, as he made clear in his celebrated essay on "Politics and the English Language." Like Bentham, Orwell believed that good prose should aim for precision, but unlike Bentham he understood precision as a kind of transparency ("good prose," he famously wrote, "is like a window pane"), which meant that Bentham's elaborate linguistic constructions, building up the truth like a series of Russian dolls, were self-defeating in Orwell's terms. As did Hobbes, Orwell preferred a robust metaphor—one that made clear exactly what its author was up to—to an intricate piece of linguistic expertise. But no metaphor, Orwell believed, should be used when it has become "worn-out," because such language has lost the power to profess its inconstancy. Dying metaphors, like what Orwell calls "pretentious diction" and "meaningless words," profess nothing of themselves, but only that "the writer is [no longer] interested in what he is saying."[11]

But what Orwell most obviously has in common with both Hobbes and Bentham is his sense that obscurantist language is most dangerous when it attempts to conceal the truth about political power. "In our time," he wrote, "political speech and writing are largely the defence of the indefensible . . . Thus

175

political language has to consist largely of euphemism, question-begging and sheer cloudy vagueness."[12] Orwell's particular hatred of the hypocrisy of left-wing intellectuals, and of their readiness to hide behind platitudes, derived from his sense that those platitudes were also serving to conceal their attitude to power. This was not true of all forms of political dishonesty, some of which, one might say, were sincerely dishonest in Orwell's terms. So, as Orwell wrote in 1945, "any large organisation will look after its own interests as best it can, and overt propaganda is not a thing to object to."[13] It did not make sense to complain that *Pravda* wouldn't print a word against Stalin, any more, as Orwell put it, "than one would expect the *Catholic Herald* to denounce the Pope."[14] But liberal opinion was not, ostensibly at least, subservient to some higher authority—it purported to speak the truth to power (that, in theory, was what made it liberal), which was why its dishonesty was so hypocritical. The problem, Orwell believed, was "that one cannot expect intelligent criticism or even plain honesty from liberal writers and journalists who are under no direct pressure to falsify their opinions."[15] It was subservient opinion passed off as though it were independent-minded, and dressed up in the trappings of intellectual probity (above all the supposed probity of value-free jargon) that posed the greatest threat to clear thinking about politics, because, Orwell claimed, "it weakens the instinct by which free peoples can tell what is and what is not dangerous."[16]

HYPOCRISY: AN ENGLISH VICE

Nevertheless, when one turns away from the forms of political expression that Orwell most despised to the forms of expression that he was willing to defend, it becomes clear that his championing of transparency did not translate into a straightforward defence of political sincerity or openness. There were various forms of political expression that Orwell was prepared to countenance in which a kind of double standard, hypocrisy, or deliberate concealment was being practiced, so long as that concealment had an element of truthfulness about it. And by this I do not mean the crudely honest dishonesty of self-professed Stalinists, to which I shall return later.[17] Rather, I am thinking of Orwell's defence of the various, complicated hypocrisies of being English. Take, for example, Orwell's treatment of two very English writers whose political views he emphatically did not share: Rudyard Kipling and P. G. Wodehouse. Orwell was willing to stick up for both of them, and in both cases it was because, whatever might be said against them, they were at least less hypocritical than those who used hypocrisy as a stick to beat them with.

Thus, while Kipling's imperialism was repugnant to Orwell—"it is no use pretending," he wrote, "that Kipling's view of life, as a whole, can be accepted or even forgiven by any civilised person"—Kipling himself was not, for a variety of different reasons.[18] First, Orwell felt that Kipling was at least open about his prejudices. He had a worldview that he was willing to defend for what it was, and as such he stood in obvious contrast to those "humanitarian" hypocrites who condemned empire while relying on its fruits to sustain their comfortable lifestyles. As Orwell puts it, in a characteristically belligerent (and over-the-top) passage from *The Road to Wigan Pier*:

> It is so easy to be witty about the British Empire. The White Man's Burden and "Rule Britannia" and Kipling's novels and Anglo-Indian bores—who could even mention such things without a snigger? . . . That is the attitude of the typical left-winger towards imperialism, and a thoroughly flabby, boneless attitude it is . . . For apart from any other consideration, the high standard of life we enjoy in England depends upon our keeping a tight hold on the Empire. Under the capitalist system, in order that England may live in comparative comfort, a hundred million Indians must live on the verge of starvation—an evil state

of affairs, but you acquiesce in it every time you step into a taxi or eat a plate of strawberries and cream.[19]

Second, Kipling's prose chimed with a truth about the world, despite the fact that it also represented a failure to face up to certain truths: "He dealt largely in platitudes," Orwell says, "and since we live in a world of platitudes, much of what he says sticks."[20] But perhaps most importantly, Orwell felt that Kipling always kept something of his own personal character in reserve, and that there was therefore always more to Kipling than the views with which he was associated. Orwell described this extra something as his essential "personal decency," and he said on Kipling's death: "It is worth remembering that he was the most widely popular English writer of our time, and yet that no one, perhaps, so consistently refrained from making a vulgar show of his personality."[21] Kipling was saved, in Orwell's eyes, by the fact that his writing, for all its robustness (and not least its robustness about power), was not fully self-revealing, in that it did not allow one to see all the way through to the man underneath.

Wodehouse, by contrast, was saved by the fact that the writing was the man—Orwell accepts that Wodehouse was "his own Bertie Wooster."[22] This is why Orwell believed it was absurd to pillory Wodehouse for the mildly treacherous radio broadcasts he made while interned by the Nazis during the Second World War (treacherous not for their content but for the fact he made them and allowed the Nazis to exploit the connection). Wodehouse was what Orwell called "a political innocent," someone whose essential stupidity about politics— "his mild facetiousness covering an unthinking acceptance [of the world he inhabited]"—rescued him from the charge of the worst sorts of hypocrisy.[23] Instead, the worst of the hypocrites were Wodehouse's critics after the war, who saw in him "an ideal whipping boy," and used him as a distraction from any attempt to expose the far more extensive collaborations and deceptions that underpinned their own war efforts. "All kinds of petty rats are hunted down," Orwell wrote in his defence of Wodehouse, "while almost without exception the big rats escape."[24]

One might say, therefore, that what Kipling and Wodehouse had in common for Orwell was that there was a kind of integrity to their double standards, though of very different kinds. Kipling deliberately concealed something of himself but did not seek to conceal the truth about the nature of imperial power; Wodehouse exposed himself, and thereby inadvertently exposed something of the double standards of the system of power in which he unthinkingly believed. Kipling, in this sense, knew what he was about and Wodehouse did not, and that was what served to rescue them respectively from the more culpable hypocrisy of their "intellectual" critics. But it is also worth noting that what rescued Kipling and Wodehouse in Orwell's eyes was that each did not share the other's vice. The easiest way to illustrate this is to consider what would have happened if their positions had been reversed. It is inconceivable that if Kipling had found himself in Wodehouse's position, broadcasting for the Nazis for the sake of a quiet life, then Orwell would have defended him; there was nothing innocent about Kipling, and therefore there was no way of imagining that he might have been self-deceived in such circumstances. Stupidity might just retain its integrity in the face of totalitarianism, but knowingness never could. Equally, it is impossible to imagine Orwell defending a P. G. Wodehouse view of British imperialism, because there was nothing innocent about imperialism, and political naivety in that context was always culpable. Kipling could write about empire because he was in no sense naive about it; what made Orwell despair of British imperialism was that it was not on the whole staffed by Kiplings, but by Bertie Woosters.

The hypocrisies of Englishness are therefore complicated: they are various, and they have their various uses (not least to expose the far worse hypocrisies of others), but they are also extremely dangerous when let loose in the wrong context. And it is this complicated attitude to hypocrisy that underpins Orwell's most famous discussion of what it means to be English, in the essays published in 1941 as *The Lion and the Unicorn*, including the one entitled "England, Your England." There are two sorts of hypocrisy described in that essay. The first is the relatively innocent hypocrisy of democracy that is underpinned in the English case by the sentimentality of the working classes and the stupidity of those who rule them. This innocent stupidity is exemplified for Orwell by the "morally sound" willingness of the English upper classes to get themselves killed in wartime. Even the Bertie Woosters of this world, who can't be relied on for much, can be relied on for this: "Bertie, a sluggish Don Quixote, has no wish to tilt at windmills, but he would hardly think of refusing to do so when honour calls."[25] Democracy, for Orwell, is a charade, but the innocence of the English version is what saves it from being a total fraud—that is, the play-acting is taken seriously, and so helps to preserve the system from the degradation that comes from merely going through the motions. "It follows," Orwell writes, "that British democracy is less of a fraud than it sometimes appears. A foreign observer sees only the huge inequality of wealth, the unfair electoral system, the governing-class control over the press, radio and education, and concludes that democracy is simply a polite name for dictatorship."[26] But democracy is more than just a name in England, because the hypocrisy is more pervasive than that would suggest. It shapes and conditions the way that people behave. "Public life in England," Orwell declares, "has never been *openly* scandalous. It has not reached the pitch of disintegration at which humbug can be dropped."[27] This, in large part, is what distinguishes English democracy from the continental versions that collapsed into, or in the face of, fascism: it is saved by its unthinking hypocrisy.

The image Orwell uses to capture the essence of English public life is as follows: it is "a society which is ruled by the sword, no doubt, but a sword which must never be taken out of its scabbard."[28] He goes on:

An illusion can become a half-truth, a mask can alter the expression of a face ... The sword is still in the scabbard, and while it stays there corruption cannot go beyond a certain point ... Even hypocrisy is a powerful safeguard ... [It is] a symbol of the strange mixture of reality and illusion, democracy and privilege, humbug and decency, the subtle network of compromises, by which the nation keeps itself in familiar shape.[29]

But this is not the whole story when it comes to the English vice of hypocrisy, which turns out to be a kind of virtue only in this particular context. There is another sort of hypocrisy at work in English life, beyond that of democratic solidarity. That is the hypocrisy of empire, and here Orwell tends to side with the foreign observers who detect in English attitudes to their empire a culpable double standard (it is no coincidence that the one place where Orwell explicitly refers to hypocrisy as "the British vice" is in his "Reflections on Gandhi"). In relation to their domestic affairs, Orwell believes that foreigners are wrong to write off the English hatred of "militarism" as merely a "decadent" form of hypocrisy. But it is impossible to ignore the fact that in relation to the politics of empire, English innocence cannot be what it appears. After all, it is in the essence of imperial power that the sword does not remain in the scabbard. The recurring images in Orwell's work that seek to capture the essence of the imperial experience are of the weapon, however blunt and however crude, being unsheathed.

Orwell himself described his personal awakening to the true nature of imperial power as occurring in Colombo harbour, during his trip out to Burma to begin his career as a military policeman. There, he witnessed a native servant, who had dropped a trunk that was being taken on board the ship, being viciously kicked on the backside by a white police sergeant, to the obvious approval of the other passengers.[30] This, for Orwell, was in essence what empire meant: inescapable brutality. But the most memorable of all Orwell's images of imperialism in action comes in perhaps the most celebrated of all his shorter pieces of writing, "Shooting an Elephant." (There is considerable controversy among Orwell's biographers about whether the event described in the essay actually happened, and therefore whether it should be classified as fiction or nonfiction; for my purposes here, I don't think it matters.) Orwell, in Burma, is called upon to shoot an elephant that is said to have killed a man, before a crowd of eager Burmese onlookers. This event, Orwell says, offers a glimpse of "the dirty work of Empire at close quarters."[31] And what it shows is that the agents of imperial authority don't know what they are doing; they are merely acting out a part over which they have lost control. "I was seemingly the leading actor in the piece," Orwell writes, "but in reality I was only an absurd puppet pushed to and fro by the will of those yellow faces behind."[32] Orwell did not wish to shoot the elephant, but he felt he had no choice. The white man on imperial duty "wears a mask and his face grows to fit it. I had got to shoot the elephant."[33] The hypocrisy of empire is revealed here as the unsheathing of the weapon by someone who does not wish to use it, and has lost all control of what can be done with it, or even of what it is for, but must go through with his part anyway.

In "Shooting an Elephant," Orwell (that is, the "Orwell" of the piece) doesn't exactly come across as Bertie Wooster—he is far too reflective for that—but he is not a million miles away from the world of P. G. Wodehouse either. Bertie Wooster would also shoot the elephant, and though in his case it might not cause him any great pangs of conscience, it would also be because he was the puppet, not the puppeteer. The stupidity of the British ruling class, which was their saving grace so far as democracy was concerned, was catastrophic in the context of empire. Kipling, who was neither stupid, nor strictly speaking a member of the British ruling class (he was, essentially, a journalist), at least did not try to pretend that the empire was something it was not. But not even Kipling was able to tell the basic truth about the British Empire: that democratic hypocrisy and imperial hypocrisy simply do not mix. Democratic hypocrisy, in Orwell's terms, is saved by the element of self-deception on which it rests, which is what turns the illusion into a half-truth, and keeps the sword in its scabbard. Imperial hypocrisy is rendered self-defeating by that very same self-deception, since the sword cannot remain in the scabbard, and will be deployed for the supposed benefit of the people it is being used to coerce, by people who are unable to be honest with themselves about the nature of that coercion.

In a way, it is easy to see what the solution is to this clash of hypocrisies: democracy needs to abandon imperialism, as Orwell was convinced that Britain needed to divest itself of its empire, and to face up to the sacrifices that that would involve. But it is important to recognise that the democracy that abandons imperialism does not abandon hypocrisy: rather, it preserves its own sustainable hypocrisy by ditching the form of power that makes a mockery of it. There is an alternative remedy, of course, which is to abandon hypocrisy altogether. This is what would happen if imperialism jettisoned democracy, rather than the other way around. An imperial order unconstrained by democratic or liberal hypocrisies, in which power can be called by its proper name, in which the sword is always unsheathed because there is never any need to conceal it, is certainly possible. Indeed, Orwell believed, it was not just possible but prevalent in the world he had come to know, and would be all-pervasive in one possible future world that he was to imagine. Imperialism without hypocrisy is called fascism, and it is one of the distinguishing marks of fascism, as of various other totalitarian regimes, that it does not need to be hypocritical.[34] Totalitarians can afford to be sincere about power. Or, as Orwell put it in his essay on Kipling: "The modern totalitarians know what they are doing and the nineteenth-century English did not know what they were doing."[35] It is out of this sincerity that we get a third quintessentially Orwellian image, to place alongside that of the unsheathed sword, and that of the young military policeman stumbling along a road in Burma, armed only with his elephant gun. The third image is of a boot, stamping on a human face forever.

HYPOCRISY AND TOTAL POWER

This brings me to the novels, to which I cannot do justice here, but which I want to use to illustrate some of the themes that come out of Orwell's nonfiction. The first is that the sincerity, or anti-hypocrisy, of fascism has its counterpart in the sincerity, or anti-hypocrisy, of anti-fascism. Orwell gives an extended glimpse of what this sincerity might look like in a passage in the novel *Coming Up for Air*, in which the hero George Bowling attends a political meeting, in the period before the outbreak of hostilities between England and Germany, and listens to a speech. Here is the passage in full:

> You know the line of talk. These chaps can churn it out by the hour. Just like a gramophone. Turn the handle, press the button, and it starts. Democracy, Fascism, Democracy. But somehow it interested me to watch him. A rather mean little man, with a white face and a bald head, standing on a platform, shooting out slogans. What's he doing? Quite deliberately, and quite openly, stirring up hatred. Doing his damnedest to make you hate certain foreigners called Fascists. It's a queer thing, I thought, to be known as "Mr So-and-so, the well-known anti-Fascist." A queer trade, anti-Fascism. This fellow, I suppose, makes his living writing books against Hitler. But what did he do before Hitler came along? And what'll he do if Hitler ever disappears? Same question applies to doctors, detectives, rat-

catchers and so forth, of course. But the grating voice went on and on, and another thing struck me. He *means* it. Not faking at all—feels every word he is saying. He's trying to work up hatred in his audience, but that is nothing compared to the hatred he feels himself. Every slogan's gospel truth to him. If you cut him open all you'd find inside would be Democracy-Fascism-Democracy. Interesting to know a chap like that in private life. But does he have a private life? Or does he only go round from platform to platform, working up hatred? Perhaps even his dreams are slogans.[36]

This scene foreshadows a better-known scene in a better-known book: the hate session in *Nineteen Eighty-Four*, in which the crowd is required to vent its fury at the hate-figure of Emmanuel Goldstein, and does so in all sincerity, even Winston Smith, who feels the hatred wash through him ("the horrible thing about the Two Minutes Hate was not that one was obliged to act a part, but that it was impossible to avoid joining in. Within thirty seconds any pretence was always unnecessary").[37] The scene from *Coming Up for Air* also foreshadows a theme of that later book, which is what it might mean not to have a private life, not to have anything held back or reserved, but simply to be the slogans that one is forced to spout through and through. In such a world, hypocrisy would not simply be valuable, it would in a sense represent the ultimate value, because its precondition is having something to hide. *Nineteen Eighty-Four* is a description of a world in which hypocrisy has become impossible. And this applies to the language of *Nineteen Eighty-Four* as well. Just as "Machiavellian" has become a facile term for any kind of political deception or double-dealing, so "double-think" (which is routinely transcribed into "double-speak") has itself become a cliché to describe any form of political expression that is not what it seems. But in Orwell's own terms, "double-think" constituted a very particular form of linguistic abuse, through which language is emptied out of all meaning, so that it becomes impossible for language to hide anything. The hypocrisies that Orwell attacks in "Politics and the English Language" are *not* the forerunners of "double-think"; instead that essay is about the deliberate concealment of the truth behind a mask of verbiage (which is what connects it to the arguments of Hobbes and Bentham). That is not what is going on in *Nineteen Eighty-Four*. Take the purest, most terrifying manifestation of double-think, the slogans that sit on top of the Ministry of Truth:

WAR IS PEACE

FREEDOM IS SLAVERY

IGNORANCE IS STRENGTH

There is nothing hypocritical about this message, because it has nothing to hide. But nor is it a metaphor. It is a lie so large and so open that it makes the terms of hypocrisy obsolete.

Let me return at this point to the author with whom I began this book, Judith Shklar. In a commemorative lecture she delivered to the American Political Studies Association in 1984 (the year she also published *Ordinary Vices*), Shklar argues that Orwell goes too far in his *Nineteen Eighty-Four*—it is a book, in her terms, without a moral centre, and so it lacks a sense of the cruelties of everyday life, and therefore of the ways cruelty can insinuate itself as a vice.[38] But Richard Rorty, in *Contingency, Irony and Solidarity*, suggests that Orwell's book offers an exemplification of the liberal understanding that, in his words (but also Shklar's), "cruelty is the worst thing we do." For Rorty, it does not matter that Orwell's account appears to stand at one remove from the world we actually inhabit, in the intensity and remorselessness of its fixation on cruelty. Rather it is to be understood as a kind of rhetorical redescription of that world, "a redescription," Rorty writes, "of what may happen or has been happening—to be compared, not with reality, but with alternative descriptions of the same events."[39] But I would go further—what Orwell is offering us is a rhetorical redescription of totalitarianism as a world in which rhetorical redescription has become impossible. The existence described in *Nineteen Eighty-Four* is not simply colourless, though it is certainly that, in all its drab, grey remorselessness; it is also one in which language has been denuded of its ability to colour reality, or indeed to cloak it as something it is not. Vices are not dressed up as virtues in *Nineteen Eighty-Four*. They are simply not dressed up at all.

What, though, of Orwell's greatest book, *Animal Farm*, of which Rorty also says: "It was not its relation to reality, but its relation to the most popular alternative description of recent events, that gave it its power"?[40] Isn't the rhetorical redescription being practiced here an exercise in the exposure of hypocrisy, rather than the exposure of a world where hypocrisy is impossible? Certainly, *Animal Farm* seems, at its most literal, to be a litany of hypocrisies: from the double standards of the pigs (changing the commandment from "No animal shall drink alcohol" to "No animal shall drink alcohol *to excess*," the day after they have discovered the joys of whisky), to the false promises of Napoleon, their Stalin-like leader, and the sanctimony of his speechifying. It is certainly not a colourless world (even at the end of the book, the animals can still be moved by the sight of the green flag of Animal Farm flying high), nor one in which language lacks the ability to colour reality (just think of the rousing terms of the song, "Beasts of England"— "Beasts of England, beasts of Ireland / Beasts of every land and clime, / Hearken well and spread my tidings / Of the golden future time").[41] But at its end, *Animal Farm* also points towards the end of hypocrisy, as the criteria by which hypocrisy might be judged themselves become unsustainable. Animal Farm is renamed Manor Farm, and it was only while it was Animal Farm that it made sense to see it as a place in which hypocrisy was being practiced. The seven commandments (including "No animal shall drink alcohol to excess," which is hypocritical, now that many of the pigs are alcoholics) are replaced by a single commandment ("All animals are equal, but some animals are more equal than others," which is not hypocritical, because it is an open and cynical absurdity). The final scene in the book describes the moment when the leading pigs are glimpsed playing cards with the humans, with whom they are now happy to do business, and drink whisky, and fight. Their faces, Orwell says, began "melting and changing." He goes on:

> Twelve voices were shouting in anger and they were all alike. No question, now, what had happened to the faces of the pigs. The creatures outside looked from pig to man, and from man to pig, and from pig to man again: but already it was impossible to say which was which.[42]

Throughout his life, Orwell, like Bentham, was obsessed with masks, including the various masks of power, and the masks worn by those who sought to hide the truth about power. It was his preoccupation with masks that makes sense of one of Orwell's most famous lines, and one of his most misunderstood. In perhaps the last thing he ever wrote, Orwell declared: "At fifty, every man has the face he deserves."[43] This does not mean, as it is so often mistakenly taken to mean, that we deserve our physical appearance; what it means is that we deserve our mask, the face we choose to show to the world, because having lived with it for so long we can no longer claim that it is merely a façade. Here, though, at the end of *Animal Farm*, is a scene in which no one is wearing a mask, because it is no longer possible to see what there is to mask. Once again, no one has anything to hide, and that is where the terror lies.

HYPOCRISY AND ANTI-HYPOCRISY

Orwell, therefore, was an anti-hypocrite for whom there were worse things than hypocrisy, which is why Rorty is right to see him as a liberal in the Shklar mould. He was also an anti-hypocrite who understood how anti-hypocrisy could itself become the vice it was supposed to be rescuing us from. Democrats who sought to confront fascism on its own terms, like "Mr So-and-So the well-known anti-Fascist" in *Coming Up for Air*, were succumbing to the temptations of sincerity that ideological conflict offers to all its participants. These are the temptations that it continues to offer to this day—Christopher Hitchens is undoubtedly sincere in his personal crusade against Islamofascism, which is what makes his attempt to corral Orwell into that all-or-nothing struggle so unconvincing. As Orwell said in March 1940 of the war then only just begun: "For Heaven's sake, let us not suppose we go into this war with clean hands. It is only while we cling to the consciousness that our hands are not clean that we retain the right to defend ourselves."[44] And as he said in February 1944 of the war whose end was still nowhere in sight: "In the last analysis, our only claim to victory is that if we win the war, we shall tell fewer lies about it than our adversaries."[45] This is not truth versus lies; it is fewer lies versus more lies, or democratic hypocrisy versus the total lie. Indeed, for Orwell, it was the hypocrisy of the English that served to ensure that they were not entirely self-deceived about the moral compromises entailed in confronting a totalitarian ideology; they at least still knew what it meant to have something to hide.

Orwell himself was not immune to the temptations of sincerity. Unlike Christopher Hitchens, I cannot claim to have read through everything Orwell wrote and found nothing of which the Orwell admirer need be embarrassed: first, because it would be hypocritical of me to claim that I have read everything, and second, because in what I have read I repeatedly found Orwell's naive faith in the "truth" of the socialist alternative to capitalism to be, at times, toe-curlingly misplaced (the most inaccurate of Orwell's predictions about the inevitable coming of socialism tend to be prefaced with the words "Everyone knows . . ."). Equally hard to take is Orwell's insistence on a kind of honest proletarian consciousness to set against the corruptions of the intellectual mind, ranging from the crass simplicities expressed in the second half of the *Road to Wigan Pier* ("A generation ago every intelligent person was in some sense a revolutionary; nowadays it would be nearer the mark to say that every intelligent person is a reactionary," etc.[46]) through to his hints in *Nineteen Eighty-Four* that the only prospect of future salvation lies with the "proles." Orwell was also wrong about the fascist tendencies of British ruling classes, in part because he appears to have ignored his own lessons about the pervasiveness of English hypocrisy. He seemed to think that there was a serious prospect that the British would divest themselves of democracy before they would divest themselves of empire, and that when it came to the crunch English blimpishness might reveal itself to have a fascist heart. P. G. Wodehouse was closer to the truth with his portrayal of the true face of English fascism, in the gimlet-eyed, palpably absurd figure of Sir Roderick Spode, the underwear tycoon. The unthinking compromises of democratic life served in the end to render homegrown fascism a kind of joke.

There is little doubt that Orwell really believed in what he said about the possibilities for a kind of "honest" socialism and about the threat posed to it by the fascist tendencies inherent in all forms of capitalism. In this respect, he was least convincing in his writing about politics when he was at his most sincere, just as his current champions are at their least convincing when they are most sincere. But he was most convincing when he was describing the perils of political sincerity, and how closely they were related to the worst sorts of hypocrisy. He understood that hypocrisy cannot simply be opposed with anti-hypocrisy; sometimes anti-hypocrisy needs to be opposed with hypocrisy instead. There are no fixed lines to be drawn in this battle. Orwell always keeps sight of the fact that hypocrisy and anti-hypocrisy are not discrete entities, and they have the potential to leak into each other. So, for example, it is not true that there are no hypocrites in *Nineteen Eighty-Four*. There is at least one—one of the few historical figures to make an appearance in that novel—glimpsed fleetingly, and at more than one remove: in Victory Square, Winston

Smith wanders past "the statue of a man on horseback which was supposed to represent Oliver Cromwell."[47] Orwell believed that Cromwell was a forerunner of the dictators of the twentieth century, in his ruthlessness and his unashamed embrace of cruelty.[48] But he also knew that Cromwell, in all his hypocrisy, stood somewhere at the foundations of English democracy as well.

His place there is symbolised by the real statue of Cromwell that still stands outside the Houses of Parliament. In his book *Roundhead Reputations*, Blair Worden devotes a chapter to the controversy surrounding this statue, which was put up in 1899. There was much party political manoeuvring before it finally received parliamentary approval (its champion on the government benches in these debates was John Morley). In the end, the project was only approved when Rosebery's government secured tacit Tory support (the Tories' tactics appear to have been not to block it so that they could subsequently mock it; they also insisted that Rosebery pay for it himself, personally). Nevertheless, the Liberals were long since out of office by the time the project was completed. Rosebery, no longer prime minister, gave a commemorative address on the day the statue was finally unveiled, the central thrust of which was to defend Cromwell against the charge of hypocrisy. It is a wonderfully disingenuous speech, and it includes this magnificent non sequitur: "We who are here tonight do not believe he was a hypocrite, or we would not be here."[49] What Rosebery might more truthfully have said is that they would not have been there had they not been hypocrites themselves, since many, including Rosebery himself (for whom the whole business had become somewhat distasteful), held deeply ambivalent views about Cromwell, which they were doing their best to conceal.

Among the subjects of dispute that delayed the completion of the statue had been the appropriate pose for its subject. Cromwell's strongest supporters wanted him in full martial pose, on horseback, as Orwell was later to imagine him in

Photo © copyright Jim Batty

Victory Square. His opponents didn't want him there at all. In the end, a compromise was reached. Cromwell is depicted not on horseback but standing on the ground, looking modestly downwards. In one hand he holds a Bible (the original plan had been for the Bible to be open but in another classic piece of English hypocrisy it was decided that it would be better if it was closed). In the other hand he holds a sword. The sword has been removed from its scabbard, which hangs behind him, but it is posed deliberately pointing downwards, with its tip touching the ground. Cromwell rests his hand lightly on the top. It is a deeply compromised image, but it is also an appropriate one. It foreshadows Orwell's understanding of the unavoidable hypocrisies of democratic power, but it echoes Hobbes as well. Here is Hobbes in *Behemoth*, describing the moment when Cromwell finally asserted the authority of Parliament to defend the people, and asserted his own authority over Parliament at the same time:

> Last of all, Cromwell himself told them, it was now expected that Parliament should govern and defend the kingdom, and not any longer let the people expect their safety from a man whose heart God had hardened; nor let those, that had so well defended the Parliament, be left hereafter to the rage of an irreconcilable enemy, lest they seek their safety in some other way. This again was threatening; as also his laying his hand upon his sword when he spake it.[50]

CONCLUSION

SINCERITY AND HYPOCRISY IN DEMOCRATIC POLITICS

The story I have tried to tell in this book is of an ongoing struggle within the English-speaking tradition of liberal political thought to escape some of the traps that the problem of hypocrisy poses for anyone who takes it seriously. All of the writers I have discussed did take the problem of hypocrisy seriously, and they all wanted to find some way round or out of it. In their attempts to do so, they encountered certain persistent difficulties but also pointed the way towards some important general lessons about how to deal with hypocrisy in politics—including the crucial question of when it's worth worrying about, and when it isn't. A number of these lessons, I believe, still hold for the politics of today. In this final chapter, I want to try to make this connection explicit, and to see what contemporary politics might learn from a history of this kind. Above all, I want to explore whether we might get a sense of perspective on our own problems by looking to the past.

If nothing else, I hope that this book has made clear some of the ways in which our current anxieties about sincerity, hypocrisy, and lies in politics have deep roots in the liberal tradition, and why therefore we do not necessarily have to step outside that tradition to gain some insight into them. We don't have to go all the way back to Machiavelli and a pre-liberal perspective, nor do we have to go all the way with Nietzsche towards an anti-liberal one. However, I would not wish to claim that the tradition of thought described in this book can be automatically assumed to run on from the book's endpoint with Orwell through to the present. It may be that we are further away from the 1940s than the 1940s were from the 1640s in relation to some of the central concerns of the authors under review. To take just one example: does anyone still really care about Oliver Cromwell's hypocrisy, apart from historians? Perhaps the last place where Cromwell's perceived defects of character might still have had the capacity to shape political argument and fashion political enmities is Northern Ireland, but even in Northern Ireland this issue is not what it was. A political climate that permits Ian Paisley and Martin McGuinness to sit down together in the same government is not one in which the question of Cromwell's hypocrisy is going to retain much heat, for a whole range of fairly obvious reasons. In this respect, as in many others, the world has moved on. Oliver Cromwell's statue outside the British Parliament is just another statue—as indeed the Parliament is now just another parliament—and its modest pose seems well suited to its status as one more piece of ceremonial stonework for people to ignore.

But it is important to resist the temptation to seek to bypass history altogether by reverting back to the genre that I warned against at the start of this book—that of maxims, with their seductive little truths about politics and character, that can be turned to any situation and made to fit any problem. One of the distinctive features of the tradition I have been discussing is that it suggests there are no easy, catch-all solutions to the difficulties we still face in deciding how to handle deceitful or dissembling politicians. At best, there are some patterns that repeat themselves in the complex weave of the past and the present, ones that we might miss if we just focussed on the small patch of political detail in front of our eyes. In what follows I will try to highlight these patterns as I see them, and to ask what they tell us about our own predicament. What is certain, though, is that it does not pay to be too dogmatic about any lessons that can be drawn here. Indeed, that is the lesson that underlies any others to follow—that there are no simple solutions to the problem of hypocrisy in politics, that it is pervasive and complex, and that the same difficulties recur in different settings.

THE TEMPTATIONS OF ANTI-HYPOCRISY

The pervasiveness of the problem of political hypocrisy, and its ability to ensnare almost any political argument, means that people will always be looking for some way to break free from it. The thinkers that I have discussed here are, in their different ways, no exception. There comes a point when almost any political thinker is liable to succumb to the temptation to seek an escape from the hypocrisy of political life by demanding a clean-up, or a clean-out, or at the very least some sort of permanent insulation from its more corrosive effects, rather than simply carrying on going round in circles. The desire to wriggle free from the hold hypocrisy has on us all is a recurring feature of even the most sophisticated discussions of its role in liberal politics. And this longing for some sort of escape is something that unquestionably still exerts its pull today. Commentators on contemporary politics can often be heard demanding that we confront the problem of political hypocrisy once and for all. However, the fact remains that this demand is incoherent, because it is self-defeating. This is the first lesson of the story I have been trying to tell: there is no way of breaking out from the hypocrisy of political life, and all attempts to find such an escape route are a delusion.

Many contemporary expressions of disgust at the slipperiness of politicians could come directly out of the pages of the past, and recognising their essential familiarity is one way of appreciating just how futile such protests really are. There is always a temptation to believe that the problem of politicians who neither say what they mean nor mean what they say keeps getting worse, and that it does so because no one has been willing to take a firm enough stand against it. But plenty of people have tried to take a firm stand against it, which is a large part of the reason why it seems to keep getting worse. Here, for example, is the political commentator Peter Oborne writing in his book *The Rise of Political Lying* (2005) about what he sees as the degradation of British public life under the government of Tony Blair, with its obsession with news management and spin:

> What Britain really needs is not just a change in the law but a change of heart. We face a choice. We can do nothing, and carry on cheating, and deceiving each other, and wait for the public anger, alienation and disgust that will follow. We can watch the gradual debasement of decent democratic politics, and the rapid rise of the shysters and the frauds and—before very long perhaps—something more sinister by far. Or we can try and act once more as moral human beings. It's a common effort. It affects us all, politicians, journalists, citizens. But there is hope. Britain has a magnificent tradition of public integrity and civic engagement, which can be reclaimed. It could even be better than before.[1]

This could come, practically word for word, from Trollope's social criticism of the 1850s. And as in Trollope's case, it is little more than a reflex cry of pain; as a line of argument about how to deal with duplicity in politics, it is going nowhere. There are two basic problems with the case Oborne makes. First, we never do face a fundamental choice of this kind. Hypocrisy and anti-hypocrisy are joined together, as Shklar said, to form a discrete system, so that it is never a question of truth versus lies; it is, at best, a choice between different kinds of truth and different kinds of lies. All-or-nothing choices are in this context always an illusion. Second, Oborne himself exemplifies the impossibility of drawing a line anywhere in this shifting heap of sand. Oborne is, among other things, a well-rewarded journalist for Associated Newspapers, in which capacity he hounds the political class from morning to night about their perceived moral turpitude, thereby making the problem he describes worse, by inflating the cycle of recrimination and counter-recrimination that produces it.

In this role, Oborne has occasionally made the news as well as simply reporting it. For instance, during the cash-for-honours affair that dogged the last days of Tony Blair's premiership, Oborne accused the prime minister's official spokesman (Tom Kelly) of lying to the press. (The point at issue was whether the police had required one of Blair's police interviews to be kept secret, and for how long—as is the way with these sorts of arguments, it is hard with the benefit of even a little bit of hindsight to see why anyone should have cared.) Oborne made his accusation against Kelly at a lobby briefing, ensuring that it was given a wide public airing. The transcript of the exchange between them shows it descending into a miserable round of hectoring, denial, accusation, counter-denial, and counter-accusation, as Oborne accuses Kelly of being a serial liar, and Kelly accuses Oborne of trading in innuendo. The exchange ends with Kelly telling Oborne that if he carries on calling him a liar, he will see him in court.[2] And as Trollope said in 1855, "the world looks on, believing none of them."

The absurdity of scavenging journalists like Oborne demanding moral renewal in public life tends to produce another, countervailing rallying cry, which is to take the side of the political classes against the journalists, and to say that the collapse of standards is the latter's fault, for making impossible demands. Trollope himself underwent a shift of this kind—from blaming the Disraelis to blaming the Quintus Slides—over the course of his own political career. The same move is visible today. It is the line taken, for instance, by John Lloyd in his self-explanatorily titled book *What the Media Are Doing to Our Politics* (2004). Lloyd's account, unlike Oborne's, is not absurd, and his argument has a good deal to be said for it—in an age of an almost limitless capacity for scrutiny of the political class, beyond anything Bentham could have dreamed of and beyond what even he might have wished for, it is reasonable to hope for some restraint from the scrutineers, in their own interests as well as ours, to prevent the cycle of masking and unmasking from collapsing into farce. But the problem with a book like Lloyd's is that it does nonetheless constitute a taking of sides, which is another of the perennial temptations when confronted by political hypocrisy.

Lloyd is not demanding a fresh start. He is acknowledging that things are never going to be perfect, and that to expect complete sincerity and honesty of politicians or journalists is a pipedream. But for that very reason he believes that it remains possible to identify some people—journalists—as clearly worse than others—politicians—because of their inability to recognise this limitation on what they do. Yet what Lloyd cannot escape from is the fact that the politicians and the journalists are locked in this together. Each side believes that they are more sinned against than sinning. So seeking to separate them out by apportioning the blame, however well intentioned the endeavour, will inevitably stoke the problem that it is designed to resolve, because the journalists will ask: why should the politicians be the ones who are allowed to get away with it?

This is a theme that has recurred throughout this book: the futility of trying to resolve the problem of political hypocrisy by taking sides, in order to say that though we may all be hypocrites, at least our hypocrisy isn't as bad as theirs (or in Lloyd's case, because he is himself a journalist, at least their hypocrisy isn't as bad as ours). Taking sides in this way requires the deployment of a kind of knowingness about politics to draw the line between the people who are in control of what they are doing and those who are not. It is a line of thought that we have seen in Mandeville, who used it to defend his own particular brand of Whiggism—Mandevillian Whigs truly understand the problem of hypocrisy, which is what makes theirs less culpable than that of their opponents. It's there, too, in Morley, who used it to defend his brand of liberalism—Morley's liberals understand the nature of political compromise, which is what makes their compromises more tolerable than those of the Tories. And it's there in a politician like Tony Blair, who has used it to defend his brand of progressivism against all those cynics and sneerers who have failed to understand just how hard it is to do good in the morally compromised world of politics. In each case, the attempt to hold this line is underpinned by a distinction between first- and second-order hypocrisy, between those whose hypocrisy is bounded by an understanding that hypocrisy is unavoidable and those whose hypocrisy has tipped over into self-deception. But the recurring problem is that to profess that one is oneself merely a first-order hypocrite is in the context of political disagreement a form of second-order hypocrisy, because it is self-exculpatory, and threatens to tip over into its own kind of self-deception. Laying out the inner dynamics of this argument can be complicated, as we have seen in Mandeville's case. So let me try to summarise the difficulty as simply as possible. In politics, saying "Well, at least I'm not as hypocritical as you" always leaves one open to the riposte "Well, you are if you really believe that" (and, of course, if you don't really believe it, then you're a hypocrite too).

In this context, it is hardly surprising that there is another perennial temptation, which is to seek to escape from the endless cycle of accusation and counter-accusation that is democratic politics by transplanting the problem of political hypocrisy into some higher realm, where it becomes manageable again. We saw something like this with Orwell, who sought an escape in his own brand of common-sense socialism, through which the basic decency of working people would be allowed to come through; with Sidgwick, who sought it in what I called "the cleaner and crisper compromises of liberal imperialism," where a philosophical approach to politics might be protected from the vagaries of politicians endlessly pandering to public opinion; and with Bentham, who sought it in his own closed world of neologism and jargon, in a final attempt to keep the fictions of political life at bay. But again, as I have sought to indicate throughout this book, in the end there is no escape. These are themselves forms of second-order hypocrisy, because they seek to overlay democratic hypocrisy with something that conceals its essential qualities. And like all forms of second-order hypocrisy, either they are evidence of the thing they are designed to counter, which makes them self-defeating, or they are evidence of self-deception, which is often worse.

All of these avenues of escape still exert their pull today, though perhaps Orwell's common-sense socialism only does so very faintly (it is striking that the current generation of neo-Orwellians have ditched the socialism in favour of a form of liberal imperialism, dressed up as democratic internationalism). Contemporary politicians have shown themselves much more prone to the last two of these temptations: seeking an escape from the messiness of democratic hypocrisy in the warm embrace of liberal imperialism, and an escape from the constant name-calling of democratic argument in the calmer waters of technocratic jargon. The attraction lies in the illusion of control—freed from the imperatives of democratic hypocrisy, politicians ought to be in a position to set their own terms for any necessary compromises with the truth. But this remains an illusion. Liberal imperialists are no more in control of what they are doing than any other kinds of democratic politicians, and the need to retain the appearance of control is liable to leave them looking more hypocritical than ever. Likewise, politicians who construe politics in terms of agendas, roll-outs, initiatives, consultations, partnerships, mechanisms, targets, performance indicators, and so on, are not insulating themselves from the name-calling of party politics; they are simply inviting more of it, because politicians who use jargon always look like they have something to hide. Politicians who try to find a way out from the horrible compromises and contortions that democratic politics demands of its practitioners simply end up looking like hypocrites to everyone that they have tried to leave behind.

THE REAL CHOICES

So in the tradition I have been discussing, there is one set of lessons, deriving from the persistence of the desire to cut oneself off from political hypocrisy—by denouncing it, or taking sides, or seeking some sort of personal insulation from it—and from the certainty with which democratic politics will suck anyone who attempts this way out back into its sticky embrace. These are essentially negative lessons, and they remind us not to approach the problem of hypocrisy with false expectations about what can be achieved. But there is another set of lessons, too, and these are the ones that offer something more positive. All the authors I have been talking about in this book, as well as sometimes succumbing to the temptations of an illusory escape from political hypocrisy, have also attempted to make sense of the discrete system of hypocrisy and anti-hypocrisy in its own terms, and rather than taking sides, to understand when and why it might become self-defeating. In this way, they have sought to distinguish between different kinds of hypocrisy, rather than simply between hypocrisy and sincerity, or between your hypocrisy and my hypocrisy. In making these distinctions, they offer some insight into many of the real choices we do in fact face. In what follows, I will attempt to highlight these choices as I see them, and to identify what they might have to do with politics as it is currently practiced. I will do so by working backwards, from Orwell to Hobbes.

Orwell

What Orwell shows us is that democratic hypocrisy and imperial hypocrisy do not mix. The reason is that they are not simply different, but opposed sorts of hypocrisy. Democratic hypocrisy involves a kind of benign self-deception—its stability depends upon people growing comfortable with the mask that conceals some of the brute facts about power, and thereby moderating the ways that those facts play themselves out. But this benign hypocrisy becomes malign in the context of imperialism, because empires cannot in the end conceal the brute coercion on which they depend. Imperial hypocrisy is the attempt to dress up coercion as something it is not, but if they are to be sustained, empires have in the end to drop their pretences about the nature of their power. In this respect, imperial power politics tends towards sincerity. But democratic politics tends towards the continuance of hypocrisy as the basis of its own sustainability. Therefore, democracy tends to make a mockery of empire, and empires tend to make a mockery of democracies.

In so far as this dilemma presents us with a choice, it ought to be no choice—we must plump for democracy over empire. But what is most striking about this way of putting the matter is that in doing so, we choose hypocrisy over sincerity. This suggests, if nothing else, that pleas of democratic sincerity in the context of early-twenty-first century liberal imperialism should set us on our guard. Democracies cannot be honest with themselves about imperial projects—about what is needed to sustain them, about what they cost in financial and moral terms—so democratic leaders who plead a sincere faith in democracy to justify their imperial adventures have justified nothing. At the same time, the more pragmatic political thinkers who have argued that democracies will only be equipped to sustain the politics of liberal empire if they accustom themselves to "double standards" need to recognised that even double standards have their own double standards. The double standards of empire are very different from the double standards of democracy.[3] If we accustom ourselves to the former, we will find it very hard to continue with the latter, and vice versa.

Of course, this is not the only way to think about the dilemmas of liberal power at the beginning of the twenty-first century. Other, practical considerations may trump the question of sincerity and hypocrisy, and there may well be better arguments both for and against liberal empire.[4] Nor would I wish to claim that this clash of democratic and imperial hypocrisy explains the immediate difficulties encountered by the neoconservative project to export democracy to Iraq by force of arms. Some may say it is too soon to judge whether that project will end in ultimate failure, and anyway, earlier empires took a long time to get going, and a long time to fall apart. Even the British Empire, whose internal contradictions Orwell dissected, did not implode, but only gradually faded away. Perhaps the clash between democratic hypocrisy and imperial hypocrisy does not necessarily spell disaster in the short-to-medium term. But Orwell at least gives us reasons to see why it might, and given that Orwell himself is so often cited in anger on the other side of these arguments, that is something worth bearing in mind.

The Victorians

Of the three writers I looked at, Trollope, the least philosophical and in his way the least consistent, understood political hypocrisy best. In *Phineas Redux* he offers us two types of political deceivers, drawn on the classic templates of Disraeli (Daubeny) and Gladstone (Gresham). One is the incautious conjurer, who is always trying to make things happen, even if that means turning reality on its head; the other is the more cautious hypocrite, who sticks to limits of the possible but in so doing sublimates many of his own personal principles. The conjurer is often sincere, but is liable to stretch the truth (as Disraeli did); the hypocrite may be honest, but is prone to dissemble about his own character (as Gladstone did). These types are still visible in politics today. Bill Clinton and Tony Blair, perhaps, are both examples of sincere conjurers who have had difficulty with the truth; Al Gore and Gordon Brown are upright hypocrites, who prefer the facts but can have difficulty persuading the public that they are what they seem. The Conservative leader David Cameron is clearly, and self-consciously, in the Blair/Clinton/Disraeli mould; Hillary Clinton, perhaps surprisingly, may be more of a Brown/Gore/Gladstone.[5] I will go further into the case of Hillary Clinton in the next section, when I consider some possible futures for American politics. The point I want to make here is that democratic politics appears to have a tendency to produce complicated, and compromised, choices of this kind—not between truth and lies, or sincerity and hypocrisy, but between politicians who are sincere but untruthful and those who are honest but hypocritical.[6]

Inevitably, some people will prefer one type and some the other—we have varying levels of tolerance for these different kinds of political deception. For some of us sincerity trumps honesty and for others honesty trumps sincerity. Equally, fashions change, and the preference for sincere liars (which has been the dominant trend in the politics of the last decade or more) may eventually produce its own reaction in favour of the upright hypocrites. But if we resist the temptation to take sides, as Trollope did, what we can learn is how much these different political types depend on each other (and it is fun to imagine what Trollope might have done with a relationship like that between the Clintons, which literally marries the two together). These types are a permanent part of the discrete system of hypocrisy and anti-hypocrisy that allows democratic politics to function. It is a false choice if we think that we need ultimately to decide between them. The real choice is between a system that can accommodate both, and one that allows either the sincere liars or the honest hypocrites to have it all their own way. So what we should be on the lookout for is not dishonesty or insincerity as such, but instead any signs that our politics have become excessively intolerant of one or the other. The real danger arises if sincerity never has to answer for itself in the face of a crabbed and hypocritical insistence on the evidence, just as it would be dangerous if reticent and secretive politicians never had to confront publicly the question of what they really believe. A politics consisting just of Daubenys would be intolerable, as would a politics consisting just of Greshams. On their own they are insufferable. We need them both as much as they each need the other.

Bentham

The political theorist John Dunn once described democracy as "the cant of the modern world."[7] What Bentham shows is that there is more than one way to cant about democracy. On the one hand, the high-flown language of democratic principle can be a mask for the power relations that lie behind it, and Bentham was always on the lookout for words that masked the workings of power. But attempts to pin democracy down, and to capture its workings in fine detail, can also constitute a kind of masking, because they conceal the extent to which democracy relies on a set of fictions about its own essential character. The way we talk about democracy can be too elevated—as when we used the word as a term of approval regardless of the desirability of the practices to which it is attached—but it can also be too fine-grained in its attempts to capture the essence of those practices, and thereby miss the bigger picture. Highfaluting cant tends to be the province of politicians; technical cant tends to the province of political scientists. In the hands of the former, democracy becomes just another "colour" term to gloss over the details of political power struggles. In the hands of the latter, it becomes distinctly colourless, but that too is a kind of gloss that serves to cover up the impossibility of denuding democracy of all ambiguity.

If the language of democracy can be either too colourful, or too colourless, is there any way of getting it just right? My reading of Bentham suggests that there is not. Attempts to retain the fictional character of democracy are always vulnerable to detailed exposure of what is really going on behind the scenes, but equally, such detailed accounts are always vulnerable to the charge that they miss what is distinctive about democracy, which is its ability to confront power in its own terms, with words that capture the sweeping claims of popular rule. Another way to put this is to say that the pursuit of the true essence of democracy is always liable to result in a form of insincerity. But it does not follow that therefore all talk about democracy is cant. Instead, we need to distinguish the purposes to which this talk is put, and it is here that Bentham provides an excellent guide. Technical language and fictional language are each capable of masking the truth about democracy, but each is also capable of exposing the other as simply a gloss on that truth. The question is not whether politicians or political thinkers are sincere in their accounts of democracy, but rather what their purpose is in using the language of democracy—are they trying to hide something, or are they trying to expose something about the inadequacies of a competing set of terms?

This connects to one of the central themes of this book: the fact that something is a mask does not mean it cannot be used to unmask something else. To talk of democracy in very general and elevated terms—to seek to confront dry and empty jargon with the unarguable claims of the people to assert themselves against their rulers—can be a means of exposing one of the masks of power. But the same language, deployed to cover up the detailed difficulties of enabling democracies to function as structures of power in a given situation, can itself be one of the masks of power that needs to be exposed. Grandiose claims for democracy have been a consistent feature of political life for much of modern history. That they are grandiose does not make them illegitimate. Sometimes—and the later years of the Cold War might have been one such time—such language is needed to remind us of the possibilities of popular rule, which the dusty terminology of political science has tended to obscure. But at other times—and the aftermath of the Cold War might be another such time—grandiose claims need to be punctured with a more considered treatment of what democracy actually means on the ground.[8] These considerations might seem to take us a long way from Bentham. Nonetheless, they relate to Bentham's insights into the choices we face, given that democratic language can be both a mask for power, and a means of removing the mask. There is no point in looking to get rid of the mask altogether. What we need to decide is what we can best use it for.

The American founders

Between them, Benjamin Franklin, John Adams, and Thomas Jefferson give us a wide panorama of the interacting dynamics of political hypocrisy and political sincerity. Of course, this is not the whole story of the American founding period, and there are other players—Washington, Hamilton, Madison—who could be added to this picture, and who would thereby introduce themes—military, economic, constitutional—that it ignores. Nevertheless, I hope that the account I have given is sufficient to indicate a few things: first, how important luck is in determining whether the appearance of sincerity can be maintained; second, how quickly contingent political arguments can spill over into more general or abstract arguments about the nature of political hypocrisy, and vice versa; and third, just how difficult it can be, for even the most seasoned political practitioners, to know where the limits of political hypocrisy should lie. The ongoing politics of hypocrisy, with all its own uncertainties and unpredictable shifts in fortune, makes it very hard to fix any durable bounds for hypocrisy in politics.

Underlying this, however, is a further consideration that I tried to bring out at the end of the chapter. The moments when politicians gain clearest insight into the limits of political hypocrisy tend to coincide with their own moments of political weakness. Adams often, Jefferson rarely, and Franklin perhaps never, came to see how important it is to separate out the kind of unavoidable hypocrisy that exists within any political system from the holding of hypocritical views about that system (and all its hypocrisies), which is much more damaging. There is a line to be drawn between first-order and second-order hypocrisy in this respect. But drawing that line can be politically incapacitating, whereas Jefferson in particular, whenever he blithely ignored it or trampled over it, found himself politically freer. This freedom connects to a certain lack of self-consciousness, and does not simply hold for politics: the best way to keep a mask in place can be to forget that one is wearing a mask. What politics brings out is the difference between living by this principle, and coming to understand it intellectually. An intellectual perspective on the problem of political hypocrisy allows the politician to see many things, but not to dispense with that degree of self-consciousness that can render the deepest insights self-defeating. Genuine freedom from the problem of hypocrisy is perhaps only to be achieved with the aid of self-deception. So there may be a hard lesson here: when it comes to sincerity and hypocrisy in politics, one can have intellectual insight, or one can have practical flexibility, but one cannot have both.

Mandeville

There is a lot to learn from Mandeville, not least how to write about political hypocrisy with humour, which is a great counsel against despair. Mandeville is one of the funniest of all serious writers about politics, and it is impossible to read him without gaining a sense of perspective on our endless anxieties about political insincerity. Laughter may really be one of the best medicines here. But Mandeville's purpose remains a serious one, and though he does not resolve the problem of political hypocrisy, he does provide us with some important considerations when trying to achieve our own accommodation with it. The first is the importance of understanding how contingent the standards of hypocrisy and sincerity are. Dealing with political hypocrisy is a question not just of recognising that politicians wear masks, but of recognising that the masks they wear must suit the age in which they find themselves. Politicians can find themselves in an age in which it is best to put on the mask of sincerity, in order to appear as though they are not wearing a mask at all; for Mandeville it was part of Cromwell's genius to understand this so clearly. It may be that we too have been living through such an age—not a Cromwellian age of enthusiasm, but rather a period of what might be called semi-confessional or faux-confessional politics (the confessional here being the daytime-TV studio). This is a world in which personal revelation is valued, reticence is derided, and openness, ease, comfort in one's own skin is what gives politicians a hold over their audiences. Any successful politician will need to adapt to this. But no politician should assume that there is anything immutable about the claims of political sincerity. There is a big difference between adapting to the demands of a faux-confessional age, and coming to believe in them—that is, believing that sincerity and openness have an independent value in justifying political action. That would be second-order hypocrisy.

In this respect, the double standards of modern politics are better understood in Mandevillian than Machiavellian terms. Mandeville highlights the contingency of all standards of political morality, and the extent to which even the most skilful politicians must be slaves to the fashions of the times. There is no scope in the Mandevillian worldview for the prince whose mastery of the secret arts of government allows him to transcend the morality of the age. Instead, even princes and prime ministers must recognise the extent to which they are not in full control of the part they are playing, and it is that recognition that can provide security against misrule. But it is not easy to achieve this sort of self-knowledge, and almost impossible to retain it—politicians who come to believe that they are self-aware about the hold that hypocrisy exercises in politics are liable to use that knowledge to make an exception for themselves. Given this inherent tendency for self-knowledge to translate into self-justification, Mandeville offers two pieces of advice that remain pertinent. The first is not to rely too much on the self-knowledge of politicians. We are used to the idea that individual politicians cannot be trusted to set the limits to their own power, and must be subject to institutional constraints. The same ought to be true of their sincerity. Even the ablest politicians—even the Cromwells, even the Jeffersons—are not in complete control of the part they have to play. So no politician's pleas of sincerity, no matter how seemingly self-aware, should be taken at face value. Much better, as Mandeville says, to assume that fifty different people could play the part of prime minister, than to assume that some are uniquely qualified for that role by dint of their self-awareness. In Mandeville's words, "a prime minister has a vast, an unspeakable advantage, barely by being so [i.e., by simply happening to be prime minister]." That ought to be enough to set us on our guard against incumbents who wish to add to their advantages by insisting on their own good faith.

Mandeville's second lesson is the closest thing there is in this tradition to a workable maxim. The worst hypocrisy arises when politicians pretend that easy things are difficult, and difficult things are easy. However, this is second-order, not first-order, advice. It is not hard to imagine circumstances in which it makes sense for politicians to misrepresent the ease or the difficulty of what they are up to: a leader whose party is cruising to election victory might do well to insist to his or her followers that every vote still remains to be fought for, in order to guard against complacency; likewise, a leader heading for crushing defeat might wish to pretend victory is still there for the taking, in order to guard against despair. But what no politicians should do is misrepresent to themselves or anyone else the ease or difficulty of taking decisions like these. It is easy to lie when you have to; much harder to judge when the lying should stop. It is hypocrisy for politicians to pretend that decisions taken out of political necessity are difficult for them personally, just as it is hypocrisy for them to pretend that knowing what counts as political necessity is ever easy for anyone.

In a faux-confessional age, politicians who go to war like to remind us that they too are human, and any decision that results in loss of life is taken with deep reluctance. That is what they mean when they talk about these as "difficult decisions." At the same time, they prefer to explain the rationale behind such decisions in terms that leave no room for doubt. That is what they mean when they talk about these as "decisions that had to be taken." But this is the wrong way around. Pangs of conscience are easy for politicians to handle; finding room for rational doubt is much harder. By putting the premium on personal sincerity, political leaders make it too easy for themselves to ignore the difficult facts.

Hobbes

Finally, underlying all of this is Hobbes's view, as I reconstructed it, that most forms of what is conventionally understood as hypocrisy don't matter, but hypocrisy about power does. One possible form of hypocrisy about power is to overstate the significance of personal sincerity—to seek to ground one's politics on the fact that one happens genuinely to believe what one says one believes. For Hobbes, modern politics is grounded on the set of institutional arrangements that can generate security in a situation in which one can never be certain what anyone really believes, though one can be certain some people will place undue weight on their personal beliefs. To over-personalise politics, to collapse the distinction between the mask and the person behind the mask, is either culpable hypocrisy, or self-delusion. And, as Hobbes suggests, one of the marks of the culpable forms of hypocrisy is how closely related they are to self-delusion, which is one of the reasons why hypocrisy and self-delusion can feed off each other.

In these circumstances, we need politicians who are sincere, but that does not mean we should wish them to be sincere believers in everything they do. Instead, we need them to be sincere about the system of power in which they find themselves, and sincere in their desire to maintain the stability and durability of that system, even if it comes at the cost of their own ability to say what they mean and mean what they say. This is as true of democratic politics as of any other kind. Democratic politicians should be sincere about maintaining the conditions under which democracy is possible, and should place a higher premium on that than on any other sort of sincerity. The system of democratic politics will require them to play a part, but they should play their part in a way that is truthful to the demands of the system itself. Their individual hypocrisy—that is, their hypocrisy judged as individuals—does not matter. Indeed, some personal hypocrisy will be inevitable for any democratic politician. What matters is whether they can be truthful, with themselves and with others, about that.

CHOOSING THE RIGHT HYPOCRITE

Thus far, I have addressed the various questions relating to sincerity, hypocrisy, and lies in modern politics by looking back, to the somewhat distant past and also, in this chapter, to the more immediate past. But I want to finish by attempting to illustrate some of these themes by looking at an event that is unfolding as I write—the 2008 U.S. presidential election. This election, like any election, raises the question of whether political hypocrisy matters, and if so, of what kind. At the time of writing, it is far from clear who will be the candidates, never mind who will be the next president. Nonetheless, the perceived hypocrisy of all the possible candidates, and how they handle it, is likely to play some role in determining the outcome (it would hardly be a democratic election if this were not the case). And in that context, I want to contrast four different kinds of hypocrisy that have the potential to figure in the politics of the election, and to connect them to wider issues that I have discussed so far in this book. This is not by way of predicting the outcome of the election, nor of saying which kinds of hypocrisy are going to prove decisive with the American electorate. Rather, it is an attempt to identify, as the authors I have been discussing in this book were attempting to identify, which kinds of hypocrisy are worth worrying about.

Hypocrisy and religion

First, there is the question of religion and personal sincerity: how much does it matter if those running for president actually believe in the "faith-based" positions any plausible candidate is required to adopt in order to win over crucial segments of the electorate? The condition of American politics means that it is difficult for candidates to be entirely sincere on questions of religion, particularly as they tack back and forth between the stance they need to adopt to secure their party's nomination, and the stance they need to adopt to win a general election. But for some, the issue of religious hypocrisy is more acute than for others, because it connects to the wider question of whether anything about their public persona is what it seems. This, for example, is Gerard Baker, the U.S. editor of the London *Times*, writing about Hillary Clinton early in 2007:

> Here is finally someone who has taken the black arts of the politician's trade, the dissembling, the trimming, the pandering, all the way to their logical conclusion. [*Baker bases this claim on a contrast between the Hillary Clinton of 15 years ago— whom he calls "a principled, if somewhat rebarbative and unelectable politician"—and the Clinton of today.—D.R.*] Now, you might say, hold on. Aren't all politicians veined with an opportunistic

streak? Why is she any different? The difference is that Mrs.
Clinton has raised that opportunism to an animating philosophy, a P.T. Barnum approach to the political marketplace. All
politicians, sadly, lie. We can often forgive the lies as the necessary price paid to win popularity for a noble cause. But the
Clinton candidacy is a Grand Deceit, an entirely artificial construct built around a person who, stripped bare of the cynicism, calculation and manipulation, is nothing more than an
enormous, overpowering and rather terrifying ego.[9]

Or, as media mogul and one-time Clinton fundraiser David
Geffen said to explain his defection to the Barack Obama
camp at around the same time: "Everybody in politics lies, but
they [the Clintons] do it with such ease it is troubling."

There are two things to be said about this: first, what Baker
says shows why it is probably wrong to run the two Clintons
together as Geffen does. All politicians lie, but some, like Bill
Clinton, are able to lie easily because they are able to persuade
others, and themselves, of their underlying sincerity. Bill Clinton was a faith-based politician, his faith being limitless faith
in his own goodness of heart. Hillary Clinton is nothing like
this; her public persona is too obviously an artificial construct,
designed to protect her from her own weaknesses as a politician and a human being (notably a lack of warmth), of which
she is clearly all too aware. This is why, in a semi-confessional
age, it will be considerably harder for her than for her husband to get elected. But it also means that there is less danger
in her case than there was in her husband's of becoming self-
deceived. With Hillary Clinton there seems little possibility
that she, any more than anyone else, will lose sight of the fact
that she is a hypocrite. Hillary Clinton appears to be a mixture of what Mandeville calls "malicious" and "fashionable"
hypocrisy, of personal ambition and a desire to pander to
the electorate. Baker, like all of her opponents, would have us
take it for granted that these are inherently bad things. But are
they? Mandeville certainly wouldn't think so. And following

Mandeville, we might say that politicians who are forced to combine these different forms of hypocrisy are less likely to be deceived about their own characters, or at least about the character of political hypocrisy, than politicians who believe themselves to be sincere.

This leads to the second point: what is Hillary's insincerity being contrasted with? The underlying contrast in Baker's attack is not with her husband, but with George W. Bush, a man who may have had his own problems with the truth, but whose underlying personality, and indeed underlying faith, is at least consistent and sincere in Baker's terms. However, as I have tried to argue throughout this book, sincerity of personal faith or belief is an overrated virtue in politics, for the reasons Hobbes makes clear. The Bush doctrine in international politics has sometimes crudely and inaccurately been characterised as a Hobbesian one.[10] Regardless of the ways in which this misapprehends Hobbes's own view of international relations, it also seems highly unlikely that Hobbes would approve of the way that Bush has allowed questions of sincerity of faith to become entangled with power politics. Religion, for Hobbes, should be at the service of politics; politics should never be subservient to religious or even semi-religious instincts. Hobbes did not want his rulers to be true believers in anything, except in the idea that politics could be organised on a rational basis. So at the risk of stretching the evidence beyond anything a historian would be remotely comfortable with, I would say that Hillary is much more obviously the model of a Hobbesian politician than George W. Bush. She is both skeptical and somewhat cynical, and therefore is bound to wear a mask; she has constructed a persona for herself in order to negotiate the world of power politics as she understands it. If that mask requires her to hide the true state of her religious beliefs, so be it. If she is sincere about anything, she is sincere about power. That at least means she is less likely than more sincere politicians to be hypocritical about the things that really matter. None of this means Hillary Clinton is certain to be elected; nor, if elected, that she is sure to be a success. But then again, that was what Hobbes most mistrusted about democracy—that it had a tendency to reward those who made a show of their personal sincerity over those who were sincere about power itself.

Hypocrisy and war

The second area in which the question of hypocrisy has been unavoidable for candidates for president in 2008 concerns their attitude to the Iraq War, and their willingness or otherwise to defend their own voting record (if they have one). Again, plausible candidates are vulnerable in one way or another here, either for having adopted positions in favour of the war on which they have subsequently felt obliged to backtrack, or for having adopted positions against the war that they have nevertheless been forced to hedge, for fear of appearing unpatriotic. Looming over them all is the baleful example of John Kerry, who was deeply compromised by his circumlocutory explanations of his complicated voting position on this question in 2004. Flexibility seems to be called for, but sincerity and integrity also appear to be required. It is nightmarishly difficult to see how to get this balance right.

As a result, there will always be the temptation to take sides on a question like this, and to say that some hypocrisies here are clearly worse than others. But which? John Edwards apologised for his vote in the Senate in 2002 authorizing war, whereas Hillary Clinton refused to apologise for hers. Barack Obama sought to emphasise that he had nothing to apologise for, glossing over the fact that he was not in the Senate in 2002, and so got off lightly. John McCain sought to emphasise his own distance from these Democratic contortions, by dint of both his loyalty to the president and his constructive criticism of the president's policy. Rudolph Giuliani emphasised the importance of personal heroism in determining integrity, glossing over his personal good fortune (from this perspective) in finding himself in charge of New York on the day the Twin Towers fell. Many people will seek to present these competing positions as fundamental moral differences, revealing of underlying differences of character: apologising for mistakes is better than not apologising; having made mistakes is better than pretending one is incapable of them; loyalty to country is better than loyalty to party; having been tested in the line of fire is the only true test of character there is; and so on. Of course, character matters, and the voters will need to decide which sort of character they prefer. But it is equally true that the attempt to portray failings of character as the worst sort of hypocrisy is simply an extension of politics, part of the endless round of constructing and deconstructing political personae that is the price that liberal democratic politics demands of its practitioners. I would hope that if the history I have been trying to tell suggests anything, it is that accusations and counter-accusations of hypocrisy are not going to settle questions of character.

But there is an extension of this question of hypocrisy when it comes to the Iraq War that poses a particular problem for Democratic candidates. This is the question of whether they really want America to win in Iraq. For example, did any of the Democratic candidates really want George Bush's 2007 troop surge in Baghdad to succeed, given that were it to do so, it would inevitably damage their own chances of winning the White House (though given the difficulty of reaching definitive agreement about such things, perhaps not irreparably)? This is a theme that has come up again and again in recent iterations of American and British politics: can opponents of the Iraq War defend themselves against the charge that deep down they want the other side to win, in order to be proved right; or, in the most toxic form of this charge, that they take pleasure in the disaster? And it goes beyond the Iraq War—it is in some ways a perennial theme of democratic politics: how can you want things to go wrong for your political opponents without appearing to want things to go wrong for the sake of it? And the answer is that you must simply dissemble. No Democratic candidate for president can ever afford to be tarred with the brush that he or she wished to offer succour to America's enemies, so all of them must deny this charge at all costs. But with some part of themselves, they are bound not to want Bush's Iraq strategy to succeed. You do not have to be a Hobbesian to recognise that this is both human nature, and in the nature of politics.

Politicians can try to justify these evasions to themselves in broadly consequential terms, arguing that a temporary success here will blind the United States to deeper, underlying problems that will bring greater difficulties down the line. But in so doing, they will be concealing the part of themselves, perhaps even from themselves, that simply wants to win power, which means the other side must lose it. Moreover, because our politics is not Hobbesian all the way through, but values contestation and dissent over straightforward obedience, this sort of concealment is the price we pay for that contestation and dissent. Here, again, is a place in our politics where sincerity would be worse than hypocrisy, because sincerity, in ruling out ill-motivated opposition, would rule out various forms of opposition altogether. There are, as Judith Shklar says, and as any careful reading of George Orwell will confirm, various forms of democratic hypocrisy that we must be sanguine about, for fear of finding something worse.

Hypocrisy and compromise

The poisonous nature of much partisan political argument about the Iraq War, and the need for all parties to stake their claim to one of the most enduringly potent colour terms of modern politics—"patriot"—inevitably provokes its own kind of backlash. There is always room in a rancorous political landscape for a candidate who states what he or she believes in, but nevertheless embodies the principles of compromise and pragmatism, in some sense above or beyond party. Sometimes these candidates literally stand outside the party system, as with privately funded, independent campaigns of the kind Michael Bloomberg would attempt were he to run in 2008 (and again, at the time of writing, it is far from clear whether he will). But such independent candidates do not have a good record of effecting a permanent shift in political values in a world that remains as dominated by party as it was in Trollope's time. Much trickier than an independent run, but also much more effective if it can succeed, is an appeal beyond the narrow limitations of partisan politics launched from within the party system itself. In their different ways, many candidates in 2008, including the Republicans McCain and Giuliani, have gestured towards such an appeal, with mixed success. But the one candidate who has made it central to his entire political persona is Barack Obama.

There is, of course, a tradition for the sort of candidature that Obama has tried to embody: the principled, free-thinking politician who nevertheless recognises that on any important question there will be an equivalent strength of feeling on the other side, and whose compromises are therefore not hypocrisy but instead a form of principled pragmatism. A *New Yorker* profile of Obama from May 2007 made the connection explicit, quoting Obama's former University of Chicago colleague Cass Sunstein:

> "Lincoln is a hero of his," Sunstein says—Obama announced his candidacy in front of the Old State Capitol in Springfield in order to draw a connection between himself and that other skinny politician from Illinois—"and in the legal culture Lincoln is famous for believing that there are some principles that you can't compromise in terms of speaking, but, in terms of what you *do*, there are pragmatic reasons and sometimes reasons of principle not to act on them. Alexander Bickel, in 'The Least Dangerous Branch,' made this aspect of Lincoln famous, and I don't know if Obama has this directly from Bickel, but if he doesn't he has it from law school." Lincoln, Bickel wrote,

"held 'that free government was, in principle, incompatible with chattel slavery.' . . . Yet he was no abolitionist." Should freed slaves become the equals of white men? "The feelings of 'the great mass of white people' would not admit of this," Bickel described Lincoln as thinking, "and hence here also principle would have to yield to necessity." Lincoln wrote, "Whether this feeling accords with justice and sound judgment, is not the sole question, if indeed, it is any part of it. A universal feeling, whether well or ill-founded, can not be safely disregarded."[11]

But, though Lincoln's is the most ringing example of this form of politics, the underlying idea that politicians can distinguish between compromising on their principles and compromising in their actions is one we have encountered before, in other contexts. Lincoln's own version of it, as well as having its roots in his legal experiences, was a deliberate refashioning of what he understood as the Jeffersonian legacy for American politics. This legacy has its own roots in a set of rationalist arguments about sincerity and compromise that reaches back into eighteenth- and seventeenth-century English political thought, all the way to Francis Bacon. As such, it is a tradition that has another, quite separate branch, running forward into the English liberal tradition, and given most prominent expression in the high Victorian period, by writers like John Morley.

Obama, as Sunstein says, has his understanding of this tradition from law school, and from the trials and tribulations of American history, not from Victorian liberal philosophy. The idiom of Obama's rhetoric is very different from anything that might come from the likes of Morley, but some of the core concerns are not. Obama has a thorough distaste for inauthentic expressions of religious faith—"the politician who shows up at a black church around election time and claps (off rhythm) to the gospel choir or sprinkles in a few biblical citations to spice up a thoroughly dry policy speech"—and a matching belief that it is only the politician who is able to speak his mind freely who knows when to compromise.[12] This is, as we have seen, a deeply attractive message for a certain type of liberal politician, allowing him to retain a partisan sense of purpose while reaching out beyond the hypocrisy of mere partisanship to embrace a spirit of principled compromise as well. But it is worth mentioning John Morley in this context, and the generation of deeply compromised liberal imperialists who fell under his spell, simply to remind us that this line of thought does not only produce Lincolns. It can also generate a form of self-deception that derives from the desire of the democratic politician to seek a form of insulation from hypocrisy in some realm that transcends it. Of course, it does not have to produce self-deception: in rare hands, like those of Lincoln, principled compromise can emerge as a form of self-knowledge. But because the problem of hypocrisy produces a series of enduring temptations that entice politicians away from a sense of their own limitations and towards a sense of their own sufficiency, such self-knowledge remains rare.

Hypocrisy and the environment

Finally, let me move away from questions of personality politics to a more global theme. An issue that is certain to dog all present and future presidential candidates in the United States and elsewhere is their approach to the problem of global warming. In the immediate context of the 2008 U.S. election, the potential candidate who had been both best placed to exploit the issue and also most vulnerable to the charge of personal hypocrisy was Al Gore. Early in 2007 newspapers on both sides of the Atlantic were full of either deeply critical or sympathetically agonised articles about whether Gore's personal hypocrisy mattered, once it was discovered that the energy needs of his private home produced a carbon footprint many times the size of others in his neighborhood. Clearly, for any possible Gore candidature this was bad politics—blatant hypocrisy of this sort always gives your enemies a stick to beat you with. On the other hand, it is not clear that this kind of hypocrisy is the obstacle it sometimes appears, because there seems to be quite wide acceptance that some personal hypocrisy of this kind (not always practicing in the private sphere what you preach in public) is unavoidable in those who seek political power: they are like us, but they are not like us, and in some aspect of their lives the gap will show.

This kind of mismatch between public pronouncements and private practice is the hypocrisy we tend to hear most about, because it is the easiest to find, and the easiest to exploit to provoke a reaction. In many settings, and above all in the more censorious branches of the media (particularly online), not practicing what you preach is what hypocrisy has come to mean, though as we have seen throughout this book, it is far from being the only way of understanding the term. But the reaction to this sort of hypocrisy is often short-lived, and frequently surprisingly tolerant. Just as the explosion of information technology has made it easier to expose any slip in a public individual's private standards, so it has also reinforced the extent to which private citizens also lead lives that require them to enact many different roles, in many different settings. Politicians are not the only ones who possess what social psychologists call "multiple selves." Perhaps for this reason, voters seem far more censorious about public inconsistencies—"flip-flopping" in the jargon—than they do about private lapses from the highest public standards. So perhaps the more serious charge of hypocrisy to which a politician like Gore is vulnerable is that he didn't do much about global warming when he was in office. But again, this hardly seems enough to preclude him from running for president (had he wanted to), since he was only vice president at the time, and he might legitimately say that someone needs to elect him president before being able to judge what he is and isn't capable of doing.

However, the real point I want to make is that the question of hypocrisy and global warming cannot, and should not, simply be about the personal hypocrisy of politicians like Al Gore.

Electoral politics can almost certainly cope with the hypocrisy of environmentalists who are not quite as good as they would like the rest of us to be. And in this area, the distinction between first- and second-order hypocrisy is both clear and workable. There is a big difference between those who do not live up to the standards they ask of others, and those who make a parade of their own ability to set an example. An environmental campaigner who travels the world by jet to spread the message that air travel is a significant cause of global warming is compromised, but such compromises may constitute the only efficient way to spread the message. Such a case is far removed from that of a politician like the British Conservative leader David Cameron, who has gone to great lengths to "green" his own personal lifestyle, and to make political capital out of that fact. When it emerged that Cameron's much publicised bicycle rides to the House of Commons involved the use of a car to ferry his personal belongings behind him, he revealed himself to be a second-order hypocrite. Second-order hypocrisy, because it makes a mockery of the whole business of public enactment, is corrosive in ways that first-order hypocrisy is not.

But even this is in a sense trivial. Far more significant than the question of whether individual politicians are hypocrites on environmental issues is the question of whether the most advanced democracies can cope with the charge of hypocrisy that is likely to be leveled against them by the rest of the world, regardless of the immediate twists and turns of their electoral politics. If global warming is as bad as most scientists fear, it will require sacrifices of everyone. But it will be easy to portray the demand by developed nations like the United States or Britain for equivalent sacrifices by developing nations that have yet to enjoy the full benefits of economic growth as a kind of hypocrisy. How then will democratic politicians in the most advanced countries be able to persuade their own electorates of the sacrifices needed if the burdens of those sacrifices are not more widely shared? It will be relatively easy for democratic politicians in the West to portray politicians elsewhere in the world (particularly in China) as hypocrites if they expect the West to take a lead in adopting growth-restricting measures while the Chinese economy continues to grow apace. But it will be relatively easy for Chinese politicians to portray democratic politicians as hypocrites if they expect the rest of the world to follow their lead without taking account of the unequal states of development of the various economies. Equal sacrifices are hard to justify in an unequal world. But unequal sacrifices will be hard to justify in the democratic world. And there lies the problem.

Of course global warming is about much more than this. Aspects of the predicament we face, particularly the problem of the commons—"that which is common to the greatest number has the least care bestowed on it"—are as old as politics itself.[13] Resolving these difficulties in the future may demand substantial technological innovations, and draw on the intellectual resources of disciplines that did not exist for much of the period covered by this book, including game theory and risk assessment. Nevertheless, at the heart of this issue lies a dilemma that the prevalence of hypocrisy poses for all forms of modern politics. Some hypocrisy seems unavoidable when it comes to environmental politics—in relation both to personal conduct, and to the behaviour of different regimes that will seek to hold each other to standards that they cannot readily meet themselves—and it would be a mistake to imagine that hypocrisy must cease before any real progress can be made. Equally, however, it would be a mistake to be too sanguine about hypocrisy in this context, given its capacity to generate political conflict, and to spill over into the most destructive forms of self-deception. So we must try to distinguish between different kinds of hypocrisy, and to decide which ones are worth worrying about.

It will not be easy—nothing about political hypocrisy ever is. But a sense of historical perspective can help. Liberal societies have always attracted accusations of hypocrisy from the outside, because of their failure to live up to their own standards. But seen from the inside, it is clear that the problem of hypocrisy in liberal politics is a good deal more complicated than this. What matters is not whether liberals are worse than they would like to appear, but whether they can be honest with themselves about the gaps that are bound to exist between the masks of politics and what lies behind those masks. This honesty cannot be taken as a given—liberal societies, particularly once they have become bound up with the requirements of democratic politics, are as capable as any others of self-deception. But liberal politics, and liberal political theory, have the advantage that they are able to probe the gaps between political appearance and political reality without either overstating them, or seeking to deny them altogether. This then is one of the resources that a history of liberal political thought has to offer. Armed with a sense of historical perspective, we can see that many forms of political hypocrisy are unavoidable, and therefore not worth worrying about, and that some others are even desirable in a democratic setting, and therefore worth encouraging. But, as Hobbes says, when hypocrisy deprives us of our ability to see what is at stake in our political life, then it still has the capacity to ruin everything for everyone.

Notes

INTRODUCTION

1. Shklar 1984: 47.
2. Ibid.: 66.
3. Ibid.: 77.
4. Grant 1997: 177.
5. Ibid.
6. For a history of the role of pretence and dissimulation in early modern religious thought and practice, see Zagorin 1990.
7. For an excellent contemporary account of the relationship between politeness and hypocrisy, see Miller 2003.
8. The open letters that President Ahmadinejad has occasionally written to President Bush are long, but can be briefly summarized—they say, "You call yourself a man of faith, but your politics of aggression make you a hypocrite" (or, as the letter of May 7, 2006 puts it: "Will you accept this invitation? That is, a genuine return to the teachings of the prophet, to monotheism and justice, to preserve human dignity and obedience to the Almighty and his prophets?"). And President Bush's unspoken responses to such invitations are easily summarised too—to be accused of hypocrisy by the president of Iran just about takes the biscuit.
9. This is a central theme of the writings of Quentin Skinner, which have profoundly influenced the way that the history of political thought has been studied for the past generation (see Skinner 2002; Brett and Tully 2006). Another consistent theme in Skinner's writing is the role played by what he calls "rhetorical redescription" in shaping political reality, and I make extensive use of this idea in what follows.
10. For an account of some of the conceptual issues surrounding current perceptions of U.S. hypocrisy in international relations, see Glazer 2006. For what has become the classic recent statement of the view that attacks on American hypocrisy are themselves hypocritical

(though the argument is not put in precisely these terms), see Kagan 2003; and for a response, see Runciman 2006a.

CHAPTER ONE
HOBBES AND THE MASK OF POWER

1. Hobbes's known writing career spanned roughly half a century: from his translation of Thucydides in 1628 through to his last piece of writing, a manuscript on the Exclusion Crisis produced shortly before his death in 1679. There is controversy about whether Hobbes was the author of some earlier pieces of writing during the 1620s—most notably a "Discourse on Tacitus" that some have attributed to him (see Hobbes 1995; Malcolm 2007).

2. On Hobbes and rhetoric, see Skinner 1996; on Hobbes's Erastianism, see Collins 2005; on Hobbes and representation, see Skinner 2005.

3. Pirated editions first started appearing in 1679, but it was only in 1682 that a version was published by William Crooke, Hobbes's usual publisher.

4. The opening paragraph of *Behemoth* is as follows: "A: If in time, as in place, there were degrees of high and low, I verily believe that the highest of time would be that which passed between the years 1640 and 1660. For he that hence, as from the Devil's Mountain, should have looked upon the world and observed the actions of men, especially in England, might have had a prospect of all kinds of injustice, and all kinds of folly, that the world could afford, and how they were produced by their dams hypocrisy and self-conceit, whereof one is double iniquity, and the other double folly." (Hobbes 1969: 1.)

5. Hume once wrote to a young friend advising him to become an Anglican clergyman notwithstanding his doubts about the articles of his faith:

> It is putting too great a respect on the vulgar and their superstitions to pique oneself on sincerity with regard to them . . . I wish it were still in my power to be a hypocrite in this particular. The common duties of society usually require it, and the ecclesiastical profession only adds a little more to an innocent dissimulation, or rather simulation, without which it is impossible to pass through the world. [Quoted in Morley 1997: 89]

6. When Cromwell makes his first appearance in the *History*, during a parliamentary debate on Popery, Hume writes: "It is amus-

ing to observe the first words of this fanatical hypocrite correspond so exactly to his character." (Hume 1983 vol. 5: 214.) Later, when Cromwell has made himself master of Parliament, Hume writes with a mixture of repulsion and admiration: "This artful and audacious conspirator conducted himself in the parliament with such profound dissimulation, with such refined hypocrisy, that he had long deceived those who, being themselves dextrous practitioners of the same arts, should naturally have entertained the more suspicions against others." (Ibid.: 335.)

7. Hobbes 1998: 54.

8. Ibid.: 48.

9. Ibid.: 54.

10. The clearest statement of this comes in *Leviathan*: "Every Soveraign hath the same Right, in procuring the safety of his People, that any particular man can have in procuring his own safety. And the same Law, that dictateth to men that have no Civil Government, what they ought to do, and what to avoid in regard of one another, dictateth the same to Common-wealths, that is, to the Consciences of Sovereign Princes." (Hobbes 1996: 244.)

11. See Hoekstra 2006b: 201. For more on Hobbes's views about democratic rhetoric and dissimulation, see Garsten 2006.

12. Much more common, as Hobbes famously puts it in *Leviathan*, is that they should adopt "the state and posture of Gladiators, having their weapons pointing, and their eyes fixed on one another." (Hobbes 1996: 90.)

13. Hobbes puts this view most bluntly in his first major statement of his political theory, *The Elements of Law* (1640): "The conscience being nothing else but a man's settled judgment and opinion, when he hath once transferred his right of judging to another, that which shall be commanded, is not less his judgment, than the judgment of that other; so that in obedience to the laws, a man doth still according to his conscience." As Richard Tuck puts it, this means "citizens have to be ready to accept the irrelevancy of their own views." (Tuck 2006: 175.)

14. Hobbes 1998: 133.

15. Ibid.

16. Ibid.: 165.

17. Hobbes 1969: 27.

18. Ibid.: 26.

19. Hobbes 1996: 72.

20. Hobbes 1969: 27. Hobbes is punning on the word "sufficiency" here, which meant both to have enough of something and

also to be well qualified for something. The parliamentarians thought that their qualifications for power were not getting enough attention from the king.

21. Ibid.: 61.

22. Though, as Maurice Goldsmith points out in his introduction to *Behemoth*, "The elder man *A* was mature during the Civil Wars; he undertakes to explain them to *B*. *B* mainly asks *A* for fuller explanations. Both *A* and *B* express Hobbesian opinions; as Wallis said of Hobbes's scientific dialogues, *Behemoth* is a conversation between Thomas and Hobbes." (Hobbes 1969: xi.)

23. Hoekstra 2006a: 49.

24. Hoekstra makes this point: "There can be a kind of practical inconsistency in publicly proclaiming the need for silence, and especially in trying to convince readers of a set of positions that includes a defence of dissimulation and deceit." (Ibid.: 46.) Hoekstra also discusses the writing of a contemporary of Hobbes, Torquato Accetto, who said something similar about his own work, admitting that "writing of dissimulation required that I dissimulate." (Ibid.: 47.)

25. Hobbes 1969: 61.

26. Ibid.: 48.

27. Ibid.

28. Ibid.: 25.

29. Ibid.: 26.

30. Quoted in Skinner 2002 vol. 2: 276.

31. Hobbes 1996: 31.

32. Its contested nature is the subject of one of Skinner's earliest accounts of the role of "evaluative-descriptive" terms in shaping political reality (see Skinner 1973).

33. See Tuck 2006; and for the response on which I draw here, see Hoekstra 2006b; Skinner 2006.

34. Hobbes 1998: 137.

35. In fact, there is some controversy as to whether "*paradiastole*" originally referred to the practice of redescription, or to the rhetorical device of exposing this practice i.e. of showing that a term was merely being used to redescribe the character of an underlying action (see Tuck 1996). Though Skinner uses it in the first sense, there is good reason to suppose that Hobbes would have understood it in the second.

36. Hobbes 1969: 2.

37. Ibid.

38. Ibid.: 104.

39. Ibid.: 103.
40. Hobbes 1996: 353.
41. See Collins 2005.
42. Hobbes 1996: 480.
43. Ibid.
44. Ibid.: 82.
45. Ibid.
46. See Hoekstra 2006a.
47. See Hobbes 1995.
48. Hobbes 1996: 112.
49. Ibid.: 62.
50. Ibid.: 418–19.

51. Mandeville gives a wonderful example of this sort of double bluff in *The Fable of the Bees, Part II*, when describing the voting in enclaves of cardinals: "Nothing is carried on without tricks and intrigues, and in them the Heart of Man is so deep and so dark an Abyss that the finest air of Dissimulation is sometimes found to have been insincere, and men often deceive one another by counterfeiting Hypocrisy." (Mandeville 1733: 35.)

52. Noel Malcolm makes this point when discussing Hobbes's distance from the prevailing currents of much reason of state theory (see introduction to Malcolm 2007).

CHAPTER TWO
MANDEVILLE AND THE VIRTUES OF VICE

1. Quoted in introduction to Mandeville 1970: 8.

2. Mandeville 1969: 332. For an extended discussion of the influences on Mandeville's work, and also on the role of theatre in his conception of society, see Hundert 1994.

3. Mandeville 1970: 98.
4. Ibid.: 88.
5. Ibid.: 107.
6. Ibid.: 106.
7. Ibid.: 76.
8. See Hont 2006.
9. Mandeville 1970: 202.
10. Ibid.: 158.
11. Ibid.: 168.
12. Ibid.: 351.
13. Ibid.: 335.

14. Mandeville 1733: 119.

15. Mandeville was also making a more narrowly political point here about what he saw as Shaftesbury's lack of political principle: why, he asks, does a man "who believes himself virtuous [not] Labour to retrieve National Losses . . . [and] make use of all his Friends and Interests to be a Lord Treasurer, that by his Integrity and Wise Management he might restore the Public Credit?" He goes on: "Virtue consists in Action, and whoever is possest of this Social Love and kind Affection to his Species, and by his Birth or Quality can claim any Post in the Publick Management, ought not to sit still when he can be Serviceable, but exert himself to the utmost for the good of his Fellow Subjects." (Ibid.: 336.) This is an attack both on John Locke, who was Shaftesbury's tutor, and also on Shaftesbury's brand of high-minded Whiggism.

16. Ibid.: 336.

17. See, for example, Davidson 2004.

18. Mandeville 1970: 256.

19. Ibid.: 296.

20. Ibid.: 155–56.

21. These characters also appear in *The Fable of the Bees Part II*, where they are described as follows: Horatio is "one of the modish People I have been speaking of but rather of the better sort of them as to morality"; Cleomenes, by contrast, is a more serious thinker, and "has been dipping into Anatomy and several parts of Natural Philosophy"; he has read a notoriously wicked book called *The Fable of the Bees*, and, determined to put its claims to the test, has found "the Insincerity of Men fully as universal as it was there represented"; Cleomenes is also described as someone who "understood perfectly well the difficulty of the task required in the Gospel." In other words, Cleomenes is Mandeville, and Mandeville writes in his introduction "that no man in his senses would think that I ought to be equally responsible for everything that Horatio says." (Mandeville 1733: xvii–xviii.)

22. Mandeville 1971: 201–2.

23. Hobbes 1969: 119.

24. Though for the view that Hobbes's light treatment of Cromwell does not reflect Hobbes's preference for Independency, see Sommerville 2003. Sommerville points out that at the end of *Behemoth* Hobbes echoes the saying that "presbyterians held him by the hayr, till the independents cut off his head" when he writes that the Presbyterians "sought only the subjection of the King, not his destruction directly," whereas the Independents "sought directly his

destruction" (Hobbes 1969: 195). Sommerville takes this as evidence that Hobbes saw both parties as equally hypocritical, but for the reasons given in the previous chapter I do not entirely share this view.

25. Hobbes 1969: 136.

26. For others, a chameleon was the definition of a hypocrite: see, for example, Robert Burton's *Anatomy of Melancholy* (1621), where he complains about seeing "a man turn himself into all shapes like a chameleon . . . to act twenty parts and persons at once for his own advantage . . . having a several face, garb and character for every one he meets" (Burton 1862: 89). This is perhaps the more conventional view, reflecting the generalised suspicion of the habits of the "stage actor" spilling over into everyday life.

27. Rousseau 1997a: 46.

28. Ibid.: 47.

29. Rousseau 1997b: 148.

30. Ibid.: 121.

31. Mandeville 1971: 162.

32. Ibid.: 230–31.

33. Ibid.: 164.

34. Ibid.

35. Ibid.: 231.

36. See Weber 1994.

37. Mandeville 1969: 384.

38. Ibid.

39. Ibid.: 376.

40. Ibid.: 390.

41. Ibid.: 408.

42. Ibid.: 382.

43. Ibid.: 386–87.

44. Mandeville 1733: 411.

45. Ibid.

46. Ibid.: 390.

47. Ibid.: 410.

48. For the details of Mandeville's personal antipathy to Walpole, which led him to greatly moderate his defence of the integrity of Whigs in government during the 1720s, see Mitchell 2003.

49. On the rhetorical redescriptions of "patriotism" in this period, see Skinner 2002: 344–67.

50. Quoted in Davis 2001: 146.

51. Mandeville 1733: 385.

52. See Hont 2006.

CHAPTER THREE
THE AMERICAN REVOLUTION AND THE ART OF SINCERITY

1. Quoted in Schama 2005: 28.

2. Jefferson 1999: 99.

3. Wills 2002: 74.

4. This is the theme of Shklar 1998b. See also Wilkins 2002.

5. See particularly Wood 1969; Pocock 1975; Pocock 1985; Kramnick 1990; Bailyn 1992.

6. American revolutionary thought was profoundly influenced by Machiavelli, though primarily as refracted through the ideas of the seventeenth-century English republican theorist, James Harrington (1611–1677). It is important to note that Harrington's Machiavelli was above all the author of the *Discourses*, not the more satirical and cynical author of *The Prince*. Machiavellianism could therefore be understood in two distinct senses in the context of American political thought: to denote a Harringtonian conception of republican virtue, or alternatively to describe a form of cynical political manipulation. In so far as they approved the first, it is by no means clear that the American revolutionaries saw themselves as the inheritors of the second (indeed, they were as ready to use the term "Machiavellian" in its pejorative sense as we are today).

7. Weinberger 2005: 287.

8. Franklin 1998: 45.

9. Ibid.: 99.

10. Ibid.: 59. Franklin misremembered the motto of his pamphlet in the *Autobiography*, adding the line "Whatever is, is right" from Pope to a passage from Dryden.

11. Thomas Hobbes, who had briefly acted as Bacon's amanuensis, may well have been the translator of at least one of them—"Of Simulation and Dissimulation"—for a Latin edition of Bacon's works published in 1638 (see Malcolm 2007: 9–10).

12. Bacon 1996: 384.

13. Franklin 1998: 231.

14. Bacon 1996: 350.

15. Simulation leads to bad habits, Bacon says, "because . . . it maketh him practise simulation in other things, lest his hand should be out of [use]"; it leads to a bad reputation, because "it puzzleth and perplexeth the conceits of many, that perhaps would otherwise cooperate with him." (Ibid.: 351.)

16. Ibid.: 350.

17. Ibid.

18. Ibid.: 351.

19. Franklin 1998: 231.

20. In "Of Simulation and Dissimulation," Bacon purposefully does not describe dissimulation as a form of cunning. Instead, he argues that dissimulation is required *because of the cunning of others,* "for men are too cunning to suffer a man to keep an indifferent carriage ... and to be secret, without swaying the balance on either side." (Bacon 1996: 350.) Dissimulation is the rational response to those who wish to pin us down in order to exploit our weaknesses; hence it is a crucial part of the armoury of the politician.

21. Franklin 1998: 230.

22. Bolingbroke 1997: 256.

23. Ibid.: 286.

24. Franklin 1998: 229.

25. Ibid.: 232.

26. Bailyn 2003: 67.

27. See Wood 2004.

28. Quoted in McCullough 2001: 20.

29. Adams 2007: www.masshist.org/digitaladams/aea/cfm/doc.cfm?id=D15.

30. Ibid.

31. Jefferson 1999: 447.

32. He also wanted these two forms of hollow distinction to be set off against each other: "The wisdom of nations has endeavoured to employ one prejudice to counteract the other: the prejudice in favour of birth, to moderate, correct or restrain, the prejudice in favour of wealth." (Adams 2000: 350.)

33. Adams 2000: 302.

34. Quoted in Thompson 1998: 224.

35. See ibid.: 117–19.

36. Adams 2000: 357.

37. Ibid.: 356.

38. Ibid: 355.

39. See Wood 1969.

40. Ibid.: 322.

41. Quoted in Thompson 1998: 186.

42. Quoted in McCullough 2001: 432.

43. Jefferson 1999: 244.

44. Ibid.: 287.

45. Paine 2000: 268.

46. Jefferson 1999: 244.

47. Ibid.: 187.

48. Ibid.: 174.
49. Ibid.: 422.
50. Ibid.: 418.
51. Ibid.: 424.
52. Ibid.: 449.
53. Ibid.: 452.
54. Ibid.: 464.
55. Ibid.: 275.
56. Quoted in McCullough 2001: 448.
57. Vidal 1973: 187.
58. Thompson 1998: 272.
59. Jefferson 1999: 420 (italics in the original). In a postscript to this letter, Jefferson added: "It is hardly necessary to caution you to let nothing of mine get before the public; a single sentence got hold of by the Porcupines [meaning the Federalist propagandists] will suffice to abuse and persecute me in their papers for months." (Ibid.)
60. Ibid.: 79.
61. Ibid.: 496.

CHAPTER FOUR
BENTHAM AND THE UTILITY OF FICTION

1. Hart 1982.
2. Bentham 1988: 21.
3. Bentham 1996: 63–64.
4. Bentham 1843: 501.
5. Bentham 1983: 279.
6. Ibid.: 268.
7. Bentham 1983: 276.
8. See Chesterfield 1992. For Bentham's comparison between Chesterfield's and his own work, see Bentham 1983: 276.
9. Ibid.: 357.
10. Ibid.
11. Burr came to know Bentham (and even briefly lived in his house) during his exile in London in 1808–09, following his acquittal in the treason trial that had been initiated against him by Thomas Jefferson.
12. Ibid.: 56.
13. Ibid.
14. Bentham 1843: 187.
15. Ibid.: 203.
16. Ibid.: 214.

17. Ibid.: 219.

18. Bentham writes of this sacrifice as follows: "In an incident thus tragical and impressive, the priesthood beheld an opportunity too favourable to be suffered to pass: an opportunity of giving the utmost possible degree of force and efficiency to an instrument, the management of which was in their hands . . . The time was a time of war. In this state of things, the authority of Jephthah, did it stand in need of check? The sort of check the priesthood were able and disposed to apply? Both questions answered in the affirmative, the price paid . . . great as it was, was perhaps not too great. The individual—the father—afflicted: another individual—the daughter—sent out of the reach of affliction—what are these evils in comparison of those of a course of unbridled and tyrannically exercised despotism?" (Ibid.: 223.) This is the voice of utilitarianism, and in the phrase "sent out of the reach of affliction" it contains its own small measure of cant.

19. Ibid.: 222.

20. Hobbes 1996: 31.

21. Ibid.

22. See Skinner 1996.

23. Hobbes 1996: 31.

24. As Noel Malcolm has put it: "Hobbes was not trying to ban metaphor as such: his warnings were chiefly against those metaphors which conceal the fact that they are metaphors." (Malcolm 2002: 227.)

25. See Bentham 2002.

26. A fuller account of the etymology of the term and its relation to the thought of the period is given in Wilson 2007.

27. Hazlitt 1988: 185.

28. See Harrison 1983.

29. Bentham 1990: 121.

30. Ibid.

31. See in particular Harrison 1983; Schofield 2006.

32. Ibid.: 123.

33. Bentham 1932: 149.

34. Ibid.: 141.

35. Bentham 1988: 53.

36. Ibid.

37. Bentham 1999: 144.

38. "There seems to be no alternative mechanism by which exposure of the causes of the beliefs of the ruling classes . . . should serve to change these beliefs, as by a kind of Freudian therapy; nor does the exposure of the causes show them to be false." (Harrison 1983: 217.)

39. See Schofield 2006: 267–68.

40. See ibid.: 294–96 and 321–22. Bentham described these juries as "Quasi-juries" in an attempt to pin down their distinctive role as mediators between real courts and the fictitious court of public opinion.

41. See Mill 1992.

42. Mill 1992: 272.

CHAPTER FIVE
VICTORIAN DEMOCRACY AND VICTORIAN HYPOCRISY

1. Quoted in Schultz 2004: 4.

2. *Phineas Redux* was first published in instalments in the *Graphic* magazine beginning in 1873, before appearing as a book a year later.

3. Henry 2001.

4. In fact, by the 1860s this image had become such a cliché that *Punch* issued a proclamation against it on 7 January 1865, as part of a list banning the use of "certain persons, objects, and things, part of the stock-in-trade of sundry literary chapmen," as "used up, exhausted, threadbare, stale and hackneyed." Henceforth "it shall not be lawful for any journalist, essayist, magazine-writer, penny-a-liner, poetaster, criticaster, public speaker, lecturer, Lord Rector, Member of Parliament, novelist, or dramatist" to use any of the list, which includes "The Bull that is always being taken by the horns . . . The British Lion . . . the Black Sheep . . . The Dodo . . . the Thin End of the Wedge," and many others. First in the list comes "Macaulay's New Zealander," and Mr. Punch remarks: "The retirement of this veteran is indispensable. He can no longer be suffered to impede the traffic over London Bridge. Much wanted at the present time in his own country. May return when London is in ruins." Many of the clichés listed in *Punch*, including that of the New Zealander, are now obsolete, but not all. Compare this to Orwell's list of "dying metaphors" in "Politics and the English Language"—"ring the changes on, take up the cudgels for, toe the line, ride roughshod over, stand shoulder to shoulder with, play into the hands of, no axe to grind, grist to the mill, fishing in troubled waters, on the order of the day, Achilles' heel, swan song, hotbed"—almost all of which are still current. Clearly, political clichés take a long time to die.

5. Trollope 1972: xii.

6. Ibid.: 20.

7. Ibid.: 130.

8. See Wilson 2008.

9. Trollope 1973.

10. Trollope 1972: 27.

11. On Disraeli's Machiavellianism, see Richmond and Smith 1998.

12. Trollope's view of the magical qualities of Disraeli's political persona is in striking contrast to his view of Disraeli's own fiction, which he loathed and saw as lacking in all magic, its contrivances and tricks being all too obvious—"the glory of the pasteboard, the wealth of tinsel, the wit of hairdressers . . . paste diamonds," as he characterised it in his *Autobiography* (see Trollope 1999: 161).

13. Hobbes 1651: 77.

14. For the evolution of Trollope's approach to utilitarianism, see Nardin 1996.

15. Morley 1903 vol. 2: 444.

16. Morley 1997: 93.

17. Ibid.: 65.

18. This for example is the view of Maurice Cowling (see Morley 1997, appendix).

19. Ibid.: 66.

20. Ibid.: 31.

21. Ibid.: 58.

22. Ibid.: 104.

23. Ibid.

24. Ibid.: 105.

25. Bacon 1996: 351.

26. Hamer 1968: 51.

27. Quoted in Schultz 2004: 223.

28. Quoted in ibid.: 269.

29. Sidgwick 1996b: 170. It is interesting to compare Sidgwick on this question with Thomas Paine's discussion in *The Age of Reason*, where he takes the opposite, more literal-minded view, that it is impossible to disprove a virgin conception, but literal ascension into heaven is something that can be witnessed, and therefore disproved: "The ascension of a dead person from the grave, and into heaven, is a thing very different, as to the evidence it admits, to the invisible conception of a child in the womb. The resurrection and ascension, supposing them to have taken place, admitted of public and ocular demonstration, like that of the ascension of a balloon, or the sun at noonday, to all Jerusalem at least . . . The whole of it falls to the ground because the evidence never was given." (Paine 2000: 272.)

30. Sidgwick 1996a: 489–90.

31. See Smart & Williams 1973.

32. Ibid.: 318.

33. It should be noted that this is a distinctively British perspective: in the United States judges tend to be more tolerant of grandstanding

by advocates; meanwhile in the European civil law tradition the relationship between magistrates and advocates is very different.

34. Sidgwick 1891: 598–99.

35. Ibid.

36. "A sincere utilitarian is likely to be an eager politician." (Sidgwick 1996a: 495.) This is a "politician" in the Bentham sense—a reformer—not the Morley sense—a compromiser.

37. Sidgwick 1996b: 81.

38. Quoted in Schultz 2004: 567.

39. Quoted in Hamer 1968: 347.

CHAPTER SIX
ORWELL AND THE HYPOCRISY OF IDEOLOGY

1. On some of the historical double standards of the medical profession, see Wootton 2006.

2. Orwell 1968 vol. 4.

3. Orwell 1968 vol.1: 2.

4. Orwell 1998a: 190–91.

5. Orwell 2006: 96.

6. See Blackburn 2005: 4–5.

7. Collini 2006: 372.

8. Hitchens 2003: 4.

9. The others include David Aaronovitch (*The Times*), Nick Cohen (*The Observer*), and John Lloyd (*The Financial Times*).

10. Orwell 1998f: 74.

11. Orwell 1984: 357.

12. Ibid.: 363.

13. Orwell 1998g: 256.

14. Ibid.

15. Ibid.

16. Ibid.: 258.

17. Orwell was very sensitive to what he saw as the varieties of dishonesty among British fellow travellers. His notorious "list" of "crypto-Communists" that he supplied to British intelligence in 1949 contained this sketch of Richard Crossman: "Political climber. Zionist (appears sincere about this). Too dishonest to be an outright F.T. [fellow traveller]." As Christopher Hitchens remarks: "Orwell had a respect for honest Leninists." (Hitchens 2003: 146.)

18. Orwell 1984: 271.

19. Orwell 1989: 147–48. As well as being over the top, this is also extremely simple-minded in economic terms (economics, as Orwell

admitted, was never his strong point). It leaves open the possibility for those Orwell accuses of hypocrisy here of responding that they only appear to be hypocritical from Orwell's blinkered and question-begging perspective. This is one of the weaknesses of *The Road to Wigan Pier*'s air of empirical and predictive as well as moral certainty.

20. Orwell 1984: 283.

21. Orwell 1968 vol. 1: 160.

22. Orwell 1984: 318.

23. Ibid.: 323.

24. Ibid.: 327.

25. Ibid.: 322.

26. Orwell 1982: 51.

27. Ibid.: 53.

28. Ibid.: 44.

29. Ibid.: 45–46. The specific reference here is to the quintessentially English institution of the "hanging judge."

30. For a description of this incident, see Orwell 1998c: 121.

31. Orwell 1968 vol. 1: 236.

32. Ibid.: 239.

33. Ibid.

34. The cases of fascism and communism are somewhat different in this respect, particularly in relation to the postwar communism of Eastern Europe, which had to pretend to be something it was not: indigenous and popular. "There was a distinctly cynical quality to Communist misrule: old-fashioned abuses were now laboriously embedded in a rhetorical cant of equality and social progress, a hypocrisy for which neither the interwar oligarchs nor the Nazi occupiers had felt the need." (Judt 2007: 194.)

35. Orwell 1984: 273.

36. Orwell 2000: 516–17.

37. Ibid.: 750.

38. In her lecture, Shklar suggests that much of the hold of Orwell's book rests with its title: there would have been no commemorative conference had the book retained its original name, *The Last Man in Europe*; it would then have had a status somewhere on a par with Arthur Koestler's *Darkness at Noon*, a book hardly anyone reads now. (See Shklar, 1998a.)

39. Rorty 1989: 173.

40. Ibid.: 174.

41. Orwell 2000: 17.

42. Ibid.: 66.

43. Orwell 1968 vol. 4: 515.

44. Orwell 1998c: 124.

45. Orwell 1998f: 89.

46. Orwell 1989: 189.

47. Orwell 2000: 810.

48. In a book review of 1944 he wrote that the "debunking of Cromwell, though probably it is not fair either, is a good antidote to the usual middle-class worship of this prototype of all the modern dictators." (Orwell 1998f: 168.)

49. Rosebery 1900: 45.

50. Hobbes 1969: 146.

Conclusion

Sincerity and Hypocrisy in Democratic Politics

1. Oborne 2005: 264.

2. See "Mr Oborne v the PMOS. Anatomy of a Westminster altercation" (February 3, 2007, www.guardian.co.uk).

3. For an account of the need for "double standards" that fails to appreciate that double standards have their own double standards, see Cooper 2003. For an extended discussion of this failure, see Runciman 2006a.

4. For, see Ferguson 2005; against, see Shapiro 2007.

5. In the early, heady days of Cameron's leadership of the Tory party, a number of commentators made the comparison with Disraeli explicit. Here, for example, is Peter Oborne, writing in *The Spectator* early in 2006: "It is not absurd or premature to start to make this comparison with Disraeli, the greatest of Tory politicians. In a very short space of time David Cameron has demonstrated the same poise, scope and towering ambition. He too is set on taking the Tory party back to Middle Britain and making it once again the natural party of government. He too is determined to recreate the political landscape. He has taken massive risks and, of course, in the end he may fail. But he will not fail for lack of courage, martial spirit or a true Conservative vision. He is a joy to behold." ("David Cameron follows in the footsteps of Benjamin Disraeli," *The Spectator*, January 7, 2006.)

6. This distinction is set out in more detail in Runciman 2006b.

7. Dunn 1979.

8. This is one possible way of thinking about the story of neo-conservatism, its recent disasters, and the inability of some of its champions to make the move from the grand vision of Cold War

confrontation to the more detailed visions required for post–Cold War reconstruction. Francis Fukuyama is the shining exception to this. See Fukuyama 2005.

9. Baker 2007.

10. See Kagan 2003. For an account of what Hobbes actually thought about international relations, see Malcolm 2002; Runciman 2006a.

11. MacFarquhar 2007.

12. Obama 2007: 216.

13. Aristotle 1996: 33.

Bibliography

Adams, John, 2000: *The political writings*, ed. George W. Carey (Washington, DC: Regnery Publishing)

Adams, John, 2007: *The diary of John Adams* (Massachusetts Historical Society, www.masshist.org/digitaladams/aea/diary/)

Arendt, Hannah, 1972: *Crises of the Republic* (New York: Harcourt, Brace, Jovanovich)

Aristotle, 1996: *The politics and the constitution of Athens*, ed. Stephen Everson (Cambridge: Cambridge University Press)

Bacon, Francis, 1996: *The major works*, ed. Brian Vickers (Oxford: Oxford University Press)

Bailyn, Bernard, 1992: *The ideological origins of the American Revolution* (Cambridge, MA: Harvard University Press, revised ed.)

Bailyn, Bernard, 2003: *To begin the world anew. The genius and ambiguities of the American Founders* (New York: Alfred A. Knopf)

Baker, Gerard, 2007: "The vaulting ambition of America's Lady Macbeth," *The Times* (January 26, www.timesonline.co.uk/comment)

Bentham, Jeremy, 1843: *Swear not at all!* in *The works of Jeremy Bentham*, vol. 5, ed. John Bowring (Edinburgh: William Tait)

Bentham, Jeremy, 1907: *An introduction to the principles of morals and legislation* (Oxford: Clarendon)

Bentham, Jeremy, 1932: *Theory of fictions*, ed. C. K. Ogden (London: Kegan Paul)

Bentham, Jeremy, 1952: *Handbook of political fallacies*, ed. Harold A. Larrabee (Baltimore: Johns Hopkins Press)

Bentham, Jeremy, 1983: *Deontology together with A table of the springs of action and The article of utilitarianism*, ed. Amnon Goldsmith (Oxford: Clarendon)

Bentham, Jeremy, 1988: *A fragment on government*, ed. Ross Harrison (Cambridge: Cambridge University Press)

Bentham, Jeremy, 1990: *Securities against misrule and other constitutional writings*, ed. Philip Schofield (Oxford: Clarendon Press)

Bentham, Jeremy, 1996: *An introduction to the principles of morals and legislation*, ed. J. H. Burns and H.L.A. Hart (Oxford: Clarendon)

Bentham, Jeremy, 1999: *Political tactics*, ed. Michael Jones, Cyprian Blamires, and Catherine Pease-Watkin (Oxford: Clarendon)

Bentham, Jeremy, 2002: *Rights, representation and reform. Nonsense upon stilts and other writings on the French Revolution*, ed. Michael Jones, Cyprian Blamires, and Catherine Pease-Watkin (Oxford: Clarendon)

Bernstein, R. B., 2003: *Thomas Jefferson* (Oxford: Oxford University Press)

Blackburn, Simon, 2005: *Truth. A guide for the perplexed* (London: Allen Lane)

Bok, Sissela, 1980: *Lying: moral choice in public and private life* (London: Quartet)

Bolingbroke, Henry, 1997: *Political writings*, ed. David Armitage (Cambridge: Cambridge University Press)

Braudy, Leo, 1970: *Narrative form in history and fiction* (Princeton: Princeton University Press)

Brett, Annabel, and James Tully (eds.), 2006: *Rethinking the foundations of modern political thought* (Cambridge: Cambridge University Press)

Burt, Shelley, 1992: *Virtue transformed. Political argument in England 1688–1740* (Cambridge: Cambridge University Press)

Burton, Robert, 1862: *The anatomy of melancholy* (New York: Sheldon and Company)

Chesterfield, Philip Dormer Stanhope, Earl of, 1992: *Letters*, ed. David Roberts (Oxford: Oxford University Press)

Claeys, Gregory, 1985: " 'The Lion and the Unicorn,' patriotism and Orwell's politics," *Journal of Politics*, 47, 186–211

Clero, Jean-Pierre, 2004: "Le personage de Cromwell dans *l'Histoire d'Angleterre* de Hume," *Cercles*, 11, 15–31

Collini, Stefan, 1991: *Public moralists. Political thought and intellectual life in Britain, 1850–1930* (Oxford: Oxford University Press)

Collini, Stefan, Donald Winch, and John Burrow, 1993: *That noble science of politics. A study in nineteenth century intellectual history* (Cambridge: Cambridge University Press)

Collini, Stefan, 2006: *Absent minds. Intellectuals in Britain* (Oxford: Oxford University Press)

Collins, Jeffrey R., 2005: *The allegiance of Thomas Hobbes* (Oxford: Oxford University Press)

Cook, Harold, 1999: "Bernard de Mandeville and the therapy of the 'clever politician,'" *Journal of the History of Ideas*, 60, 101–24

Cooper, Robert, 2003: *The breaking of nations. Order and chaos in the twenty-first century* (London: Atlantic Books)

Creppell, Ingrid, 2003: "The democratic element in Hobbes's *Behemoth*," *Filozofski Vestnik*, 24, 7–36

Crosby, Travis, 1997: *The two Mr Gladstones. A study in psychology and history* (New Haven: Yale University Press)

Davidson, Jenny, 2004: *Hypocrisy and the politics of politeness. Manners and morals from Locke to Austen* (Cambridge: Cambridge University Press)

Davis, J. C., 2001: *Oliver Cromwell* (London: Hodder Arnold)

Dienstag, Joshua Foa, 2006: *Pessimism. Philosophy, ethic, spirit* (Princeton: Princeton University Press)

Dunn, John, 1979: *Western political theory in the face of the future* (Cambridge: Cambridge University Press)

Elster, Jon (ed.), 1996: *The multiple self* (Cambridge: Cambridge University Press)

Fénelon, François de, 1994: *Telemachus*, ed. Patrick Riley (Cambridge: Cambridge University Press)

Ferguson, Niall, 2005: *Colossus. The rise and fall of the American empire* (London: Penguin)

Forbes, Duncan, 1975: *Hume's philosophical politics* (Cambridge: Cambridge University Press)

Frankfurt, Harry, 2005: *On bullshit* (Princeton: Princeton University Press)

Franklin, Benjamin, 1998: *Autobiography and other writings* (Oxford: Oxford University Press)

Frost, Samantha, 2001: "Hobbes's thinking-bodies and the ethics of dissimulation," *Political Theory*, 29, 30–57

Fukuyama, Francis, 2005: *State building. Governance and world order in the twenty-first century* (London: Profile Books)

Galston, William A., 2005: *The practice of liberal pluralism* (Cambridge: Cambridge University Press)

Garsten, Bryan, 2006: *Saving persuasion. A defence of rhetoric and judgment* (Harvard: Harvard University Press)

Ginzburg, Benjamin, 1922: "Hypocrisy as a pathological symptom," *International Journal of Ethics*, 32, 160–66

Glazer, Daryl, 2006: "Does hypocrisy matter? The case of U.S. foreign policy," *Review of International Studies*, 32, 251–68

Glover, Jonathan (ed.), 1990: *Utilitarianism and its critics* (New York: Macmillan)

Goodin, Robert E., 1980, *Manipulatory politics* (New Haven: Yale University Press)

Goodin, Robert E., 1991: "Government House utilitarianism," in *The utilitarian response. The contemporary viability of utilitarian political philosophy*, ed. Lincoln Allison (London: Sage)

Grant, Ruth W., 1997: *Hypocrisy and integrity. Machiavelli, Rousseau, and the ethics of politics* (Chicago: Chicago University Press)

Green, T. H., 1883: *Prolegomena to ethics*, ed. A. C. Bradley (Oxford: Clarendon Press)

Green, T. H., 1895: *Lectures on the principles of political obligation* (London: Longmans)

Green, T. H., 1912: *Four lectures on the English Revolution* (London: Longmans)

Greenblatt, Stephen, 1973: *Sir Walter Ralegh. The Renaissance man and his roles* (New Haven, Yale University Press)

Greenblatt, Stephen, 1980: *Renaissance self-fashioning. From More to Shakespeare* (Chicago: Chicago University Press)

Halperin, John, 1977: *Trollope and politics* (London: Macmillan)

Hamer, D. A., 1968: *John Morley. Liberal intellectual in politics* (Oxford: Clarendon)

Hamilton, Alexander, James Madison, and John Jay, 2003: *The Federalist. With Letters of "Brutus,"* ed. Terence Ball (Cambridge: Cambridge University Press)

Hampshire, Stuart, 1989: *Innocence and experience* (Harvard: Harvard University Press)

Harrison, Ross, 1983: *Bentham* (London: Routledge)

Harrison, Ross, 2004: *Hobbes, Locke, and confusion's masterpiece* (Cambridge: Cambridge University Press)

Hart, H.L.A., 1982: *Essays on Bentham: philosophy and jurisprudence* (Oxford: Oxford University Press)

Hazlitt, William, 1988: *The selected writings of William Hazlitt*, vol. 9 (*Uncollected essays*), ed. Duncan Wu (London: Pickering and Chatto)

Henry, Nancy, 2001: "George Eliot and politics," in *Cambridge companion to George Eliot*, ed. George Levine (Cambridge: Cambridge University Press)

Herzog, Don, 2006: *Cunning* (Princeton: Princeton University Press)

Himmelfarb, Gertrude, 1968: *Victorian minds* (New York: Knopf)

Hitchens, Christopher, 2003: *Orwell's victory* (London: Penguin Press)

Hobbes, Thomas, 1651: "The answer of Mr. Hobbes to Sir Will. D'Avenant's Preface before Gondibert," in Sir William D'Avenant, *Gondibert* (London: Thomas Newcomb)

Hobbes, Thomas, 1969: *Behemoth*, ed. Ferdinand Tönnies (London: Frank Cass)

Hobbes, Thomas, 1995: *Three discourses. A critical modern edition of newly identified work of the young Hobbes*, ed. Noel B. Reynolds and Arlene W. Saxonhouse (Chicago: Chicago University Press)

Hobbes, Thomas, 1996: *Leviathan*, ed. Richard Tuck (Cambridge: Cambridge University Press)

Hobbes, Thomas, 1998: *On the citizen*, ed. Richard Tuck and Michael Silverthorne (Cambridge: Cambridge University Press)

Hoekstra, Kinch, 2006a: "The end of philosophy. The case of Hobbes," *Proceedings of the Aristotelian Society*, 106, 23–60

Hoekstra, Kinch, 2006b: "A lion in the house. Hobbes and democracy," in *Rethinking the foundations of modern political thought*, ed. Annabel Brett and James Tully (Cambridge: Cambridge University Press)

Hollis, Martin, 1982: "Dirty hands," *British Journal of Political Science*, 12, 385–98.

Hont, Istvan, 2006: "The early Enlightenment debate on commerce and luxury," in *The Cambridge history of eighteenth-century political thought*, ed. Mark Goldie and Robert Wokler (Cambridge: Cambridge University Press)

Hume, David, 1975: *Enquiries concerning human understanding and concerning the principles of morals*, ed. L. A. Selby-Bigge (Oxford: Clarendon)

Hume, David, 1983: *The history of England from the invasion of Julius Caesar to the Revolution in 1688*, vols. 5 and 6 (Liberty Classics: Indianapolis)

Hume, L. J., 1981: *Bentham and bureaucracy* (Cambridge: Cambridge University Press)

Hundert, E. J., 1994: *The Enlightenment's fable. Bernard de Mandeville and the discovery of society* (Cambridge: Cambridge University Press)

Hundert, E. J., 1995: "Bernard de Mandeville and the Enlightenment maxims of modernity," *Journal of the History of Ideas*, 56, 577–93

Hundert, E. J., 2000: "Sociability and self-love in the theatre of the moral sentiments: Mandeville to Adam Smith," in *Economy, polity, and society*, ed. Stefan Collini, Richard Whatmore, and Brian Young (Cambridge: Cambridge University Press)

Isaacson, Walter, 2003: *Benjamin Franklin. An American life* (New York: Simon & Schuster)

James, Susan, 1997: *Passion and action. The emotions in seventeenth-century philosophy* (Oxford: Oxford University Press)

Jefferson, Thomas, 1999: *Political writings*, ed. Joyce Appleby and Terence Ball (Cambridge: Cambridge University Press)

Jenkins, Roy, 1995: *Gladstone* (London: Macmillan)

Johnson, Peter, 1988: *Politics, innocence and the limits of goodness* (London: Routledge)

Judt, Tony, 2007: *Postwar. A history of Europe since 1945* (London: Pimlico)

Kagan, Robert, 2003: *Paradise and power. America and Europe in the new world order* (London: Atlantic Books)

Klein, Lawrence E., 1994: *Shaftesbury and the culture of politeness. Moral discourse and cultural politics in early eighteenth-century England* (Cambridge: Cambridge University Press)

Kramnick, Isaac, 1990: *Republicanism and bourgeois radicalism. Political ideology in late eighteenth-century England and America* (New York: Cornell University Press)

Laache, R., 1917: "A letter by Holberg concerning Cromwell," *English Historical Review*, 32, 412–15

Lieberman, David, 2000: "Economy and polity in Bentham's science of legislation," in *Economy, polity, society*, ed. Stefan Collini, Richard Whatmore, and Brian Young (Cambridge: Cambridge University Press)

Lloyd, John, 2004: *What the media are doing to our politics* (London: Constable & Robinson)

Lucas, Philip, and Anne Sheeran, 2006: "Asperger's Syndrome and the eccentricity and genius of Jeremy Bentham," *Journal of Bentham Studies*, 8 (www.ucl.ac.uk/Bentham-Project/journal/jnl _2006.htm)

Lund, William, 2003: "Neither *Behemoth* nor *Leviathan*. Explaining Hobbes's illiberal politics," *Filozofski Vestnik*, 24, 59–84

MacFarquhar, Larissa, 2007: "The conciliator. Where is Barack Obama coming from?" *The New Yorker*, May 7 (www.newyorker .com/reporting/2007/05/07/07050fa_fact_macfarquahr)

Machiavelli, Niccolo, 1988: *The prince*, ed. Quentin Skinner and Russell Price (Cambridge: Cambridge University Press)

Malcolm, Noel, 2002: *Aspects of Hobbes* (Oxford: Clarendon)

Malcolm, Noel, 2003: "*Behemoth latinus*. Adam Ebert, Tacitism and Hobbes," *Filozofski Vestnik*, 24, 85–120

Malcolm, Noel, 2007: *Reason of state, propaganda and the Thirty Years' War. An unknown translation by Thomas Hobbes* (Oxford: Oxford University Press)

Mandeville, Bernard de (Anonymous), 1733: *The fable of the bees, part II* (London: J. Roberts)

Mandeville, Bernard de, 1969: *Free thoughts on religion, the Church and national happiness* (facsimile edition, Stuttgart: Friedrich Frommann Verlag)

Mandeville, Bernard de, 1970: *The fable of the bees*, ed. Philip Harth (Harmondsworth: Penguin)

Mandeville, Bernardde, 1971: *An enquiry into the origin of honour and the usefulness of Christianity in war*, ed. M. M. Goldsmith (London: Frank Cass)

Manin, Bernard de, 1997: *The principles of representative government* (Cambridge: Cambridge University Press)

McCullough, David, 2001: *John Adams* (New York: Simon & Schuster)

Mill, James, 1992: *Political writings*, ed. Terence Ball (Cambridge: Cambridge University Press)

Mill, John Stuart, 1989: *Autobiography*, ed. John M. Robson (Harmondsworth: Penguin)

Miller, William Ian, 2003: *Faking it* (Cambridge: Cambridge University Press)

Mitchell, Annie, 2003: "Character of an Independent Whig—'Cato' and Bernard Mandeville," *History of European Ideas*, 29, 291–311

Morley, John, 1900: *Oliver Cromwell* (London: Macmillan)

Morley, John, 1903: *The life of William Ewart Gladstone*, 3 vols. (London: Macmillan)

Morley, John, 1997: *On compromise*, ed. John Powell (Edinburgh: Keele University Press)

"Mr Oborne v the PMOS. Anatomy of a Westminster altercation," 2007: *Guardian Unlimited*, February 3 (www.guardian.co.uk)

Nardin, Jane, 1996: *Trollope and Victorian moral philosophy* (Athens, OH: Ohio University Press)

Obama, Barack, 2007: *The audacity of hope. Thoughts on recapturing the American dream* (Edinburgh: Canongate)

Oborne, Peter, 2005: *The rise of political lying* (London: The Free Press)

Oborne, Peter, 2006: "David Cameron follows in the footsteps of Benjamin Disraeli," *The Spectator*, January 7

Orwell, George, 1968: *The collected essays, journalism and letters*, 4 vols., ed. Sonia Orwell and Ian Angus (London: Secker & Warburg)

Orwell, George, 1982: *The lion and the unicorn. Socialism and the English genius* (London: Penguin Books)

Orwell, George, 1984: *The Orwell reader. Fiction, essays, and reportage* (San Diego: Harcourt)

Orwell, George, 1989: *The Road to Wigan Pier* (London: Penguin Books)

Orwell, George, 1998a: *A kind of compulsion 1903–36*, ed. Peter Davison (London: Secker & Warburg)

Orwell, George, 1998b: *Facing unpleasant facts 1937–39*, ed. Peter Davison (London: Secker & Warburg)

Orwell, George, 1998c: *A patriot after all 1940–41*, ed. Peter Davison (London: Secker & Warburg)

Orwell, George, 1998d: *All propaganda is lies 1941–42*, ed. Peter Davison (London: Secker & Warburg)

Orwell, George, 1998e: *Two wasted years 1943*, ed. Peter Davison (London: Secker & Warburg)

Orwell, George, 1998f: *I have tried to tell the truth 1943–44*, ed. Peter Davison (London: Secker & Warburg)

Orwell, George, 1998g: *I belong to the left 1945*, ed. Peter Davison (London: Secker & Warburg)

Orwell, George, 2000: *The complete novels* (London: Penguin Books)

Orwell, George, 2006: *The lost Orwell*, ed. Peter Davison (London: Timewell Press)

Paine, Thomas, 2000: *Political writings*, ed. Bruce Kucklick (Cambridge: Cambridge University Press)

Pettit, Philip, 2008: *Made with words. Hobbes on language, mind and politics* (Princeton: Princeton University Press)

Plato, 2003: *The republic*, ed. G.R.F. Ferrari (Cambridge: Cambridge University Press)

Pocock, J.G.A., 1975: *The Machiavellian moment. Florentine thought and the Atlantic republican tradition* (Princeton: Princeton University Press)

Pocock, J.G.A., 1985: *Virtue, commerce and history* (Cambridge: Cambridge University Press)

Priestley, Joseph, 1993: *Political writings*, ed. Peter Miller (Cambridge: Cambridge University Press)

Randall, William Sterne, 1994: *Thomas Jefferson. A life* (London: HarperPerennial)

Richmond, Charles, and Paul Smith (eds.), 1998: *The self-fashioning of Disraeli, 1818–1851* (Cambridge: Cambridge University Press)

Rochefoucauld, François, Duc de la, 1959: *Maxims*, ed. Leonard Tancock (Harmondsworth: Penguin)

Rodden, John (ed.), 2007: *The Cambridge companion to George Orwell* (Cambridge: Cambridge University Press)

Rorty, Richard, 1989: *Contingency, irony and solidarity* (Cambridge: Cambridge University Press)

Rosebery, Archibald, Philip, Primrose, Earl of, 1900: "On Cromwell," *The Critic*, 36, 43–51

Rosen, Frederick, 1983: *Jeremy Bentham and representative democracy. A study of the Constitutional Code* (Oxford: Clarendon)

Rousseau, Jean-Jacques, 1997a: *The discourses and other early political writings*, ed. Victor Gourevitch (Cambridge: Cambridge University Press)

Rousseau, Jean-Jacques, 1997b: *"The social contract" and other later political writings*, ed. Victor Gourevitch (Cambridge: Cambridge University Press, 1997)

Runciman, David, 2006a: *The politics of good intentions. History, fear and hypocrisy in the new world order* (Princeton: Princeton University Press)

Runciman, David, 2006b: "Liars, hypocrites and crybabies," *London Review of Books*, 28:21, November 2 (www.lrb.co.uk/v28/n21/runc01)

Ryerson, Richard Alan (ed.), 2001: *John Adams and the founding of the Republic* (Boston: Massachusetts Historical Society)

Schama, Simon, 2005: *Rough crossings. Britain, the slaves and the American Revolution* (London: BBC Books)

Schofield, Philip, 2006: *Utility and democracy.: The political thought of Jeremy Bentham* (Oxford: Oxford University Press)

Schultz, Bart, 2002: "Eye of the universe. Henry Sidgwick and the problem public," *Utilitas*, 14, 155–88

Schultz, Bart, 2004: *Henry Sidgwick. Eye of the universe* (Cambridge: Cambridge University Press)

Scott, Jonathan, 2004: *Commonwealth principles. Republican writing of the English Revolution* (Cambridge: Cambridge University Press)

Searle, G. R., 2004: *A new England? Peace and war 1886–1918* (Oxford: Clarendon)

Shaftesbury, Anthony Ashley Cooper, Earl of, 1999: *Characteristicks of men, manners, opinions, times*, ed. Philip Ayres, 2 vols. (Oxford: Clarendon)

Shannon, Richard, 1999: *Gladstone. Heroic minister 1865–1898* (London: Allen Lane)

Shapiro, Ian, 2007: *Containment. Rebuilding a strategy against global terror* (Princeton: Princeton University Press)

Shklar, Judith, 1984: *Ordinary vices* (Cambridge, MA: Bellknap Press)

Shklar, Judith, 1998a: *Political thought and political thinkers*, ed. Stanley Hoffmann (Chicago: University of Chicago Press)

Shklar, Judith, 1998b: *Redeeming American political thought*, ed. Stanley Hoffmann and Dennis F. Thompson (Chicago: University of Chicago Press)

Sidgwick, Henry, 1891: *Elements of politics* (London: Macmillan)

Sidgwick, Henry, 1996a: *Methods of ethics* (Bristol: Thommies Press)

Sidgwick, Henry, 1996b: *Practical ethics. A collection of addresses and essays* (Bristol: Thoemmes)

Sidgwick, Henry, 1996c: *Miscellaneous essays 1870–1899* (Bristol: Thoemmes)

Silver, Victoria, 1996: "Hobbes on rhetoric," in *The Cambridge companion to Hobbes*, ed. Tom Sorrell (Cambridge: Cambridge University Press)

Skinner, Quentin, 1973: "The empirical theorists of democracy and their critics: A plague on both their houses," *Political Theory*, 1, 287–305

Skinner, Quentin, 1996: *Reason and rhetoric in the philosophy of Thomas Hobbes* (Cambridge: Cambridge University Press)

Skinner, Quentin, 2002: *Visions of politics*, 3 vols. (Cambridge: Cambridge University Press)

Skinner, Quentin, 2005: "Hobbes on representation," *European Journal of Philosophy*, 13, 155–84

Skinner, Quentin, 2006: "Surveying *The Foundations*. A retrospect and reassessment," in *Rethinking the foundations of modern political thought*, ed. Annabel Brett and James Tully (Cambridge: Cambridge University Press)

Slomp, Gabriella, 2003: "Hobbes's *Behemoth* on ambition, greed and fear," *Filozofski Vestnik*, 24, 189–204

Smart, J.J.C., and Bernard Williams, 1973: *Utilitarianism. For and against* (Cambridge: Cambridge University Press)

Smith, Adam, 1976: *The theory of moral sentiments*, ed. D. D. Raphael and A. L. Macfie (Oxford: Clarendon)

Sommerville, Johann P., 2003: "Hobbes, *Behemoth*, church-state relations and political obligation," *Filozofski Vestnik*, 24, 205–22

Springborg, Patricia, 2003: "*Behemoth* and Hobbes's 'science of just and unjust,'" *Filozofski Vestnik*, 24, 243–66

Strachey, Lytton, 2003: *Eminent Victorians* (Oxford: Oxford University Press)

Strauss, Leo, 1959: *What is political philosophy? And other studies* (Glencoe: Free Press)

Taylor, D. J., 2003: *Orwell. The life* (London: Chatto & Windus)

Thompson, C. Bradley, 1998: *John Adams and the spirit of liberty* (Lawrence: University of Kansas Press)

Thompson, Dennis F., 2005: 'Hypocrisy and democracy' in *Restoring responsibility. Ethics in business, healthcare and government* (Cambridge: Cambridge University Press)

Trollope, Anthony, 1972: *The New Zealander* (Oxford: Clarendon)

Trollope, Anthony, 1973: *Phineas Redux* (Oxford: Oxford University Press)

Trollope, Anthony, 1983: *The letters of Anthony Trollope*, 2 vols., ed. N. John Hall (Stanford: Stanford University Press)

Trollope, Anthony, 1994: *The way we live now*, ed. Frank Kermode (Harmondsworth: Penguin)

Trollope, Anthony, 1999: *Autobiography* (Bath: Trollope Society)

Tuck, Richard, 1993: *Philosophy and government 1572–1651* (Cambridge: Cambridge University Press)

Tuck, Richard, 1996: "Hobbes's moral philosophy," in *The Cambridge companion to Hobbes*, ed. Tom Sorrell (Cambridge: Cambridge University Press)

Tuck, Richard, 2000: "Hobbes and Tacitus," in *Hobbes and history*, ed. G.A.J. Rogers and T. Sorrell (London: Routledge)

Tuck, Richard, 2006: "Hobbes and democracy," in *Rethinking the foundations of modern political thought*, ed. Annabel Brett and James Tully (Cambridge: Cambridge University Press)

Vidal, Gore, 1973: *Burr* (New York: Random House)

Wall, Stephen, 1988: *Trollope and character* (London: Faber and Faber)

Weber, Max, 1994: *Political writings*, ed. Peter Lassman and Ronald Speirs (Cambridge: Cambridge University Press)

Weinberger, Jerry, 2005: *Benjamin Franklin unmasked. On the unity of his moral, religious and political thought* (Lawrence: University Press of Kansas)

Wilkins, Roger, 2002: *Jefferson's pillow. The founding fathers and the dilemma of black patriotism* (Boston: Beacon Press)

Williams, Bernard, 2002: *Truth and truthfulness* (Princeton: Princeton University Press)

Williams, Bernard, 2005: *In the beginning was the deed. Realism and moralism in political argument*, ed. Geoffrey Hawthorn (Princeton: Princeton University Press)

Williamson, Chilton, 1955: "Bentham looks at America," *Political Science Quarterly*, 70, 543–51

Wills, Garry, 2002: *Inventing America. Jefferson's Declaration of Independence* (New York: Houghton Mifflin)

Wilson, Bee, 2008: *Swindled. From poison sweets to counterfeit coffee— the dark history of the food cheats* (London: John Murray)

Wilson, Ben, 2007: *Decency and disorder. The age of cant 1789–1837* (London: Faber & Faber)

Wolin, Sheldon, 2004: *Politics and vision. Continuity and innovation in Western political thought* (expanded edition, Princeton: Princeton University Press)

Wood, Gordon S., 1969: *The creation of the American Republic 1776–1787* (Chapel Hill: University of North Carolina Press)

Wood, Gordon S., 2004: *The Americanization of Benjamin Franklin* (London: Penguin)

Wootton, David, 1986: Introduction to *Divine right and democracy. An anthology of political writing in Stuart England*, ed. David Wootton (Harmondsworth: Penguin)

Wootton, David, 1993: "David Hume 'the historian,'" in *The Cambridge companion to Hume*, ed. David Fate Norton (Cambridge: Cambridge University Press)

Wootton, David, 2006: *Bad medicine. Doctors doing harm since Hippocrates* (Oxford: Oxford University Press)

Worden, Blair, 2001: *Roundhead reputations. The English Civil War and the passions of posterity* (London: Penguin)

Zagorin, Perez, 1990: *Ways of lying. Dissimulation, persecution and conformity in early modern Europe* (Cambridge, MA: Harvard University Press)

Zagorin, Perez, 1998: *The English Revolution. Politics, events, ideas* (Aldershot: Ashgate)

Index

259